Books by Christopher Isherwood

NOVELS
A Meeting by the River
A Single Man
Down There on a Visit
The World in the Evening
Prater Violet
Goodbye to Berlin
The Last of Mr. Norris
(English title: *Mr. Norris Changes Trains*)
The Memorial
All the Conspirators

AUTOBIOGRAPHY
My Guru and His Disciple
Christopher and His Kind
Kathleen and Frank
Lions and Shadows

BIOGRAPHY
Ramakrishna and His Disciples

PLAYS (with W. H. Auden)
On the Frontier
The Ascent of F6
The Dog beneath the Skin

TRAVEL
The Condor and the Cows
Journey to a War (with W. H. Auden)

COLLECTION
Exhumations

TRANSLATIONS
The Intimate Journals of Charles Baudelaire
(and the following with Swami Prabhavananda)
The Yoga Aphorisms of Patanjali
Shankara's Crest-Jewel of Discrimination
The Bhagavid-Gita

CHRISTOPHER AND HIS KIND

CHRISTOPHER AND HIS KIND

CHRISTOPHER ISHERWOOD

University of Minnesota Press
Minneapolis

First University of Minnesota Press edition, 2001

Published by the University of Minnesota Press
111 Third Avenue South, Suite 290
Minneapolis, MN 55401-2520
http://www.upress.umn.edu

Library of Congress Cataloging-in-Publication Data

Isherwood, Christopher, 1904–1986
Christopher and his kind / Christopher Isherwood. —
1st University of Minnesota Press ed.
p.   cm.
ISBN 978-0-8166-3863-5 (pbk. :alk paper)
1. Isherwood, Christopher, 1904–1986.   2. Auden, W. H. (Wystan
Hugh), 1907–1973—Friends and associates.   3. Authors, English—
20th century—Biography.   4. Gay men—Great Britain—
Biography.   I. Title.
PR6017.S5 Z498 2001
823'.912—dc21
[B]
2001037031

Printed in the United States of America on acid-free paper

The University of Minnesota is an equal-opportunity educator
and employer.

15 14 13 12 11 10 09 08   10 9 8 7 6 5 4 3 2

TO DON BACHARDY

MY THANKS

to my brother Richard and to Don Bachardy, for the help they
gave me while I was writing this book;

to John Lehmann, Stephen Spender, and Edward Upward, for
letting me quote from their letters to me;

to Professor Edward Mendelson, literary executor of the estate
of W. H. Auden, for letting me quote from Auden's
unpublished writings;

to the Provost and Scholars of King's College, Cambridge, for
letting me quote from E. M. Forster's letters to me;

to P. N. Furbank, Forster's biographer, for answering my
questions about him;

to Rudolph Amendt, for answering my questions
about pre-Hitler Berlin;

to Werner and Susanne Rosenstock, for giving me information
about the life of Wilfrid Israel;

to Babette Deutsch, for permission to quote from her
translation of Ilya Ehrenburg's poem "The Sons of Our Sons,"
included in *A Treasury of Russian Verse*,
edited by Avrahm Yarmolinsky

C.I. July 1976

CHRISTOPHER AND HIS KIND

ONE

There is a book called *Lions and Shadows,* published in 1938, which describes Christopher Isherwood's life between the ages of seventeen and twenty-four. It is not truly autobiographical, however. The author conceals important facts about himself. He overdramatizes many episodes and gives his characters fictitious names. In a foreword, he suggests that *Lions and Shadows* should be read as if it were a novel.

The book I am now going to write will be as frank and factual as I can make it, especially as far as I myself am concerned. It will therefore be a different kind of book from *Lions and Shadows* and not, strictly speaking, a sequel to it. However, I shall begin at the point where the earlier book ends: twenty-four-year-old Christopher's departure from England on March 14, 1929, to visit Berlin for the first time in his life.

Christopher had been urged to come to Berlin by his friend and former schoolmate Wystan Hugh Auden—who is called Hugh Weston in *Lions and Shadows.* Wystan, then aged twenty-two, had been on a study holiday in Germany since taking his degree at Oxford.

While in Berlin, Wystan had met the anthropologist John Layard—Barnard in *Lions and Shadows.* Layard had once been a patient and pupil of Homer Lane, the American psychologist. He had introduced Wystan to Lane's revolutionary teachings, thus inspiring him to use them as a frame of reference for his poems. Wystan had now begun to write lines which are like the slogans of a psychiatric dictator about to seize control of the human race: "Publish each healer . . . It is time for the destruction of error . . . Prohibit sharply the rehearsed response . . . Harrow the house of the dead . . . The game is up for you and for the others . . . Love . . . needs death . . . death of the old gang . . . New styles of architecture, a change of heart."

According to Lane-Layard:

There is only one sin: disobedience to the inner law of our own nature. This disobedience is the fault of those who teach us, as children, to control God (our desires) instead of giving Him room to grow. The whole problem is to find out which is God and which is the Devil. And the one sure guide is that God appears always unreasonable, while the Devil appears always to be noble and right. God appears unreasonable because He has been put in prison and driven wild. The Devil is conscious control, and is, therefore, reasonable and sane.

Life-shaking words! When Christopher heard them, he was even more excited than Wystan had been, for they justified a change in his own life which he had been longing but not quite daring to make. Now he burned to put them into practice, to unchain his desires and hurl reason and sanity into prison.

However, when *Lions and Shadows* suggests that Christopher's chief motive for going to Berlin was that he wanted to meet Layard, it is avoiding the truth. He did look forward to meeting Layard, but that wasn't why he was in such a hurry to make this journey. It was Berlin itself he was hungry to meet; the Berlin Wystan had promised him. To Christopher, Berlin meant Boys.

At school, Christopher had fallen in love with many boys and been yearningly romantic about them. At college he had at last managed to get into bed with one. This was due entirely to the initiative of his partner, who, when Christopher became scared and started to raise objections, locked the door, and sat down firmly on Christopher's lap. I am still grateful to him. I hope he is alive and may happen to read these lines.

Other experiences followed, all of them enjoyable but none entirely satisfying. This was because Christopher was suffering from an inhibition, then not unusual among upper-class homosexuals; he couldn't relax sexually with a member of his own class or nation. He needed a working-class foreigner. He had become clearly aware of this when he went to Germany in May 1928, to stay with an elderly cousin who was the British consul at Bremen. He had no love adventures while there, but he looked around him and saw what he was missing. The Bremen trip isn't even mentioned in *Lions and Shadows* because Christopher was then unwilling to discuss its sexual significance. It is described in a novel written many years later, *Down There on a Visit,* but with too much fiction and too little frankness.

Christopher's first visit to Berlin was short—a week or ten days—but that was sufficient; I now recognize it as one of the decisive events of my life. I can still make myself faintly feel the delicious nausea of initiation terror which Christopher felt as Wystan pushed back the heavy leather door curtain of a boy bar called the Cosy Corner and led the way inside. In the autumn of 1928, Christopher had felt a different kind of nauseated excitement, equally strong and memorable, when, as a medical student, he had entered an operating theater in St. Thomas's Hospital to watch his first surgical operation. But the door of the operating theater, unlike that of the Cosy Corner, led him nowhere.

Within six months, he had given up medicine altogether.

At the Cosy Corner, Christopher met a youth whom I shall call Bubi (Baby). That was his nickname among his friends, because he had a pretty face, appealing blue eyes, golden blond hair, and a body which was smooth-skinned and almost hairless, although hard and muscular. On seeing Bubi, Christopher experienced instant infatuation. This wasn't surprising; to be infatuated was what he had come to Berlin for. Bubi was the first presentable candidate who appeared to claim the leading role in Christopher's love myth.

What was this role? Most importantly, Bubi had to be the German Boy, the representative of his race. (Bubi was actually Czech, but that could be overlooked since German was the only language he spoke.) By embracing Bubi, Christopher could hold in his arms the whole mystery-magic of foreignness, Germanness. By means of Bubi, he could fall in love with and possess the entire nation.

That Bubi was a blond was also very important—and not merely because blondness is a characteristic feature of the German Boy. The Blond—no matter of what nationality—had been a magical figure for Christopher from his childhood and would continue to be so for many years. And yet I find it hard to say why . . . John Layard would have encouraged me to invent an explanation, never mind how absurd it sounded. He would have said that *anything* one invents about oneself is part of one's personal myth and therefore true. So here is the first explanation which occurs to me: Christopher chose to identify himself with a black-haired British ancestor and to see the Blond as the invader who comes from another land to conquer and rape him. Thus the Blond becomes the masculine foreign *yang* mating with Christopher's feminine native *yin* . . . This makes a kind of Jungian sense—but I can't by any stretch of the imagination apply it to the relations between Bubi and Christopher. Bubi

4

had been, among other things, a boxer, so he must have been capable of aggression. But with Christopher he was gentle, considerate, almost too polite.

In addition to being able to play the German Boy and the Blond, Bubi had a role which he had created for himself; he was the Wanderer, the Lost Boy, homeless, penniless, dreamily passive yet tough, careless of danger, indifferent to hardship, roaming the earth. This was how Bubi saw himself and how he made Christopher and many others see him. Bubi's vulnerability, combined with his tough independence, was powerfully attractive and at the same time teasing. You longed to protect him, but he didn't need you. Or did he? You longed to help him, but he wouldn't accept help. Or would he? Wystan wasn't at all impressed by Bubi's performance as the Wanderer. Yet, largely to please Christopher, he wrote a beautiful poem about Bubi, "This Loved One."

Throughout Christopher's stay in Berlin, Bubi spent a few hours with him every day. For Christopher, this was a period of ecstasy, sentimentality, worry, hope, and clock-watching, every instant of it essentially painful. Christopher wanted to keep Bubi all to himself forever, to possess him utterly, and he knew that this was impossible and absurd. If he had been a savage, he might have solved the problem by eating Bubi—for magical, not gastronomic, reasons. As for Bubi himself, he was the most obliging of companions; but there was nothing he could do, in bed or out of it, to make Christopher feel any more secure.

They went shopping together and bought Bubi small presents, mostly shirts, socks, and ties; he refused to let Christopher be extravagant. They ate wiener schnitzels and whipped-cream desserts at restaurants. They went to the zoo, rode the roller coaster at Luna Park, and swam in the Wellenbad, a huge indoor pool which had a mechanism for making waves. At the movies, they saw Pudovkin's *Storm over Asia* and Pabst's Wedekind film, *Pandora's Box.*

The latter was highly educational entertainment for Christopher, as Wystan unkindly pointed out, since it shows the appalling consequences of trying to own someone who is naturally promiscuous. Christopher did indeed start to make a scene when Bubi broke a date with him. After being coached by Wystan, he painstakingly repeated a short speech which began: *"Ich bin eifersuechtig"* (I am jealous). Bubi listened patiently. Perhaps he even sympathized with Christopher's feelings; for he himself, as Wystan found out later, had a weakness for whores and would pursue them desperately, giving them all the money he had. He then answered at some length, laying his hand on Christopher's arm and speaking in a soothing tone. But Christopher's German was still scanty and he couldn't understand whatever lies Bubi was telling him.

All was soon forgiven, of course. When Christopher left for London, Bubi pulled a cheap gold-plated chain bracelet out of his pocket—probably an unwanted gift from some admirer—and fastened it around Christopher's wrist. This delighted Christopher, not only as a love token but also as a badge of his liberation; he still regarded the wearing of jewelry by men as a daring act, and this would be a constant reminder to him that he was now one of the free. When he got home, he displayed the bracelet challengingly. But his mother, Kathleen, wasn't shocked, only vaguely puzzled that he should care to wear anything so common.

Despite his preoccupation with Bubi, Christopher had found the time to see John Layard in Berlin. Under any other circumstances, he would have been fascinated by Layard's X-ray eyes, his mocking amusement, his stunning frankness, and his talk about Lane. But Layard's theory had seemed academic, just then, compared with Bubi's practice.

However, the next year, during a visit to England, Christopher met Layard again. They became friends and Layard taught him a great deal. He even cured Christopher—or, rather, made him cure himself—of an intimate physical shame. Christopher had been ashamed of the patch of hair which had sprouted out of an old acne scar on his left shoulder blade. Layard explained that this was a conflict between instinct—the hairy left shoulder—and conscious control—the hairless right one. God and the Devil were at it again. "You see, your instinct's trying to get your animal nature out of jail, trying to force you to recognize it. So it's growing *fur!* I like it, it's beautiful!" And Layard actually kissed the hairy shoulder, to show he meant what he said. Christopher giggled with embarrassment. But gradually, from that day on, he stopped being conscious of the hair, even when he had his shirt off in public.

Soon after getting back from Berlin, Christopher had a more than usually severe attack of tonsillitis. In those days, he was subject to sore throats. Wystan called them "the liar's quinsy" and reminded him that Lane had said they are symptoms of a basic untruthfulness in one's life. Christopher was quite willing to admit that his life in England was basically untruthful, since it conformed outwardly to standards of respectability which he inwardly rejected and despised. But Lane had also said, "Every disease is a cure, if we know how to take it," and Christopher was now sure that he knew how to make his life truthful again. He studied German hard—from Hugo's *German in Three Months without a Master.* He wrote letters in German to Bubi, which Bubi answered with tactful requests for money. And, as soon as he could afford the trip, he went back to Germany. This was in early July.

Wystan was now at a village called Rothehuette in the Harz Mountains, surrounded by forests. The air smelled of resin and echoed romantically with jangling cowbells. At the end of the day, when the cows came down from the high pastures into the village, they would separate from the herd of their own accord and find their ways to their respective farms. It was easy to pretend to yourself that they were human beings bewitched, for the whole place could have been a setting for one of Grimm's fairy tales, except that it had a railway station.

Wystan was staying at the inn with a cheerful, good-natured youth he had brought with him from Berlin. He had already made himself completely at home. His room was like every other room he had ever lived in, a chaos of books and manuscripts; he was reading and writing with his usual impatient energy. He welcomed Christopher as one welcomes a guest to one's household; he had the air of owning the village and the villagers. Certainly he must have been the chief topic of their conversation. He entertained them by thumping out German popular songs and English hymn tunes on a piano in the refreshment room of the railway station and intrigued them by wrestling naked with his friend in a nearby meadow.

At Christopher's request, Wystan had phoned Bubi in Berlin and told him to come and join them the day after Christopher arrived. But two days passed and he didn't appear. Christopher became frantic. He decided to go to Berlin and look for Bubi. To help Christopher in his search, Wystan gave him the address of an Englishman he knew there, named Francis. And Francis did help, by coming with him to the Cosy Corner and other bars and translating when he questioned boys who knew Bubi. Thus Christopher found out that Bubi was wanted by the police and that he had disappeared.

So Christopher returned mournfully to Rothehuette. And, the next day, the police arrived. They must have been tipped off by somebody in one of the Berlin bars that Bubi might be expected to join Christopher at this mountain hideout. While the police were questioning him and Wystan, a letter was handed to Christopher by the innkeeper. It had a Dutch stamp on it. It was from Bubi. Christopher read it under their very noses. Bubi wrote that he was in Amsterdam and about to ship out as a deck hand on a boat to South America. Could Chris-

8

topher send him some money as quickly as possible, poste restante? Bubi added that he wasn't giving the address where he was staying because he was in Holland illegally and this letter might fall into the wrong hands. As for the money, Bubi had sworn to himself never to ask for any more, because Christopher had been so generous already. But now here he was, amongst strangers, all alone. There was no one he could trust in the whole world. Except Christopher, his last dear true friend . . . The letter thrilled Christopher unspeakably. As he read, he began to feel that he himself had become an honorary member of the criminal class. Now he must be worthy of the occasion. He must respond recklessly. He must leave for Amsterdam at once and see Bubi before he sailed.

Meanwhile, the police, not wanting to go away empty-handed, were checking up on Wystan's friend. They asked for his identity papers—and, alas, his papers were not in order. (Boys would say, "My papers aren't in order," and "My stomach isn't in order," in the same plaintive tone, as though both were ailments.) The police soon made him admit that he was a fugitive from a reform school. Then they took him off with them.

As soon as they were gone, Christopher showed Wystan the letter and Wystan agreed to come to Amsterdam too, although he wasn't feeling kindly toward Bubi, who was indirectly to blame for his friend's arrest. When they left Rothehuette, the innkeeper was still friendly, despite the scandal of having had the police on his premises. He said to Wystan, with a tolerant grin, "I expect a lot of things happen in Berlin which we wouldn't understand."

In Amsterdam, they ran into Bubi almost at once; he was going into the post office to see if Christopher had sent him a letter. Bubi's astonishment and delight were all that Christopher had hoped for. Even more gratifying, after their first joyful embraces, was his sudden sadness: "We have so little time left, to be together." Bubi was a true German in his enjoyment of emotional partings.

9

He turned this short reunion with Christopher into a continuous farewell; they went for farewell walks, ate farewell meals, drank farewell toasts, made farewell love. Then the day came for Bubi's ship to sail. His eyes brimmed with tears of heartfelt pity for the lonely Wanderer, as he wrung Christopher's and Wystan's hands, saying, "Who knows if we shall ever meet again!"

(They did meet again, many times, in many different places. When Christopher next saw Bubi he was in Berlin, about three years later. Christopher found it very odd to be able to chatter away to him in German—odd and a little saddening, because the collapse of their language barrier had buried the magic image of the German Boy. Bubi seemed an entirely different person, not at all vulnerable, amusingly sly. Christopher felt wonderfully at ease with him and absolutely uninfatuated.)

Christopher and Wystan stayed on an extra day in Amsterdam, before Christopher went back to England. They were both in the highest spirits. It was such a relief and happiness to be alone with each other. They took a trip through the canals and the harbor in a tourist launch, deep in an exchange of private jargon and jokes, barely conscious of their surroundings. On disembarking, all the passengers were asked to sign a guest book. Beside their two signatures, Wystan wrote a quotation from Ilya Ehrenburg's poem about the Russian Revolution:

> *Read about us and marvel!*
> *You did not live in our time—be sorry!*

In August, Christopher left London for a remote seaside village where he had been engaged to tutor a small boy or at least keep him occupied during his school holidays. While Christopher was there, he had his first —and last—complete sex experience with a woman. After dark, in that tiny place, there was nothing social to do but play cards, get drunk, or make love. They were both drunk. She was five or six years older than he was, easygoing, stylish, humorous. She had been married. She liked sex but wasn't in the least desperate to get it. He started kissing her without bothering about what it might lead to. When she responded, he was surprised and amused to find how easily he could relate his usual holds and movements to this unusual partner. He felt curiosity and the fun of playing a new game. He also felt a lust which was largely narcissistic; she had told him how attractive he was and now he was excited by himself making love to her. But plenty of heterosexuals would admit to feeling that way sometimes. What mattered was that he was genuinely aroused. After their orgasm, he urged her to come to his room, where they could take all their clothes off and continue indefinitely. She wouldn't do this because she was now sobering up and getting worried that they might be caught together. Next day, she said, "I could tell that you've had a lot of women through your hands."

What did all this prove? That he had gained enormously in self-confidence. That sex, as sex, was becoming more natural to him—in the sense that swimming is natural when you know how to swim and the situation demands it. This he owed to Bubi.

He asked himself: Do I now want to go to bed with more women and girls? Of course not, as long as I can have boys. Why do I prefer boys? Because of their shape and their voices and their smell and the way they move. And boys can be romantic. I can put them into my myth and fall in love with them. Girls can be absolutely beautiful but never romantic. In fact, their utter lack of romance is what I find most likable about them. They're so sensible.

Couldn't you get yourself excited by the shape of girls, too—if you worked hard at it? Perhaps. And couldn't you invent another myth—to put girls into? Why the hell should I? Well, it would be a lot more convenient for you, if you did. Then you wouldn't have all these problems. Society would accept you. You wouldn't be out of step with nearly everybody else.

It was at this point in his self-examination that Christopher would become suddenly, blindly furious. Damn Nearly Everybody. Girls are what the state and the church and the law and the press and the medical profession endorse, and command me to desire. My mother endorses them, too. She is silently brutishly willing me to get married and breed grandchildren for her. Her will is the will of Nearly Everybody, and in their will is my death. *My* will is to live according to my nature, and to find a place where I can be what I am . . . But I'll admit this—even if my nature were like theirs, I should still have to fight them, in one way or another. If boys didn't exist, I should have to invent them.

Psychologists might find Christopher's admission damaging to his case, and his violence highly suspicious. They might accuse him of repressed heterosexuality. Wystan sometimes half jokingly did this, telling Christopher that he was merely "a heter with good taste," and expressing fears that he would sooner or later defect. Nearly fifty years have passed, since then; and Wystan's fears have been proved groundless.

Wystan was now back in England. Soon he would start work as a schoolmaster. Bubi was somewhere in South America; he never wrote. Layard had left Berlin. On November 29, Christopher set out on his third visit to Germany that year. Only, this time, he wasn't putting any limits on his stay. This might even become an immigration. When the German passport official asked him the purpose of his journey, he could have truthfully replied, "I'm looking for my homeland and I've come to find out if this is it."

On the morning after his arrival, he went to call on Francis, who was now the only English-speaking person he knew in Berlin. Francis lived on a street called In den Zelten. It had a view across the Tiergarten park. As the huge house door boomed shut behind him, Christopher ran upstairs with his characteristic nervous haste to the second or third floor—I now forget which it was—and rang.

The door of the apartment flew open and Francis appeared, tousled, furious, one hand clutching the folds of his crimson silk robe. Instantly he started screaming in German. Christopher understood the language better now; he knew that he was being told to go away and never come back or Francis would call the police. The screaming ended and the door was slammed in his face. He stood staring at it, too astonished to move. Then he shouted, "Francis—it's me, Christopher!"

The door reopened and Francis reappeared. "I say, how awful of me! I *do* apologize! I felt certain you must be the boy who came home with me last night. Just because I was drunk, he thought he could steal everything in the place. I caught him at it and threw him out . . . But you don't even look like him . . . Why, I *know* you, don't I?"

"I was over here in the summer, looking for someone. You were so kind, taking me round the bars. As a matter of fact, I've just got back from England—"

"Won't you come in? I'm afraid this place is in an awful mess. I'm never up at the unearthly hour they want to clean it. Is this your first visit to Berlin?"

"Well, no—I told you, I was here in the summer—"

"Do forgive me, lovey—my mind's a total blank before I've had lunch. I suppose you wouldn't care to have lunch here, would you? Or is that more than you can face?"

13

What Christopher was being asked to face was the ordeal of having lunch with the staff and some of the patients of Dr. Magnus Hirschfeld's Institut fuer Sexual-Wissenschaft—Institute for Sexual Science—which occupied the adjoining building. A sister of Dr. Hirschfeld lived in this apartment and let out two of its rooms to Francis. It so happened that she had a third room which was vacant just then and which she charged less for, because it was small and dark. By the time lunch was over, Christopher had decided to move into it.

TWO

The building which was now occupied by the Hirschfeld Institute had belonged, at the turn of the century, to the famous violinist Joseph Joachim; its public rooms still had an atmosphere which Christopher somehow associated with Joachim's hero, Brahms. Their furniture was classic, pillared, garlanded, their marble massive, their curtains solemnly sculpted, their engravings grave. Lunch was a meal of decorum and gracious smiles, presided over by a sweetly dignified lady with silver hair: a living guarantee that sex, in this sanctuary, was being treated with seriousness. How could it not be? Over the entrance to the Institute was an inscription in Latin which meant: Sacred to Love and to Sorrow.

Dr. Hirschfeld seldom ate with them. He was represented by Karl Giese, his secretary and long-time lover. Also present were the doctors of the staff and the patients or guests, whichever you chose to call them, hiding their individual problems behind silence or polite table chatter, according to their temperaments. I remember the shock with which Christopher first realized that one of the apparently female guests was a man. He had pictured transvestites as loud, screaming, willfully unnatural creatures. This one seemed as quietly natural as an animal and his disguise was accepted by everyone else as a matter of course. Christopher had been telling himself that he had rejected respectability and that he now regarded it with amused contempt. But the Hirschfeld kind of respectability disturbed his latent puritanism. During those early days, he found lunch at the Institute a bit uncanny.

Christopher giggled nervously when Karl Giese and Francis took him through the Institute's museum. Here were whips and chains and torture instruments designed for the practitioners of pleasure-pain; high-heeled, intricately decorated boots for the fetishists; lacy female undies which had been worn by ferociously masculine Prussian officers beneath their uniforms. Here were the lower halves of trouser legs with elastic bands to hold them in position between knee and ankle. In these and nothing else but an overcoat and a pair of shoes, you could walk the streets and seem fully clothed, giving a camera-quick exposure whenever a suitable viewer appeared.

Here were fantasy pictures, drawn and painted by Hirschfeld's patients. Scenes from the court of a priapic king who sprawled on a throne with his own phallus for a scepter and watched the grotesque matings of his courtiers. Strange sad bedroom scenes in which the faces of the copulators expressed only dismay and agony. And here was a gallery of photographs, ranging in subject matter from the sexual organs of quasi-hermaphrodites to famous homosexual couples—Wilde with Alfred Douglas, Whitman with Peter Doyle, Ludwig of Bavaria with Kainz, Edward Carpenter with George Merrill.

Christopher giggled because he was embarrassed. He was embarrassed because, at last, he was being brought face to face with his tribe. Up to now, he had behaved as though the tribe didn't exist and homosexuality were a private way of life discovered by himself and a few friends. He had always known, of course, that this wasn't true. But now he was forced to admit kinship with these freakish fellow tribesmen and their distasteful customs. And he didn't like it. His first reaction was to blame the

Institute. He said to himself: How can they take this stuff so *seriously?*

Then, one afternoon, André Gide paid them a visit. He was taken on a tour of the premises personally conducted by Hirschfeld. Live exhibits were introduced, with such comments as: "Intergrade. Third Division." One of these was a young man who opened his shirt with a modest smile to display two perfectly formed female breasts. Gide looked on, making a minimum of polite comment, judiciously fingering his chin. He was in full costume as the Great French Novelist, complete with cape. No doubt he thought Hirschfeld's performance hopelessly crude and un-French. Christopher's Gallophobia flared up. Sneering, culture-conceited frog! Suddenly he loved Hirschfeld—at whom he himself had been sneering, a moment before—the silly solemn old professor with his doggy mustache, thick peering spectacles, and clumsy German-Jewish boots . . . Nevertheless, they were all three of them on the same side, whether Christopher liked it or not. And later he would learn to honor them both, as heroic leaders of his tribe.

When Hirschfeld founded the Institute in 1919, he was just over fifty years old and notorious all over Western Europe as a leading expert on homosexuality. Thousands of members of the Third Sex, as he called it, looked up to him as their champion because, throughout his adult life, he had been campaigning for revision of Paragraph 175 of the German Criminal Code. This paragraph dealt with the punishment of homosexual acts between men. (By not including lesbian acts, it expressed a basic contempt for women which has been shared by the lawmakers of many other nations.)

When young, Hirschfeld had been a middle-of-the-road socialist. Now he was being drawn into alliance with the Communists. This was because the Soviet government, when it came into power in 1917, had declared that all forms of sexual intercourse between consenting individuals are a private matter, outside the law. The German Communist Party, of course, took the same stand. The emerging Nazi Party, on the other hand, was announcing that it would stamp out homosexuality because "Germany must be virile if we are to fight for survival." Hitler denounced homosexuals, leftists, and Jews as traitors who had undermined Germany's will to resist and caused the military defeat of 1918.

Hirschfeld was a representative of all three groups. While lecturing in Munich in 1920, he was beaten up by Nazi-inspired members of his audience. Characteristically, he returned to Munich next year and got beaten up again; this time his skull was fractured and he was left for dead. But 1922 found him still unliquidated and in combat. He was even allowed to present the grievances of the Third Sex in a speech to some members of the Reichstag. To be sometimes treated with official respect, sometimes threatened with death; to be alternately praised and lampooned by the press; to be helped by those who would later lose their nerve and betray him— such was his nobly insecure position.

The Institute was by no means exclusively concerned with homosexuality. It gave advice to couples about to marry, based on research into their hereditary backgrounds. It offered psychiatric treatment for impotence and other psychological problems. It had a clinic which dealt with a variety of cases, including venereal disease. And it studied sex in every manifestation.

However, the existence of the Institute did enable Hirschfeld to carry on his campaign against Paragraph 175 much more effectively than before. It was a visible guarantee of his scientific respectability which reassured the timid and the conservative. It was a place of education for the public, its lawmakers, and its police. Hirschfeld could invite them to the sex museum and guide them through a succession of reactions—from incredulous disgust to understanding of the need for penal reform. Meanwhile, the Institute's legal department advised men who were accused of sex crimes and represented them in court. Hirschfeld had won the right to give them asylum until their cases were heard. Some of the people Christopher met at lunch belonged to this category.

(I have a memory of Christopher looking down from a room in the Institute and watching two obvious plainclothes detectives lurk under the trees which grow along the edge of the park. They hope that one of their wanted victims will be tempted to venture out of Hirschfeld's sanctuary for a sniff of fresh air. Then, according to the rules of the police game, he can be grabbed and carried off to prison.)

The year Christopher arrived at the Institute, Hirschfeld and his allies seemed about to win a victory. Earlier in 1929, the Reichstag Committee had finished drafting a penal-reform bill. According to this bill, consensual sex acts between adult males would no longer be crimes. The vote which decided this point had been close and it had only been won through the support of the Communists. The bill had been presented to the Reichstag and seemed likely to be passed into law. Then, in October, came the U.S. Stock Market crash, causing a period of panic and indecision in Europe which was unfavorable to reform of any kind. The Reichstag postponed discussion of the bill indefinitely.

Christopher's room, like the two rooms occupied by Francis, was just inside the front door of the apartment. You and your visitors could come and go at any hour without ever running into the landlady; no doubt, she tactfully used a rear exit. She lived far away at the back, somewhere, within a clearing in a Black Forest of furniture. If sex-connected sounds did reach her now and then, she never complained. Perhaps she even approved of them, on principle. After all, she was Hirschfeld's sister.

Francis's rooms had a view of the park. Christopher's room looked down into an interior courtyard; that was why it was dark and cheap. On one wall of this courtyard, Hirschfeld had caused to be printed in Gothic lettering a stanza by Goethe:

> *Seele des Menschen,*
> *Wie gleichst du dem Wasser!*
> *Schicksal des Menschen,*
> *Wie gleichst du dem Wind!*

Spirit of Man, how like thou art to water! Fate of Man, how like thou art to wind! Never before in his life had Christopher had a room with a view of a poem. In his present state of mind, he much preferred his view to Francis's view of the Tiergarten trees. Just as changes in the light make trees look different, so Christopher's varying moods made the poem speak in different tones of voice: joyful, cynical, tragic. But always, whatever his mood, it reminded him: You are in Germany. The featureless walls of the courtyard, the neutral puddles of rain water on its floor, the patch of international sky above it—all were made utterly German by the presence of these German words.

Months later, when Christopher began giving English lessons, he would try to convey to his German pupils something of his own mystique about the German language. "A table doesn't *mean* 'ein Tisch'—when you're learning a new word, you must never say to yourself *it means.* That's altogether the wrong approach. What you must say to yourself is: Over there in England, they have a thing called a table. We may go to England and look at it and say, 'That's our Tisch.' But it isn't. The resemblance is only on the surface. The two things are essentially different, because they've been thought about differently by two nations with different cultures. If you can grasp the fact that that thing in England isn't merely *called* a table, it really *is* a table, then you'll begin to understand what the English themselves are like. They are the sort of people who are compelled by their nature to think about that thing as a table; being what they are, they couldn't possibly call it anything else ... Of course, if you cared to buy a table while you were in England and bring it back here, it would become *ein Tisch*. But not immediately. Germans would have to think about it as *ein Tisch* and call it *ein Tisch* for quite a long while, first."

When Christopher talked like this, most of his pupils would smile, finding him charmingly whimsical and so English. Only a few decided that he was being metaphysical and therefore listened with respect. Having listened, they would question him and then argue, taking his statements with absolute literalness, until he became tired and tongue-tied.

How could he possibly explain himself to these people? They wanted to learn English for show-off social reasons, or to be able to read Aldous Huxley in the original. Whereas he had learned German simply and solely to be able to talk to his sex partners. For him, the entire German language—all the way from the keep-off-the-grass signs in the park to Goethe's stanza on the wall —was irradiated with sex. For him, the difference between a table and *ein Tisch* was that a table was the dining table in his mother's house and *ein Tisch* was *ein Tisch* in the Cosy Corner.

Christopher had made up his mind that as soon as he was settled in Berlin he would start revising his novel, *The Memorial.* He had finished the first draft of it about six months before this. Since then, he had scarcely looked at it.

So now, every morning, with his manuscript under his arm, he walked along In den Zelten and sat down in one of its cafés; indoors if the weather was cold or wet, out of doors in his overcoat if it was mild. He didn't come here merely because the room in his apartment was dark. To work in this public atmosphere seemed better suited to his new way of life. He wanted to be in constant contact with Germans and Germany throughout the day, not shut up alone.

With his manuscript in front of him, a tall glass of beer on his right, a cigarette burning in an ashtray on his left, he sipped and wrote, puffed and wrote. The beer, of course, was German: Schultheiss-Patzenhofer. The cigarette was a Turkish-grown brand especially popular in Berlin: Salem Aleikum. Bubi had introduced him to both, so the taste of the one and the smell of the other were magically charged. And how strange and delightful it was to be sitting here, with Turkish smoke tickling his nostrils and German beer faintly bitter on his tongue, writing a story in the English language about an English family in an English country house! It was most unlikely that any of the people here would be able to understand what he was writing. This gave him a soothing sense of privacy, which the noise of their talk couldn't seriously disturb; it was on a different wave length. With them around him, it was actually easier to concentrate than when he was by himself. He was alone and yet not alone. He could move in and out of their world at will. He was beginning to realize how completely at home one can be as a foreigner.

The beer, taken in tiny doses, put Christopher into a state of gradually increasing relaxation which he found he could safely prolong for about two and a half hours. All this while, his pencil moved over the paper with less and less inhibition, fewer and fewer pauses. But then, somewhere in the middle of the fourth glass, his attention lost its grip upon his theme. He wrote lines which made him grin to himself, knowing, as he did so, that they wouldn't seem so clever—maybe not clever at all—when he reread them later. He was getting a bit silly. He must stop. He picked up his papers, left the money for the waiter, and walked slowly home, thinking to himself: This is what freedom is. This is how I ought always to have lived.

And now he must wake Francis and tell him to dress for lunch. Francis seldom actually needed waking. Usually, Christopher would find him reading and smoking, propped on pillows, on the outer side of his bed. On the inner side, snuggled against the wall, the back of the head of a boy would be visible. And sometimes another boy would be asleep on the couch, under a pile of coats and rugs.

When Christopher entered the bedroom, Francis would give him a faintly embarrassed smile which was like a halfhearted apology for the untidiness of the room and of his life. Christopher had no wish to make Francis feel apologetic. But he had to admit to himself that this daily encounter did make him feel smug. He had been working all morning; Francis hadn't.

In *Down There on a Visit*, Francis appears as a character called Ambrose and is described as follows:

His figure was slim and erect and there was a boyishness in his quick movements. But his dark-skinned face was quite shockingly lined, as if Life had mauled him with its claws. His hair fell picturesquely about his face in wavy black locks which were already streaked with grey. There was a gentle surprise in the expression of his dark brown eyes. He could become frantically nervous at an instant's notice—I saw that; with his sensitive nostrils and fine-drawn cheekbones, he had the look of a horse which may bolt without warning. And yet there was a kind of inner contemplative repose in the midst of him. It made him touchingly beautiful. He could have posed for the portrait of a saint.

This is true to life, more or less, except for the last three sentences, which relate only to the fictitious part of Ambrose. Photographs of Francis at that time show that he was beautiful, certainly, but that he had the face of a self-indulgent aristocrat, not a contemplative ascetic. I can't detect the inner repose. He could be surprisingly patient, however; he never minded being kept waiting if he had a drink to wait with. He seemed almost unaware of discomfort. If anyone complained of it, Francis would reprove him mildly for being "fussy." Now and then, he had to spend a day in bed; he was an invalid, though an incredibly tough one. He was perhaps suffering from side effects of the treatment for syphilis which he was then undergoing at the Institute. This was a tedious process. Francis was weary of it, all the more so now that he had been told he was no longer infectious. The doctors had warned him against giving up the treatment prematurely, but he probably would, as soon as he left Germany and started to travel in countries with fewer medical conveniences.

It wasn't long before Christopher realized that Francis harbored an aggression—usually well concealed but occasionally obvious—against all those who had never had syphilis. He appeared to feel that it was their self-righteousness and cowardice which had prevented them from having it, and that they therefore *ought* to have it, for the good of their souls. Perhaps, in his fantasies, he even imagined himself tricking such people into going to bed with infected partners.

Theoretically, Christopher rather sympathized with this attitude. He saw Francis as an unwitting missionary of the gospel of Homer Lane, trying to teach the world that prophylaxis is one of the Devil's devices. Nevertheless, though he knew he was being priggish and squeamish, Christopher begged to be excused; he did want to defy the Devil but he didn't want to do it by getting syphilis, if that could possibly be avoided. Francis tolerated Christopher's squeamishness good-humoredly. No doubt he felt confident that syphilis would catch up with Christopher sooner or later, because of his sexual promiscuity.

They got along well together. Francis's life was such that he seldom had the chance of talking to a fellow countryman who was like-minded in many respects. Christopher was eager to know everything that Francis could tell him about Berlin, including the weird idioms of Berlinerisch slang. Francis wasn't really interested in Germany, however. He never felt truly at home, he said, except in the countries of the Eastern Mediterranean. It was there that he could pull himself together and work. Christopher, who had seen him only in an atmosphere of disorder and self-indulgence, was surprised to discover that he had a serious profession—although, admittedly, he practiced it by fits and starts. He was a trained archaeologist. He had directed archaeological digs in Palestine and elsewhere and written articles on his findings for scientific journals. Francis knew a vast amount about prehistoric Greece. He spoke of it often, with a quiet understated passion which Christopher found curiously moving. It was as if part of his mind dwelt continually in that world.

As the short winter afternoon began to darken, they would visit Karl Giese for coffee and gossip. The atmosphere of Karl's sitting room had none of the Institute's noble seriousness; it was a cozy little nest, lined with photographs and souvenirs.

In repose, Karl's long handsome face was melancholy. But soon he would be giggling and rolling his eyes. Touching the back of his head with his fingertips, as if patting bobbed curls, he would strike an It-Girl pose. This dedicated, earnest, intelligent campaigner for sexual freedom had an extraordinary innocence at such moments. Christopher saw in him the sturdy peasant youth with a girl's heart who, long ago, had fallen in love with

Hirschfeld, his father image. Karl still referred to Hirschfeld as "Papa."

He told Christopher that all working-class boys who are homosexual have a natural urge to get themselves educated; therefore, they have to climb into the middle class. This was what Karl had done. Christopher felt shocked by his statement and didn't want to admit that it was true. Why couldn't a working-class boy become educated without acquiring bourgeois airs and graces? If his nature required him to be a queen, why couldn't he be a working-class queen? The fact was that Christopher, the upper-class boy, was now trying to disown his class. Because he hated it, he despised the middle class for aping its ways. That left him with nothing to admire but the working class; so he declared it to be forthright, without frills, altogether on the path of truth. Karl had no such illusions.

One of Karl's friends—the one Christopher liked best —was not only homosexual and fairly well educated but unashamedly proletarian. This was Erwin Hansen. He was a big muscular man with blond hair close-cropped, Army-style. He had been a gymnastic instructor in the Army; now he did various jobs around the Institute and was running to fat. He was good-humored, with rough and ready manners and pale roving blue eyes. He used to grin sexily at Christopher and sometimes pinch his bottom. Erwin was a Communist, so perhaps his unbourgeois behavior wasn't altogether spontaneous but a part of his political persona.

Nearly all the friends who looked in on Karl in the afternoons were middle-class queens. They had a world of their own which included clubs for dancing and drinking. These clubs were governed by the code of heterosexual middle-class propriety. If two boys were sitting together and you wanted to dance with one of them, you bowed to both before asking, "May I?" Then, if the boy said yes, you bowed again to the other boy, as though he

26

were the escort of a girl and had just given you his permission to dance with her.

Soon after Christopher's arrival, Karl had given him a photograph of himself on which he had written: "From one who would like to be your friend." The inscription was an appeal. Karl wanted to win Christopher away, before it was too late, from Francis—whom he regarded, with sad affection, as a hopeless case—and from what Francis represented: low life, drunkenness, scandals. Karl hoped to convert Christopher to a way of life more worthy of the Third Sex by introducing him to some nice boy with steady habits who had clean fingernails and wore a collar and tie. Christopher was touched by Karl's concern for him. He really liked Karl, and respected everything about him but his respectability.

Like the young man with female breasts and everyone else who entered the domain of the Institute, Christopher had automatically become a museum specimen, subject to Hirschfeld's diagnosis and classification. Karl told him, in due course, that Hirschfeld had classified him as "infantile." Christopher didn't object to this epithet; he interpreted it as "boyish." You couldn't call him a pretty boy—his head and his nose were too big—but he did look young for his age, with his fresh pink complexion, inherited from Kathleen, bright eyes, and glossy dark-brown hair flopping down over his right cheek. He also had a boyish grin, full of clean white teeth. Far better to be boyish, he thought, than effeminate. He could never join the ranks of Karl's friends and play at nicey-nice third-sexism, because he refused utterly to think of himself as a queen. Wystan was much more mature than Christopher, in this respect. Labels didn't scare him.

When night came, Christopher was off with Francis to the bars. Here Francis was, of course, a well-known figure. The boys' version of his name was Franni. And since, in

German, you can put the definite article before a friend's name—thus making it into a title like that of a saga hero —they also often called Francis "Der Franni," The Franni. Christopher and Wystan anglicized Franni into Fronny in their letters to each other. The name appears in several of Wystan's poems, and the Fronny character is present, though unnamed, in the published version of *The Dance of Death.* He is one of the roles mimed by the Dancer. As the paralyzed patron of a boy bar, he is wheeled onto the stage, makes his will, orders drinks all round, and dies.

In the bars, Christopher used to think of Francis and himself as being like traders who had entered a jungle. The natives of the jungle surrounded them—childlike, curious, mistrustful, sly, easily and unpredictably moved to friendship or hostility. The two traders had what the natives wanted, money. How much of it they would get and what they would have to do to get it was the subject of their bargaining. The natives enjoyed bargaining for bargaining's sake; this Francis understood profoundly. He was never in a hurry. Indeed, his patience outwore theirs. Francis bought them drinks but promised nothing, and the night grew old. "I never get the really attractive ones," he used to say. "The ones I finish up with are the ones who haven't anywhere else to sleep." Actually, Francis didn't care who he finished up with; he wasn't much interested in making love. What did fascinate him —and what began, more and more, to fascinate Christopher, looking at it through Francis's eyes—was the boys' world, their slang, their quarrels, their jokes, their outrageous unserious demands, their girls, their thefts, their encounters with the police.

Dazed with drink, smiling to himself, lighting cigarette after cigarette with shaky hands, arguing obstinately with the boys about nothing in indistinct German, Der Franni meandered from bar to bar, waiting for the moment when he would feel ready to go home and sleep. It was characteristic of Christopher that he would accompany

Francis every evening on his Journey to the End of the Night, yet always leave him one third of the way through it, going home quite sober at ten, with or without a bedmate, so as to wake up fresh in the morning to get on with his novel. Seldom have wild oats been sown so prudently.

For Christopher, the Cosy Corner was now no longer the mysterious temple of initiation in which he had met Bubi; Berlin was no longer the fantasy city in which their affair had taken place. Their affair had been essentially a private performance which could only continue as long as Wystan was present to be its audience. Now the performance was over. Berlin had become a real city and the Cosy Corner a real bar. He didn't for one moment regret this. For now his adventures here were real, too; less magical but far more interesting.

The Cosy Corner (Zossenerstrasse 7) and most of the other bars frequented by Francis and Christopher were in Hallesches Tor, a working-class district. Such places depended on their regular customers. They were small and hard to find and couldn't afford to advertise themselves, so casual visitors were few. Also, many homosexuals thought them rough and felt safer in the high-class bars of the West End, which only admitted boys who were neatly dressed.

In the West End there were also dens of pseudo-vice catering to heterosexual tourists. Here screaming boys in drag and monocled, Eton-cropped girls in dinner jackets play-acted the high jinks of Sodom and Gomorrah, horrifying the onlookers and reassuring them that Berlin was still the most decadent city in Europe. (Wasn't Berlin's famous "decadence" largely a commercial "line" which the Berliners had instinctively developed in their competition with Paris? Paris had long since cornered the straight girl-market, so what was left for Berlin to offer its visitors but a masquerade of perversions?)

The Berlin police "tolerated" the bars. No customer risked arrest simply for being in them. When the bars were raided, which didn't happen often, it was only the boys who were required to show their papers. Those who hadn't any or were wanted for some crime would make a rush to escape through a back door or window as the police came in.

Nothing could have looked less decadent than the Cosy Corner. It was plain and homely and unpretentious. Its only decorations were a few photographs of boxers and racing cyclists, pinned up above the bar. It was heated by a big old-fashioned iron stove. Partly because of the great heat of this stove, partly because they knew it excited their clients *(die Stubben)*, the boys stripped off their sweaters or leather jackets and sat around with their shirts unbuttoned to the navel and their sleeves rolled up to the armpits.

They were all working class and nearly all out of work. If you chose to describe them as male prostitutes *(Pupen-jungen)* you had to add that they were mostly rank amateurs, compared with the more professional boys of the West End. They were greedy but not calculating, temperamentally unable to take thought for the morrow. When they stole they stole stupidly and got caught. Although it would have been in their own interests to have their clients fall in love with them, they did nothing to encourage this. If you mooned over them they became bored and soon began to avoid you. Beyond keeping their hair carefully combed, they showed few signs of vanity. They didn't seem able to picture themselves as objects of desire. Their attitude was an almost indifferent "take me or leave me." Their chief reason for coming to the bars was of course to get money, but they also came because this was a club where they could meet other boys and gossip and play cards. Often, if you wanted one of them to join you at your table, he would tell you to wait until he had finished his game.

Christopher's relations with many of the boys soon

became easy and intimate. Perhaps they recognized and were drawn to the boyishness in him. He felt a marvelous freedom in their company. He, who had hinted and stammered in English, could now ask straight out in German for what he wanted. His limited knowledge of the language forced him to be blunt and he wasn't embarrassed to utter the foreign sex words, since they had no associations with his life in England.

And what did he want? Hirschfeld had rightly called him infantile. He wanted to go back into the world of his adolescent sexuality and reexperience it, without the inhibitions which had spoiled his pleasure then. At school, the boys Christopher had desired had been as scared as himself of admitting to their desires. But now the innocent lust which had fired all that ass grabbing, arm twisting, sparring and wrestling half naked in the changing room could come out stark naked into the open without shame and be gratified in full. What excited Christopher most, a struggle which turned gradually into a sex act, seemed perfectly natural to these German boys; indeed, it excited them too. Maybe because it was something you couldn't do with a girl, or anyhow not on terms of physical equality; something which appealed to them as an expression of aggression-attraction between a pair of males. Maybe, also, such mildly sadistic play was a characteristic of German sensuality; many of them liked to be beaten, not too hard, with a belt strap. Of course it would never have occurred to any of them to worry about the psychological significance of their tastes.

This rough athletic sexmaking was excellent isometric exercise. It strengthened Christopher's muscles more than all his years of joyless compulsory games at school. He felt grateful to his partners for his new strength. There was much love in his contact with their sturdy bodies; love which made no demands beyond the pleasure of the moment.

Christopher was delighted with his way of life and with himself for living it—so much so that he became bumptious, and actually wrote to a woman he knew in England, telling her: "I am doing what Henry James would have done, if he had had the guts." The woman foolishly reported this statement to Christopher's former literary mentor, an Irish authoress who had been a friend of his father, Frank, and whom Frank had nicknamed Venus. (See *Kathleen and Frank.*) Venus, a devout Jamesian, was not amused. She replied loftily: "Christopher has become either a silly young ass or a dirty young dog, and I am interested in neither animal."

Christopher wasn't angry with Venus—she soon forgave him—and he wasn't in the least abashed by her rebuke. But, before long, he began to feel that he had done enough exploring of his rediscovered adolescence. What he wanted now was a more serious relationship, expressed by a different kind of lovemaking.

Since he no longer needed his former sex partners, he could afford to regard them objectively and to moralize over them. Wasn't it basically wrong to hire other human beings to have sex with you? Weren't you exploiting them, degrading them? Christopher had found it charming to watch Francis bargaining with the natives of the jungle. Francis himself didn't have the ugliness of an exploiter because his own state of degradation put him on a level with the natives and made him sympathetically picturesque. But this was a colonial situation, nevertheless. The behavior of many Cosy Corner clients was ugly because it was sentimental. Not content with hiring the boys' bodies—which was at least a straightforward commercial transaction—they sentimentally expected gratitude, even love, thrown into the bargain. Not getting either, they turned nasty, called the boys whores and begrudged the money they had spent on them. One of the least sentimental of the clients used to tell a story against himself: In the midst of a quarrel with a boy, he had heard himself exclaim: "I don't give a damn about the money—it's *you* I want!" He had involuntarily said what he had been wishing the boy would say to *him*.

There was one thing the boys had to offer that very few clients wanted: their friendship. Most boys dreamed of a Friend—that sacred German concept. This friend would help them with money, of course, but he would also— and this was far more important to them—offer them serious interest, advice, encouragement. Sometimes, when a client had shown him unexpected kindness, a boy would put this concept into awkward words. The client might indulge him in his friendship talk, but as one indulges a sufferer from a terminal illness. From the average client's point of view, these boys had no future; therefore, one couldn't allow oneself to care what became of them.

During the Christmas season, a great costume ball was held in one of the dance halls of In den Zelten: a ball for men. Many of them wore female clothes. There was a famous character who had inherited a whole wardrobe of beautiful family ball gowns, seventy or eighty years old. These he was wearing out at the rate of one a year. At each ball, he encouraged his friends to rip his gown off his body in handfuls until he had nothing but a few rags to return home in.

Christopher went to the ball with Francis. He had dressed himself in some clothes lent him by a boy from the Cosy Corner—a big sweater with a collar and a pair of sailor's bell-bottomed trousers. It gave him an erotic thrill to masquerade thus as his own sex partner. A little makeup applied by Francis took the necessary five years off his age; the effect was so convincing that a friend of Karl Giese, who didn't know Christopher, later protested to Karl that Francis had really gone too far— bringing a common street hustler into this respectable social gathering.

The respectability of the ball was open to doubt. But it did have one dazzling guest: Conrad Veidt. The great film star sat apart at his own table, impeccable in evening tails. He watched the dancing benevolently through his monocle as he sipped champagne and smoked a cigarette in a long holder. He seemed a supernatural figure, the guardian god of these festivities, who was graciously manifesting himself to his devotees. A few favored ones approached and talked to him but without presuming to sit down.

Veidt had appeared in two films dealing with the problems of the homosexual; hence the appropriateness of his presence at this ball. The first of these films was *Anders als die Andern* (Different from the Others), produced in 1919. Performances of it had often been broken up by the Nazis. In Vienna, one of them had fired a revolver into the audience, wounding several people. The second film, *Gesetze der Liebe* (Laws of Love), was produced in 1927. This was, in many respects, a remake of *Anders als die Andern*.

Christopher had been shown one of these films at the Institute, or perhaps both, I can't be sure. Three scenes remain in my memory. One is a ball at which the dancers, all male, are standing fully clothed in what seems about to become a daisy chain. It is here that the character played by Veidt meets the blackmailer who seduces and then ruins him. The next scene is a vision which Veidt has (while in prison?) of a long procession of kings, poets, scientists, philosophers, and other famous victims of homophobia, moving slowly and sadly with heads bowed. Each of them cringes, in turn, as he passes beneath a banner on which "Paragraph 175" is inscribed. In the final scene, Dr. Hirschfeld himself appears. I think the corpse of Veidt, who has committed suicide, is lying in the background. Hirschfeld delivers a speech—that is to say, a series of subtitles—appealing for justice for the Third Sex. This is like the appearance of Dickens beside the corpse of Jo, in *Bleak House,* to deliver the splendid diatribe which begins: "Dead, your Majesty . . ."

Early in the New Year of 1930, Francis left Berlin, en route for warmer southern lands. So now Christopher was quite alone with the Germans.

THREE

On February 6, 1930, Christopher wrote to Stephen Spender:

> I'm very apathetic here. It's all so pleasant and I have utterly lost any sense of strangeness in being abroad. I even don't particularly care when I see England again. And when I read in my diary about my life at home, it's like people on the moon.

Two weeks later, he was back in London. The cause of his unforeseen return was Henry Isherwood, Christopher's elder uncle. Henry was the only member of the family who could be described as wealthy; he had inherited the Isherwood estates and money when his father died in 1924. Soon after this event, Christopher had decided to become Uncle Henry's favorite nephew; and he had done so instantaneously, by making it clear to Henry that they had the same sexual nature. Henry's brothers and sisters had always known about his homosexuality and had made unkind jokes behind his back, of which he was well aware. So Henry was delighted to discover a blood relative who shared his tastes—using the slang expressions of his generation, he referred to himself as being "musical" or "so."

Once they had reached this understanding, it hadn't been hard for Christopher to introduce a benevolent idea into Henry's head. Since Henry was separated from his wife after a childless marriage; since, as a good Catholic, he couldn't remarry; since, being what he was, he didn't want to; since the estates were entailed and Christopher was the heir presumptive—why shouldn't Christopher be given a small allowance now, at a time of life when he really needed the money?

Christopher was proud of the diplomacy he had employed to achieve this objective. He boasted of it to his friends. They envied him and weren't in the least shocked; in his shoes, they said, they would have done the same thing. I suspect that Henry saw through Christopher's amateur maneuvers from the start and was amused by them. When young, he himself had squeezed money from his father at every opportunity.

Christopher couldn't have afforded to live in Berlin without Henry's allowance. Henry had promised to pay it every three months. Christopher was expected to reciprocate by writing to him regularly and by dining with him when they were both in London. Writing the letters was a weary task, because Henry had to be thanked for his bounty over and over again, and reassured that he was the Model Uncle. The dinners were more fun, because you could get drunk. Henry demanded to be told every detail of Christopher's sex life; Christopher obliged, exaggerating wildly. Then Henry described his guardsmen and other favorites. "Oh, he's what I call a tearer—a regular tearin' bugger, don't you know?" He had once paid a young man not to wash himself for a month. "At the end of the month, he came to see me and he smelt exactly like a *fox!* Delicious!" Henry waved his beringed hands and uttered his harsh parrot laugh. Christopher found his coarseness bracing and sympathetic. But Henry was also a snob and a Fascist. He adored the titled ladies of Roman society, amongst whom he spent most of the winter, and praised Mussolini for having made Italy more comfortable for foreign visitors like himself. Christopher had to keep his mouth shut, project sparkling interest, and smile flatteringly at this aging beauty—it was as if he were a courtier of Queen Elizabeth I. And yet, from time to time, despite all Christopher's efforts, Henry would capriciously fail to pay up. As he had on this occasion.

Thus Christopher was reminded that he wasn't a free spirit, as he liked to think, but a captive balloon. Coming down to earth with a humiliating bump, in an evil humor and suffering from one of his sore throats, he found himself in the midst of a domestic battle. His brother Richard, now eighteen, had been making an attempt to assert himself and prove to their mother, Kathleen, that she couldn't go on treating him as a schoolboy. Richard's attempt was clumsy—in order to avoid being sent back to the tutor who was cramming him for Oxford, he had pretended that he had found himself a job. But Kathleen's reaction, when she discovered he was lying, was clumsier: "If your father was alive," she told him, "you wouldn't dare behave like this!" The two of them were victims of a classic situation, forced to become enemies against their will. Christopher must surely have understood this, and known that it was his duty to play the affectionate peacemaker and help them work out a new way of living with each other. But, instead, he sided with Richard against Kathleen.

So there were bitter sessions in which he revenged himself on the tired tearful woman for all the humiliations he had endured at the hands of others. He accused her of having tried to wreck his life and of being now determined to wreck Richard's. She had tried to turn Christopher into a Cambridge don, he said, to gratify her selfish daydream of the kind of son she wanted him to be. And since he had foiled her, by getting himself thrown out of college, she was trying to turn Richard into an Oxford don, against his will.

Christopher told her coldly and aggressively about his life in Berlin. He made his acts of homosexual love sound like acts of defiance, directed against Kathleen. I don't think Kathleen was shocked. What he described was totally unreal to her. How could there be real sex without women? All she was aware of was the hate in his voice. So she wept and wrote in her diary that this was the end of "the nice era of peace." She was obstinate, willfully stupid, and maddeningly pathetic. Yet, in the midst of her misery, she never yielded a single point. It wasn't even that she thought she was in the right. When Christopher called in John Layard and he talked to her with his usual bluntness, she agreed meekly that she had made many mistakes. Layard impressed her favorably. She referred to him in her diary as "very striking and unusual." But she wasn't about to change her attitude—she was incapable of changing—as Christopher now began to realize.

At length, a letter arrived from Henry Isherwood, who was somewhere abroad. Kathleen described it by saying that "Henry did the heavy uncle in grand style"—which I take to mean that he advised Christopher to stop wasting time in Berlin, settle down in London, and get a job. Henry never did pay that quarter's allowance. Three weeks later, he sent Christopher fifteen pounds which he had won at Monte Carlo, making it clear that this was to be regarded as an advance on the *next* quarter. This episode was typical of Henry's queenly arrogance. Christopher excused it, as always. He couldn't take Henry seriously enough to be angry with him.

A few days after Christopher's arrival in London, Wystan had to undergo an operation for a rectal fissure. His announcement of this, on a postcard, was characteristically terse. It ended with a T. S. Eliot quotation: "Pray for Boudin." Christopher went up to Birmingham twice to be with him, before leaving England.

Wystan suffered from the aftereffects of this operation for several years. They inspired him to write his "Letter to a Wound," which forms part of *The Orators.*

Christopher went back to Berlin on May 8, having told Kathleen that he could never live in her house again. According to her diary, "he begged that I should refuse to have him again even if he suggested coming." He did come back, but not until ten months later. And, of the next three and a half years, he was to spend only five months in England.

The only good which came of this unhappy visit was that Christopher and Richard became intimate. Up to that time, they had been almost strangers, because of the rareness of their meetings and the seven-year age gap between them. Richard had been dreading Christopher's return from Berlin, since he felt sure Christopher would agree with Kathleen that he must go back to his hated tutor. So, when Christopher disagreed with her and sympathized with his point of view, Richard was correspondingly grateful. Before the visit was over, they had become friends. Richard was often rash and childish in his dealings with the outside world, but the eyes with which he observed it were searching and mature and his comments were as candid as Layard's. Christopher realized, with surprise and pleasure, that he had a brother to whom he could tell absolutely anything about himself without shame.

During his years in Germany, Christopher kept a diary. As he became aware that he would one day write stories about the people he knew there, his diary entries got longer. They later supplied him with most of the material which is used to create period atmosphere in *Mr. Norris* and *Goodbye to Berlin*.

After those two books had been written, Christopher burned the diary. His private reason for doing this was that it was full of details about his sex life and he feared that it might somehow fall into the hands of the police or other enemies.

Christopher's declared reason for burning his Berlin diary was unconvincing. He used to tell his friends that he had destroyed his real past because he preferred the simplified, more creditable, more exciting fictitious past which he had created to take its place. This fictitious past, he said, was the past he wanted to "remember." Now that I am writing about Christopher's real past, I sadly miss the help of the lost diary and have no patience with this arty talk. The Berlin novels leave out a great deal which I now want to remember; they also falsify events and alter dates for dramatic purposes. As for the few surviving letters written at that time by Christopher and his friends to each other, they usually have no dates at all. I get the impression that their writers regarded letter dating as something beneath their dignity as artists— something bank clerkly, formal, and mean-spirited. My most reliable source of information proves, ironically, to be the diaries of Kathleen, whom Christopher was trying to exclude from his Berlin life altogether. Kathleen picked up scraps of news from friends who had visited him there and from his occasional grudging letters. I bless her for having recorded them.

It was probably in May 1930, soon after Christopher's return from London, that he met the youth who is called Otto Nowak in *Goodbye to Berlin*. He was then sixteen or seventeen years old.

Otto has a face like a very ripe peach. His hair is full and thick, growing low on his forehead. He has small sparkling eyes, full of naughtiness, and a wide disarming grin, which is much too innocent to be true. When he grins, two large dimples appear in his peach-bloom cheeks . . . Otto moves fluidly, effortlessly; his gestures have the savage, unconscious grace of a cruel elegant animal . . . Otto is outrageously conceited . . . Otto certainly has a superb pair of shoulders and chest for a boy of his age—but his body is nevertheless somehow slightly ridiculous. The beautiful ripe lines of the torso taper away too suddenly to his rather absurd little buttocks and spindly, immature legs. And these struggles with the chest-expander are daily making him more and more top-heavy.

This is how Otto is described by "Christopher Isherwood," the narrator of the novel. The fictitious Isherwood takes the attitude of an amused, slightly contemptuous onlooker. He nearly gives himself away when he speaks of "the beautiful ripe lines of the torso." So, lest the reader should suspect him of finding Otto physically attractive, he adds that Otto's legs are "spindly." Otto's original in life had an entirely adequate, sturdy pair of legs, even if they weren't quite as handsome as the upper half of his body.

Otto—as he will be called in this book, also—was a child of the borderland. His family came from what was then known as the Polish Corridor, the strip of Germany which had been ceded to Poland by the Treaty of Versailles, after World War I. Like many other families in that area, the Nowaks had moved west and settled in Berlin, rather than lose their German nationality. Yet Otto himself seemed Slav rather than German, in his looks and temperament. His sensual nostrils and lips reminded Christopher of a photograph he had once seen of a Russian dancer.

When Otto was in a good mood, Christopher would be enchanted by his eagerness to enjoy himself. He delighted in watching movies and eating meals and making love. Like Christopher, he was a play actor. In the midst of their lovemaking, he would exclaim, in a swooning tone, "This is how I'd like to die—doing this!" Once, when they had seen a film about a psychopathic killer, he turned to Christopher and said solemnly, "Let's thank God, Christoph, we're both normal!" And he told stories, with immense tragic gusto. Of how, for example, he was haunted by a huge spectral black hand. He had seen it twice already, once in childhood, once in his early teens. "One day soon, I'll see that Hand again—and then it'll be all over with me." Otto would say this with his eyes full of tears. And there would be tears in Christopher's eyes too, from laughing.

For Christopher, during their first months together, Otto's physical presence seemed part of the summer itself. Otto was the coming of warmth and color to the drab cold city, bringing the linden trees into leaf, sweating the citizens out of their topcoats, making the bands play outdoors. Christopher rode on the bus with him to the great lake at Wannsee, where they splashed together in the shallow water amidst the holiday crowds, then wandered off into the surrounding woods to find a spot where they could be alone. Otto was the exciting laughter of the crowd and the inviting shadow of the woods. But the crowd and the woods were also full of menace to Christopher; within them lurked those who might lure Otto away from him.

Otto preferred women to men, but he was a narcissist first and foremost. Therefore, the degree of his lust was largely dependent upon that of his partner. Christopher could compete successfully with most women by showing more lust, more shamelessly, than they would. (Older women were a greater threat than young ones.) "I love the way you look when you're hot for me," Otto used to say to him. "Your eyes shine so bright." Otto was perpetually admiring his body and calling Christopher's attention to its muscles and golden smoothness—"just feel, Christoph, as smooth as silk!" When winter returned and

43

Otto revealed himself bit by bit as he pulled off layers of thick clothes, his nakedness aroused both of them even more. His body became a tropical island on which they were snugly marooned in the midst of snowbound Berlin.

Although Otto's attractiveness was very much a matter of taste—he certainly wasn't conventionally handsome—Christopher always felt proud to be seen with him in public. When they went to their favorite cabaret, which was also a restaurant, Christopher would keep looking away from the stage to see if people at other tables were admiring Otto. And he loved to watch the performance as it was reflected in Otto's eyes.

Christopher spent more money on Otto than he could well afford, but Otto was careful not to go too far in his demands, or rather, wheedlings. When Otto was coaxing Christopher into buying him a new suit, Christopher enjoyed the game in spite of his misgivings. It was a kind of seduction and it always ended erotically as well as financially.

Certainly, Otto was selfish. But so was Christopher, as is pointed out in *Goodbye to Berlin*. (I have changed a name and some pronouns from the ones used in the novel, in order not to confuse the reader of this book.)

> Christopher's selfishness is much less honest, more civilised, more perverse. Appealed to in the right way, he will make any sacrifice, however unreasonable and unnecessary. But when Otto takes the better chair as if by right, then Christopher sees a challenge which he dare not refuse to accept . . . Christopher is bound to go on fighting to win Otto's submission. When, at last, he ceases to do so, it will merely mean that he has lost interest in Otto altogether.

This is an attempt to describe the relationship between Christopher and Otto as it may have appeared to a third party, Stephen Spender. Stephen was then living in Hamburg, and they went to visit him there for a few days, that summer. (I remember Stephen's explosive laugh as he greeted Christopher—the laugh of a small boy who has done something forbidden: "I've just written the most marvelous poem!" A pause. Then, with sudden anxiety: "At least, I hope it is.")

In Stephen's presence—and indeed in the presence of any of his English friends—Christopher's attitude to Otto became one of apology and embarrassment. He felt himself being pulled in two opposite directions. His way of apologizing to Stephen for Otto's existence was to play the martyred, masochistic victim of a hopeless passion— a character like Maugham's Philip Carey in *Of Human Bondage,* who becomes the slave of Mildred, the faithless, rapacious teashop waitress. This was deliberate farce. Even when Christopher felt genuinely jealous, genuinely furious with Otto, he continued to play for Stephen's amusement. Otto, being a natural actor, knew this instinctively and entered into the performance; he didn't object to taking the unsympathetic role. Here is another scene from *Goodbye to Berlin,* with names and pronouns changed, as before:

Suddenly, Christopher slapped Otto hard on both cheeks. They closed immediately and staggered grappling about the room, knocking over the chairs. Stephen looked on, getting out of their way as well as he could. It was funny and, at the same time, unpleasant, because rage made their faces strange and ugly. Presently, Otto got Christopher down on the ground and began twisting his arm: "Have you had enough?" he kept asking. He grinned: at that moment he was really hideous, positively deformed with malice. Stephen knew that Otto was glad to have him there, because his presence was an extra humiliation for Christopher.

Nevertheless, Otto wanted Christopher's friends to like him. He tried to approach them by the only method he knew: flirtation. This didn't usually displease them but it did make them decide that he was a quite ordinary boy of his kind, unworthy of their further curiosity. So they went back to talking English with Christopher. Otto, who didn't understand the language, was obliged to read their faces, gestures, and tones of voice as an animal does— with the result that he ended by knowing a great deal more about them than they knew about him.

From time to time, Christopher was apt to become suddenly angered by his own embarrassment over Otto. Then he would blame his friends for it and punish them by exposing them even more mercilessly to the annoyance of Otto's presence. Those whose ultimatum is "love me, love my dog" are using their pets in the same aggressive manner.

When defending Otto, I must beware of making Christopher seem too sinister. He was well aware of his masochism and his domineering will; they were part of his survival technique as a writer. He needed to be made to suffer; otherwise, he would have lapsed into indifference and never noticed or cared about anybody or anything. And he needed his will; without it, he would have stopped working and probably have become an alcoholic. His will was a psychological muscle which had been overdeveloped in his struggle with sloth. But too much muscle is better than none at all.

At the end of June, Wystan came out to Berlin on a short visit. He had brought with him a proof copy of his first volume of poems, which was to be published that September. The poems were publicly dedicated to Christopher, and Wystan had also composed a personal dedication to him, in dog German full of private jokes. Christopher later lent the proof copy to Stephen, who accidentally crumpled its flimsy paper jacket. Before returning it, Stephen himself inscribed it: "Written by

46

Wystan, dedicated to Christopher, damaged by Stephen Spender.''

Wystan wasn't greatly interested in Otto but he did at least pay Otto the compliment of treating him as a metaphysical concept. In a poem which he wrote for Christopher's birthday in 1931, Otto is the prize for which Christopher is fighting against the powers of Hell. And Wystan declares—with more politeness, perhaps, than genuine optimism:

> *The plants have one whole cycle run*
> *Since your campaign was first begun,*
> *Though still the peace-map is not drawn*
> *It stands recorded*
> *That most of Otto has been won*
> *To you awarded.*

Edward Upward (who is called Allen Chalmers in *Lions and Shadows*) also visited Christopher in Berlin in 1930, toward the end of August. Edward was Christopher's closest heterosexual male friend—they had met at their public school and had become constant companions while up at Cambridge. Their friendship had grown out of their admiration for each other as writers. Since both of them were essentially novelists, they shared the experience of writing more completely than Christopher and Wystan ever did. From Christopher's point of view, Wystan's poems were like rabbits he produced from a hat; they couldn't be talked about before they appeared.

Because of the difference in their sexual tastes, Edward and Christopher had tended to keep their sex lives in the background of their conversation, to be referred to with apologetic humor. They talked about homosexuality, of course; but Christopher was conscious that Edward trod carefully. When he spoke of "buggers" and "buggery"

47

—these were Christopher's preferred epithets at that time—he did so in exactly the right tone of voice.

Here in Berlin, Edward felt himself to be on buggers' territory and obliged to tread more carefully than ever. He did his best to treat both the Hirschfeld Institute and Otto with respect. When they saw how good-looking Edward was, Karl Giese and his friends archly decided that he and Christopher must once have been lovers, despite Christopher's denials. As for Otto, he flirted with Edward because Edward was Christopher's friend. Christopher was uneasily aware that Otto's presence was spoiling their reunion. Yet his obsession was such that he couldn't bring himself to tell Otto to disappear until Edward's visit was over. He was afraid that Otto might disappear altogether.

Christopher had always regarded Edward as his literary mentor; and now it seemed that he might become Christopher's political mentor, too. For Edward was now a convert to Marxism, although he hadn't, as yet, joined the Communist Party. Christopher found no difficulty in responding to Communism romantically, as the brotherhood of man. But he was well aware that Edward's involvement wasn't romantic, it was altogether sane and serious; it was a change in his whole way of life. This change implied an austerity which both attracted and scared Christopher. He began to regard Edward as a conventionally pious Catholic might regard a friend who had made up his mind to become a priest.

Edward returned to England at the end of the month. On September 2, he went to see Kathleen, at her invitation. Formerly, she had disapproved of Edward as a subversive influence on Christopher in college. (She always thought in terms of "influences.") But now she turned to Edward instinctively, no doubt feeling that, as a heterosexual, he couldn't be part of Berlin's influence on Christopher. ("That hateful Berlin," she exclaimed in her diary, "and all it contains!")

Edward reported on the meeting in a letter to Christopher:

I have betrayed everything, but very diplomatically. My only blunder was letting her know that you were paying for Otto. I was properly trapped. And I'm far from sure that I managed to convince her that buggery isn't unnatural. However, I insisted that you were more terrific than ever in England.

After Edward's visit, Christopher became increasingly aware of the kind of world he was living in. Here was the seething brew of history in the making—a brew which would test the truth of all the political theories, just as actual cooking tests the cookery books. The Berlin brew seethed with unemployment, malnutrition, stock-market panic, hatred of the Versailles Treaty, and other potent ingredients. On September 20, a new one was added; in the Reichstag elections, the Nazis won 107 seats as against their previous 12, and became for the first time a major political party.

At the beginning of October, Christopher moved out of his In den Zelten room and went to live with Otto and his family. The Nowaks had a flat in a slum tenement in the Hallesches Tor district: Simeonstrasse 4. (In *Goodbye to Berlin,* the name of the street is given as the Wassertorstrasse, the Water Gate Street, because Christopher thought it sounded more romantic. The Wassertorstrasse was actually a continuation of the Simeonstrasse.)

The Nowaks' flat consisted of a tiny kitchen, a living room, and a small bedroom. The living room contained two large double beds, a dining table, six chairs, and a sideboard. These pieces of furniture must have come from a larger home and a more prosperous period; there was barely space to move around them. The bedroom had two single beds in it.

Christopher's arrival caused a rearrangement of sleeping space which, characteristically, inconvenienced everybody in the family but Otto. Otto's elder brother, Lothar, had to give up his bed in the bedroom to Christopher and move into one of the double beds in the living room, sharing it with their twelve-year-old sister, Grete. Frau Nowak, who had been sleeping with Grete, had to share the other double bed with her husband. Frau Nowak probably didn't mind this—though she complained of Herr Nowak's snoring—because Christopher, as a lodger, was bringing extra money for his bed and board into the household. Herr Nowak certainly didn't mind; he drank enough beer every night to be able to sleep like a hog, regardless of his bedmate. Grete can't have minded, either; she was at an age when such changes are fun. Lothar probably did mind. He was a serious, hard-working boy of twenty who had been converted to National Socialism; he must therefore have disapproved of Christopher as a degenerate foreigner who had turned him out of his bed in order to have perverse sex with his brother.

This was one of the attic flats, so it overlooked the rooftops and got plenty of daylight, at least. The lower flats stared at each other across the deep pit of the courtyard and their gloom was perpetual. The Nowaks' chief disadvantage was that the roof of the building leaked and the rain water seeped through their ceiling. There was only one toilet to every four flats, and the Nowaks had to walk down a flight of stairs to reach theirs, unless they preferred to use the bucket in the kitchen. To wash properly—that is to say, not in the kitchen sink—they had to go to the nearest public baths.

When the kitchen stove was alight, the flat got smelly and stuffy; when it wasn't, you shivered. And, no matter what the temperature was, the sink stank. Because of the leaky roof and the overcrowding, the Nowaks had been told by the housing authorities that they mustn't go on living here. Dozens of other families in this district had been told the same thing; but there was nowhere for them to move to.

In *Goodbye to Berlin,* "Isherwood" goes to live with the Nowaks in the autumn of 1931, not 1930. There were two reasons for this falsification. First, from a structural point of view, it seemed better to introduce some of the more important characters—Sally Bowles, Frl. Schroeder, and her lodgers—before the Nowaks. Second, since "Isherwood" is not overtly homosexual, he has to be given another reason for knowing Otto and another motive for going to live with his family. In the novel, "Isherwood" meets Otto through an Englishman named Peter Wilkinson who is Otto's lover; and the meeting takes place merely because they happen to be staying at the same boarding house in a seaside village (Sellin) on the island of Ruegen in the Baltic. Then Peter goes back to England, having broken with Otto, and Otto and "Isherwood" return to Berlin—but not together.

In September 1931, the British government was forced to abandon the gold standard, thereby lowering the value of the pound in relation to foreign currencies and impoverishing British nationals who were living abroad on British money. In the novel, this gives "Isherwood" a respectable motive for going to live with the Nowaks; he becomes their lodger because he is poor, not because he wants to share a bedroom with Otto.

Christopher's In den Zelten room did cost a little more than he could easily afford. But when he left it, he didn't do so because he had suddenly become poorer; his move to the Nowaks' flat was due to Otto's coaxing. Otto had decided that it would be fun if they all lived together, and Christopher agreed; such slumming seemed a thrilling adventure. By the time the British pound fell, a year later, Christopher was almost able to balance his loss with the German money he was earning by giving English lessons. He could always have afforded something a little better than the Simeonstrasse.

Quite aside from the novelty of the experience, Christopher enjoyed living with the Nowaks. He soon became very fond of Frau Nowak. Her cheeks were flushed prettily and the big blue rings under her eyes made her look sick but strangely young for her age; she had tuberculosis. There was something touchingly girlish and gay and even naughty about her—she knew all about his relationship with Otto and, though she never referred to it, Christopher was sure that it didn't shock her. She loved the excitement of having him as a visitor. Christopher also got along well with Herr Nowak, a sturdy little furniture remover who called him Christoph and slapped him on the back. Grete he found tiresome but endearingly silly. He had done his best to make friends with Lothar and had, several times, tried addressing him with the familiar *du* (thou). Working-class men would call each other *du* even when they were strangers. Herr Nowak had said *du* to Christopher from the beginning, though Frau Nowak had told him that it was no way to speak to a gentleman. But Lothar had quietly snubbed Christopher by replying to him with the formal *Sie* (you). The flat was uncomfortable, certainly; there was nowhere to put anything down. But, as far as Christopher was concerned, the discomforts were easily bearable, like those of a camping trip which could be brought to an end whenever he wished.

I doubt if Christopher managed to do any writing while he was with the Nowaks. True, there is a passage in *Goodbye to Berlin:*

Sunday was a long day at the Nowaks. There was nowhere to go in this wretched weather. We were all of us at home . . . I was sitting on the opposite side of the table, frowning at a piece of paper on which I had written: "But, Edward, can't you *see?*" I was trying to get on with my novel. It was about a family who lived in a large country house on unearned incomes and were very unhappy. They spent their time explaining to each other why they couldn't enjoy their lives; and some of the reasons—though I say it myself—were most ingenious. Unfortunately, I found myself taking less and less interest in my unhappy family; the atmosphere of the Nowak household was not very inspiring.

But here "Isherwood" is playing to the gallery. The novel he seems to be referring to, *The Memorial,* is described with willful inaccuracy—none of its characters are unhappy for "ingenious" reasons; they are bereaved and lonely and in need of love, as people often are on any social level. "Isherwood," merely because he has moved to the Simeonstrasse, feels that he has broken with his bourgeois literary past. Anything written about the upper classes is simply not worth reading, he implies. The rich *ought* to be happy—that is the least they can be—since they are living on money they've stolen from the poor; if they are miserable, that's just too tiresome. In any case, their lives can never be meaningful, as the lives of the Nowaks are—and as "Isherwood" 's life is, now that he is living with them.

Such was a side effect of Christopher's political awakening. But Edward Upward can't be blamed for it. He was utterly incapable of such silliness. And Christopher himself knew better, despite his occasional lapses. Indeed, I remember how, in the later thirties, he used to tell people that he had written about the Nowaks in order to debunk the cult of worker worship as it was being practiced by many would-be revolutionary writers.

As it turned out, Christopher didn't stay much more than a month at the Simeonstrasse. His immediate reason for leaving was that Frau Nowak was being sent to a sanatorium; but he would have left soon in any case. Slumming had lost its novelty for him, and he and Otto were on bad terms. His next move, sometime in November, was to lodgings in the Admiralstrasse—number 38. This was in the neighboring district of Kottbusser Tor, also a slum. But Christopher now had a room to himself and was in comparative comfort. When he went to register with the police—you had to do this whenever you changed your address—they told him that he was the only Englishman living in that area. Christopher's vanity was tickled. He liked to imagine himself as one of those mysterious wanderers who penetrate the depths of a foreign land, disguise themselves in the dress and customs of its natives, and die in unknown graves, envied by their stay-at-home compatriots; like Waring in Browning's poem, or like Bierce, who vanished forever into Mexico.

In the early stages of our friendship, I was drawn to him by the adventurousness of his life. His renunciation of England, his poverty, his friendship, his independence, his work, all struck me as heroic. During months in the winter of 1930, when I went back to England, I corresponded with him in the spirit of writing letters to a Polar explorer.

Thus writes Stephen Spender, serio-comically, in his autobiography, *World within World.* Stephen had adopted Wystan and Christopher as his mentors while he was still at Oxford. Christopher had been eager to welcome Stephen as a pupil; he enjoyed preaching Lane-Layard to him and he briskly took charge of Stephen's problems as a writer: "Don't be put off by what any don says about Form. What does C." (referring to an internationally famous scholar and critic) "know about Form? *I* tell you it is a good well-constructed piece of work. Isn't that enough for you?"

It was more than enough. Stephen responded in the spirit of wholehearted pupilship:

How many years will it take before I can emerge from the waters at the point where you have emerged. It is as though I had to *swim* that rotten Channel. I have always been trying to build tunnels under it. Now I give up. I see it has got to be swum.

After their meeting in Hamburg in the summer of 1930, Stephen began visiting Christopher in Berlin. Christopher let him have a glimpse of the rigors of the Simeonstrasse, and he was suitably impressed. (Writing to me more than forty years later, Stephen observed satirically: "This was your most heroic period of poverty and sacrificing everything to buying new suits for Otto.") Stephen was naturally generous and also conscious that, compared to Christopher, he was well off. Christopher didn't discourage this idea. He accepted money from Stephen and occasionally from Edward. Sometimes he paid it back, sometimes he didn't. Stephen also showered him with books and other gifts.

As pupil, Stephen had to endure Christopher's moods, his hypochondria, his sulks, and his domestic crises; but he seemed content to do this as long as he could enjoy Christopher's play-acting and dogmatic pronouncements. I can only suppose that Christopher's performance was worth the trouble. Christopher seems to have had a remarkable power of dramatizing his predicament at any given moment, so that you experienced it as though you were watching a film in which you yourself had a part. Stephen possessed this power also, and soon he would begin to outshine his mentor. Which led to difficulties, later.

Mentor and pupil must have made an arresting pair, as they walked the streets and parks of Berlin together. Stephen, at twenty-one, still fitted pretty well the description of him at nineteen, as Stephen Savage in *Lions and Shadows:*

He burst in upon us, blushing, sniggering loudly, contriving to trip over the edge of the carpet—an immensely tall shambling boy with a great scarlet poppy-face, wild frizzy hair and eyes the violent color of bluebells. His beautiful resonant voice . . . would carry to the farthest corners of the largest restaurant the most intimate details of his private life.

According to *World within World,* Christopher had:

a neatness of the cuffs emphasized by the way in which he often held his hands extended, slightly apart from his body.

(I myself think that Christopher had unconsciously copied this from the pose of a fighter in a Western movie who is just about to draw his guns.)

His hair was brushed in a boyish lick over his forehead, below which his round shining eyes had a steadiness which seemed to come from the strain of effort . . . They were the eyes of someone who, when he is a passenger in an aeroplane, thinks that the machine is kept in the air by an act of his will . . . The mouth, with its deep vertical lines at the corners, was that of a tragi-comic Christ.

The Pupil, striding along beside the brisk, large-headed little figure of the Mentor, keeps bending his beautiful scarlet face downward, lest he shall miss a word, laughing in anticipation as he does so. There are four and a half years between their ages and at least seven inches between their heights. The Pupil already has a stoop, as all tall people must who are eager to hear what the rest of the world is saying. And maybe the Mentor, that little tormentor, actually lowers his voice at times, to make the Pupil bend even lower.

FOUR

In December 1930, Christopher moved again—westward, from working-class into middle-class Berlin. His new room was in a flat at Nollendorfstrasse 17. The Nollendorfstrasse lay just south of the Nollendorfplatz, on which there were cafés and a big cinema. From the Nollendorfplatz, by way of the Kleiststrasse, you entered the West End of the city with its expensive shops. The zoo was there and the Kaiser Wilhelm Memorial Church. (This church was fated to become a memorial twice over. When Berlin was rebuilt after World War II, it was left in its ruined state, as a reminder of the bombings.)

The Nollendorfstrasse was neither elegant nor in good repair, but it was middle-class-shabby, not slum-shabby. It is described in *Goodbye to Berlin:*

From my window, the deep solemn massive street. Cellar-shops where the lamps burn all day, under the shadow of top-heavy balconied façades, dirty plaster frontages embossed with scrollwork and heraldic devices. The whole district is like this: street leading into street of houses like shabby monumental safes crammed with the tarnished valuables and second-hand furniture of a bankrupt middle class.

"Isherwood" sits looking out of the window. According to the time scheme of the novel, he has only just arrived in Germany. He is the detached foreign observer, getting his first impressions. "I am a camera," he says to himself, "quite passive, recording, not thinking."

This phrase, *I am a camera,* was the title John van Druten chose for the play he made out of the novel, in 1951. Taken out of its context, it was to label Christopher himself as one of those eternal outsiders who watch the passing parade of life lukewarm-bloodedly, with wistful impotence. From that time on, whenever he published a book, there would always be some critic who would quote it, praising Mr. Isherwood for his sharp camera eye but blaming him for not daring to get out of his focal depth and become humanly involved with his sitters.

In the next paragraph, "Isherwood" listens to the whistling of young men down in the street below. It is after eight o'clock, so all the house doors have been locked, according to regulation, and the men must whistle until their girls throw down a house key for them to enter with and come upstairs.

Because of the whistling, I do not care to stay here in the evenings. It reminds me that I am in a foreign city, alone, far from home.

"Isherwood" is playing to the gallery again. As little Mr. Lonelyheart, with nobody to whistle for him, he invites the sympathy of the motherly or fatherly reader. In real life, the whistling would only have worried Christopher on some occasion when a boy *was* whistling for him and he was afraid that Otto, who had a key, might show up unexpectedly and find them together and make a scene.

Christopher's landlady at the Nollendorfstrasse, Frl. Meta Thurau, appears as Frl. Lina Schroeder in both *Mr.*

Norris and *Goodbye to Berlin.* Of all the chief characters in the two books, this one is least distorted from its original.

All day long she goes paddling about the large dingy flat. Shapeless but alert, she waddles from room to room, in carpet slippers and a flowered dressing-gown pinned ingeniously together, so that not an inch of petticoat or bodice is to be seen, flicking with her duster, peeping, spying, poking her short pointed nose into the cupboards and luggage of her lodgers. She has dark, bright, inquisitive eyes and pretty waved brown hair of which she is proud. She must be about fifty-five years old.

When Frl. Thurau read this description many years later, in a German translation, she objected to nothing except the statement that she "waddled." Like many thousands of other middle-class victims of the inflation, Frl. Thurau had known wealthier days and still felt a sour amusement at finding herself forced to do menial, un-ladylike work. ("If you were a German woman of your class," Christopher once said severely to Kathleen when he was angry with her, "you'd probably be running a brothel, right at this moment!") Poor Frl. Thurau would have been far better off with a brothel than she was with her flatful of sleazy lodgers—Bobby the bartender, Frl. Kost the streetwalker, Frl. Mayr the out-of-work Nazi-minded *jodlerin.* They were all of them apt to get behind with the rent.

Frl. Thurau and Christopher took to each other from the start. On her side, this was because she decided that he was what she called a real gentleman, someone who wouldn't damage the furniture or throw up on the carpet and who would pay his rent on time. She addressed him, coyly and courteously, as "Herr Issyvoo." Christopher found Frl. Thurau sympathetic, even adorable, for a reason which he could never explain to her: she strongly resembled a character in his childhood mythology—Beatrix Potter's Mrs. Tiggy-winkle, the hedgehog-lady who does laundry for the other animals in her neighborhood.

Frl. Thurau would brew cups of coffee or tea and chat with him at any hour of the day. She was fond of exclaiming against the depraved state of Berlin's moral life, but in practice she was nearly unshockable. She had a low opinion of Otto because she regarded him as a parasite who lived off Christopher; but she never objected to what they did together in her flat. She slept on a sofa in the central living room and could therefore hear almost everything which went on in the neighboring bedrooms. When Christopher looked in to say good morning to her, after having enjoyed himself with more than usual energy and noise, she would roll her eyes and say archly, "How sweet love must be!" As for Frl. Kost, Frl. Thurau only disapproved of her profession when she was angry with Frl. Kost for some other reason. An establishment like Frl. Thurau's, where you could do just as you pleased sexually, was described by Berliners as being *sturmfrei* (storm-free).

I wish I could remember what impression Jean Ross—the real-life original of Sally Bowles in *Goodbye to Berlin*—made on Christopher when they first met. But I can't. Art has transfigured life and other people's art has transfigured Christopher's art. What remains with me from those early years is almost entirely Sally. Beside her, like a reproachful elder sister, stands the figure of Jean as I knew her much later. And both Sally and Jean keep being jostled to one side of my memory to make way for the actresses who have played the part of Sally on the stage and on the screen. These, regardless of their merits, are all much more vivid to me than either Jean or Sally; their boldly made-up, brightly lit faces are larger than life.

(Sally Bowles's second name was chosen for her by Christopher because he liked the sound of it and also the looks of its owner, a twenty-year-old American whom he

60

met in Berlin in 1931. The American thought Christopher treated him with "good-humored condescension"; Christopher thought the American aloof. Christopher wasn't then aware that this young man was in the process of becoming a composer and novelist who would need nobody's fiction character to help him make his second name famous. His first name was Paul.)

Studying early photographs of Jean—that long thin handsome white face, that aristocratic nose, that glossy dark hair, those large brown eyes—I can see that she was full of fun and quite conscious of herself as a comic character. Once, a few years later in London, she told Christopher that she was going over to Ostende for the weekend. He asked: "Why on earth—?" She answered, with her brilliant grin: "So I can come back here and be the Woman from Ostende." I wouldn't care to risk letting Sally say that line. If a fiction character is allowed to play-act so self-consciously, there is a danger that the mask may stick to its face. It may lose its identity altogether.

Jean was more essentially British than Sally; she grumbled like a true Englishwoman, with her grin-and-bear-it grin. And she was tougher. She never struck Christopher as being sentimental or the least bit sorry for herself. Like Sally, she boasted continually about her lovers. In those days, Christopher felt certain that she was exaggerating. Now I am not so certain. But when Julie Harris was rehearsing for the part of Sally in the American production of *I Am a Camera,* John van Druten and Christopher discussed with her the possibility that nearly all of Sally's sex life is imaginary; and they agreed that the part should be played so that the audience wouldn't be able to make up its mind, either way. Julie achieved an exquisite ambiguity in her delivery of such lines as:

I had a wonderful, voluptuous little room—with no chairs. That's how I used to seduce men.

One never knew *exactly* what she meant by "seduce."

John van Druten's Sally wasn't quite Christopher's Sally; John made her humor cuter and naughtier. And Julie contributed much of herself to the character. She seemed vulnerable but untouchable (beyond a certain point), quickly moved to childlike delight or dismay, stubbornly obedient to the voices of her fantasies; a bohemian Joan of Arc, battling to defend her way of life from the bourgeoisie. In the last scene but one, the battle appeared to be lost; Julie was about to go back to England in the custody of her domineering mother, defiant but defeated. In token of her humiliation, she wore a frumpy expensive British coat which her mother had made her put on. She looked as miserable as Joan of Arc must have looked when she was forced to stop dressing as a man. Then, in the last scene, Julie entered in the costume she had worn throughout most of the play—a black silk sheath with a black tam-o'-shanter and a flame-colored scarf, the uniform of her revolt. Seeing it, one knew, before she spoke, that her mother had retired routed from the battlefield. The effect was heroic. Bohemia had triumphed. The first-night audience cheered with joy. Julie became a star. And the play became a hit, because of her.

The leading male character in the play is called Christopher Isherwood. In dealing with his sex life or, rather, the lack of it, John used a scene from the novel. Sally asks Christopher if he is in love with her. He answers, "No." Sally replies that she is glad he isn't, "I wanted you to like me from the first minute we met. But I'm glad you're not in love with me. Somehow or other, I couldn't possibly be in love with you." The "somehow or other" may be taken to suggest that Sally knows instinctively that Christopher is homosexual—or it may not. As for Christopher, he once says vaguely that he has wasted a lot of time "hunting for sex," but he doesn't say which kind.

In the film of *I Am a Camera,* Christopher gets drunk and tries to rape Sally. She resists him. After this, they are

62

just good friends. In the musical play *Cabaret,* the male lead is called Clifford Bradshaw. He is an altogether heterosexual American; he has an affair with Sally and fathers her child. In the film of *Cabaret,* the male lead is called Brian Roberts. He is a bisexual Englishman; he has an affair with Sally and, later, with one of Sally's lovers, a German baron. At the end of the film, he is eager to marry Sally. But Sally reminds him of his lapse and hints that there may be others in the future. Brian's homosexual tendency is treated as an indecent but comic weakness to be snickered at, like bed-wetting.

In real life, Jean and Christopher had a relationship which was asexual but more truly intimate than the relationships between Sally and her various partners in the novel, the plays, and the films. Jean moved into a room in the Nollendorfstrasse flat after she met Christopher, early in 1931. Soon they were like brother and sister. They amused each other greatly and enjoyed being together, but both of them were selfish and they often quarreled. Jean never tried to seduce him. But I remember a rainy, depressing afternoon when she remarked, "What a pity we can't make love, there's nothing else to do," and he agreed that it was and there wasn't. Nevertheless, on at least one occasion, because of some financial or housing emergency, they shared a bed without the least embarrassment. Jean knew Otto and Christopher's other sexmates but showed no desire to share them, although he wouldn't have really minded.

I don't think that Jean stayed for more than a few months at the flat. Frl. Thurau was tremendously intrigued by her looks and mannerisms, her makeup, her style of dressing, and, above all, her stories about her love affairs. But she didn't altogether like Jean. For Jean was untidy and inconsiderate; she made a lot of extra work for her landladies. She expected room service and would sometimes order people around in an imperious tone, with English upper-class rudeness. Frl. Thurau preferred male lodgers, anyway.

63

Unlike "Isherwood" and Sally, Christopher and Jean didn't part forever when she left Berlin. Circumstances separated them for long intervals, but they continued to meet, as affectionate friends, throughout the rest of Jean's life. She died in 1973.

Through Stephen Spender, Christopher got to know another of his chief characters-to-be: Gisa Soloweitschik. She was a young Jewish girl who lived with her wealthy parents. Stephen had first met her in Switzerland, some years previously.

In *Goodbye to Berlin,* Gisa is called Natalia Landauer:

She had dark fluffy hair, far too much of it—it made her face, with its sparkling eyes, appear too long and too narrow. She reminded me of a young fox. She shook hands straight from the shoulder in the modern student manner. "In here, please." Her tone was peremptory and brisk.

Natalia is presented as a bossy bluestocking, desperately enthusiastic about culture, sexually frigid and prudish. She takes "Isherwood" in hand immediately, deciding what books he must read, what concerts he must go to, what picture galleries he must visit. At first, "Isherwood" remains mockingly passive toward her attempts to run his life; then he counterattacks by introducing her to Sally Bowles. He does this to test Natalia, not Sally; for he knows in advance how Sally will behave. Sally, as usual, boasts about her lovers; and Natalia is prudishly shocked. She has failed Christopher's test. After this, he and Natalia become temporarily estranged.

In real life, Jean and Gisa never met, so there was no test. But I am sure Gisa could have passed it; she might even have made friends with Jean. Indeed, the Natalia character is a mere caricature of Gisa, as Stephen Spender pointed out to Christopher in a reproachful letter:

64

Gisa always seemed to me a very passionate character, childish in a way, more Russian almost than Jewish, generous and deeply interested in other people. The essential fact to me about your relationship with Gisa is that you talked to her continually about Otto. When you did this, tears of sympathy started into Gisa's eyes. Of course, the actual nature of the relationship was never discussed, but surely Gisa understood and deeply sympathized.

Since "Isherwood" in the novel is never emotionally involved with Otto or with anyone else, it would have been impossible for him to reveal such feelings to Natalia, and thereby give her a chance to show her own warmth and sympathy. Christopher himself was aware that he hadn't given the Natalia character enough warmth. He tried to make up for this toward the end of the story, when Natalia appears transformed by being in love.

In the same letter, Stephen reproached Christopher for his sneers at Natalia's culture worship: "After all, the Nazi attitude towards concerts and culture and Jews is in some respects like yours."

It is true that Christopher was still, at that time, violently prejudiced against culture worship. This prejudice had been formed long before he came to Germany, while he was living in the world of the London studios, salons, and concert halls as secretary to the violinist André Mangeot (called Cheuret in *Lions and Shadows*). There he had grown to hate the gushings of concert audiences and the holy atmosphere of concerts.

But Christopher and the Nazis didn't see eye to eye. The Nazis hated culture itself, because it is essentially international and therefore subversive of nationalism. What they called Nazi culture was a local, perverted, nationalistic cult, by which a few major artists and many minor ones were honored for their Germanness, not their talent. The rest were condemned as alien and decadent and as representing the culture of the Jews. Christopher himself worshipped culture, but his was a very exclusive religion, to be shared only with fellow artists. No one, he said, should dare to praise a work of art unless he himself is a practicing artist. Christopher therefore condemned the vast majority of culture worshippers as being ignorant, presumptuous, and probably insincere—whether they were Jews or non-Jews was irrelevant.

Christopher outgrew this prejudice as he continued to publish books and began to acquire enthusiastic readers. It is not in human nature to condemn your own worshippers, even when they aren't fellow artists.

In *Goodbye to Berlin,* Natalia Landauer has a cousin, Bernhard Landauer. Bernhard helps to run the department store which is owned by Natalia's father. The original of Bernhard Landauer was Wilfrid Israel. Wilfrid Israel and Gisa Soloweitschik weren't related to each other. Their families had no business connections. Wilfrid did, however, help to run a department store founded by his own family. It was one of the biggest in Berlin.

Wilfrid was tall, pale, dark-eyed, soft-spoken, precise in his speech, a smiler who seldom laughed. He looked young for his age. When Christopher met him in 1931, he was thirty-two years old.

As Bernhard in the novel, his profile is described as "over-civilized, finely drawn, beaky":

He smiled and his face was masked with exhaustion: the thought crossed my mind that he was perhaps suffering from a fatal disease.

Again and again, Bernhard is presented as being tired, apathetic. He is evidently quite able to meet the obligations of his important executive job, but he regards it with weary irony. He even confesses to "Isherwood" that the store itself seems unreal to him at times, perhaps part of an hallucination from which he is suffering. This may not be meant literally, but Bernhard certainly is expressing a sense of the meaninglessness of his business life and of himself as a businessman. And he goes much further. When "Isherwood" asks him if he thinks there will be a Nazi Putsch or a Communist revolution, he answers that the question seems to him "a little trivial." He produces a letter from a fanatical anti-Semite, threatening him with death, and remarks that he gets three or four such letters a week. "Isherwood" exclaims: "Surely you'll tell the police?" Bernhard smiles another of his tired smiles:

> My existence is not of such vital importance to myself or to others that the forces of the Law should be called upon to protect me . . .

a reply which suggests apathy rather than courage.

I am quite sure that these aspects of Bernhard's character weren't invented, that they were founded on Christopher's observation of Wilfrid in real life. But a very different Wilfrid appears in *World within World.* Stephen tells how, when the two of them were walking together on Ruegen Island, during a summer holiday in 1932, Wilfrid surprised him

> by outlining a plan of action for the Jews when Hitler seized Germany—an event which he seemed to anticipate as certain. The Jews, he said, should close their businesses and go out into the streets, remaining there, as a protest, and refusing to go home even if the Storm Troopers fired on them. It was only such a united action, within a hopeless situation, which would arouse the conscience of the world.

This was no mere theoretical talk. Less than a year later, when Hitler came to power, Wilfrid began to show himself capable of great courage and firmness of purpose.

Wilfrid's mother had been English and he himself had been born in England. He was a British subject and could therefore leave Germany and settle in England whenever he chose to do so. Instead, he chose to remain in Berlin for seven more years. As it became increasingly clear that no concerted action could be taken against the Nazis by the Jews or by any other group, Wilfrid concentrated on more limited objectives, including the defense of the department store itself, for as long as that might be possible.

The store, like all other Jewish stores, was boycotted from time to time. Wilfrid himself was threatened, arrested, cross-examined, and (I have heard) temporarily imprisoned. Nevertheless, though repeatedly ordered to do so, he refused to dismiss his Jewish employees. He even refused to placate the authorities by making the token gesture of flying the swastika flag over the store building. Meanwhile, he worked to arrange the emigration of as many Jews as possible to foreign countries. A Jew could often be released from a concentration camp on condition that he emigrated immediately. But someone else would have to find the money for this because his own property would have been confiscated already. At length, in 1939, the firm of Israel was taken over by non-Jews; it was the last of its kind to change hands. Wilfrid thus lost most of his power to help others. Just before the outbreak of war, his friends persuaded him to leave for England.

I can understand why Wilfrid chose to discuss his problems as a Jew with Stephen rather than with Christopher. Stephen's parentage was partly Jewish as well as Anglo-German; Wilfrid may well have felt more akin to him. But Stephen must have told Christopher about their conversation. And Christopher, before the time came to write about Wilfrid, must have heard at least something of his defiance of the Nazis.

68

Then why is this aspect of Wilfrid left out of the portrait of Bernhard? Even though the novel had to end in 1933 with "Isherwood"'s departure from Berlin, there could have been a final scene with Bernhard in which his future attitude to the Nazis is foreshown; in which, perhaps, "Isherwood" realizes that he has misunderstood and underestimated Bernhard from the beginning, and feels guilty. Instead, "Isherwood"'s final scene with Bernhard—it is set in the spring of 1932—ends on a note of escapism. Bernhard has been talking about China, saying that in Peking he felt at home for the first time in his life. "Isherwood" suggests that he go back there. The suggestion sounds slightly contemptuous; it seems to equate Peking with the culture worship which "Isherwood" despises. For Bernhard is a culture devotee like Natalia, though an infinitely more sophisticated one. Bernhard replies calmly yes, he will go to Peking, but on condition that "Isherwood" comes with him as his guest and that they start that very evening. "Isherwood" makes excuses. He takes Bernhard's offer as a joke, anyway. It is only much later, after Bernhard is dead, that "Isherwood" becomes convinced that the offer was serious, after all. "I recognize it as Bernhard's last, most daring, and most cynical experiment upon us both." In other words, Bernhard has played an inverted form of Russian roulette, in which five of the chances are death and only the sixth chance an escape from death into a faraway land —a land where he can believe in his own existence.

Christopher was accustomed to say that he never wrote about people he didn't like—because, when he disliked someone, he simply didn't find him interesting. This was a show-off remark, typical of Christopher in his arrogant mood. Christopher did find Wilfrid intensely interesting, despite the fact that there was a great deal of hostility between them. Nevertheless, his hostility may well have prevented him from seeing and describing Wilfrid as a hero.

69

He is sympathetic, charming. But his gestures, offering me a glass of wine or a cigarette, are clothed in arrogance, the arrogant humility of the East.

"Isherwood" stresses the "Oriental" aspect of Bernhard. In this case, the epithet seems to refer to the Chinese. But Christopher had a prejudice, at that period in his life, against another Oriental race, the Hindus. He found something repellent—that is to say, personally disturbing—in Hindu humility and passivity and the arrogance he felt that it concealed. As a matter of principle, he sided with the Hindus against the British raj and agreed that they had every right to treat their English conquerors with arrogance. Still, he identified instinctively with the English. And so he found deeply disturbing the picture of himself confronted by one of these humble-arrogant figures, a Hindu, or a Wilfrid—someone who "knew" about life and whose knowledge might be superior to his. "He is not going to tell me what he is really thinking or feeling, and he despises me because I do not know." This prejudice of Christopher's, I now realize, sprang from fear—fear of the unknown something which the Hindus knew, the something which he might one day have to accept and which might change his life. As a kind of mock-Hindu, Wilfrid aroused that prejudice.

Earlier in their relationship, there has been a brief, inconclusive showdown between "Isherwood" and Bernhard. "Isherwood" accuses him of showing hostility by adopting this mock-humble attitude. "Actually, you're the least humble person I ever met." Bernhard replies with "Oriental" obliqueness:

I wonder if you are right . . . I think not altogether. But partly . . . Yes, there is some quality in you which attracts me and which I very much envy, and yet this very quality also arouses my antagonism.

70

Bernhard sums himself up by adding: "I'm afraid that I am a quite unnecessarily complicated piece of mechanism." Which may be taken to imply that he thinks "Isherwood" quite unnecessarily crude.

There is an enigmatic remark in a letter written by Christopher to Stephen Spender in November 1932. After telling Stephen that he has seen Wilfrid lately but only once, Christopher adds: "He is kind. But he condemns me in his heart." What did Christopher think Wilfrid condemned him for? I believe Christopher suspected that Wilfrid was a severely repressed homosexual and that, as such, he condemned Christopher for his aggressive frankness about his own sex life. If Christopher did indeed suspect this, it would have been characteristic of him to be extra frank with Wilfrid, in order to jolt him into frankness about himself.

In the novel, it seems to be implied that what Bernhard is hiding is a romantic attachment to "Isherwood." The shared trip to China which Bernhard proposes is made to sound like an elopement. Whether Wilfrid was or wasn't homosexual is neither here nor there. Of one thing I am certain, he wasn't in love with Christopher. I therefore find the hint contained in the novel offensive, vague as it is, and I am embarrassed to know that Wilfrid read it.

The story of Bernhard Landauer ends with the news of Bernhard's death. "Isherwood" overhears two men talking about it at a restaurant in Prague, in the spring of 1933, just after he himself has left Germany for good. One of them has read in a newspaper that Bernhard has died of heart failure and both take it for granted that he has really been killed by the Nazis.

The killing of Bernhard was merely a dramatic necessity. In a novel such as this one, which ends with the outbreak of political persecution, one death at least is a must. No other major character in *Goodbye to Berlin* has been killed, and Bernhard is the most appropriate victim, being a prominent Jew. The timing of his death, so early in the persecution, is unconvincing, however—unless he was murdered by mistake. The Nazis would surely have waited long enough to prepare some false charges against him. The liquidation of such an important figure in the business world would have caused a lot of bad publicity abroad. Wilfrid himself survived for years, despite his defiance. The Nazis did kill him in the end—but that, one can almost say, was by accident.

Having settled in England, Wilfrid devoted himself to helping his fellow refugees. After the French defeat, many of them were temporarily interned. When Wilfrid visited the internment camps he used to say, "This is where I ought to be, too." But, as a British subject, he was free. He enlisted in the Civil Defence.

By 1943, there were many Jews who had escaped from Germany and Austria and found their way to Spain and Portugal. In March of that year, Wilfrid flew to Portugal to arrange for some of the younger refugees to emigrate to Palestine. Within two months, he had done this. On June 1, he boarded a plane to fly back to London. Among his fellow passengers was the famous actor Leslie Howard.

Over the Bay of Biscay, three hundred miles off Cape Finisterre, their plane met eight Nazi fighters. It is almost certain that the fighters came upon them by chance, while returning from an unsuccessful attempt to locate two of their own U-boats. Unarmed airliners flying between Lisbon and London were very seldom attacked, though they often carried important people. But, on this occasion, the Nazis had some reason to suspect that Churchill himself might be on board; they knew that he would be flying back from a conference in Algiers at about that time. There were no survivors.

Christopher first met Gerald Hamilton in the winter of 1930–31. At that period, Gerald's social position was solidly respectable; he was the sales representative of the London *Times* for Germany and had his office in Berlin.

In *Mr. Norris and I,* one of Gerald's several autobiographical books, he describes how he obtained this job:

This serves to show with what ease anybody can today obtain a responsible position, no matter what his past life might have been. I was able to provide the usual references; I did not have to tell a single lie, and I found myself suddenly launched into this most respectable and responsible post. The ease with which I obtained it is only another illustration of the vast scale of hypocrisy upon which the standards of our civilization really depend.

Good old, bad old Gerald! One can't help admiring his tactics. He asks *The Times* for a job. *The Times* gives him one and is promptly denounced for its hypocrisy. How dare it pretend to have standards of right and wrong if it hires people like Gerald, who outrage those standards? How dare it pretend ignorance of, for example, these two facts?

That, during the First World War, Gerald had been imprisoned and later interned in England because of his "openly expressed pro-German and anti-British sentiments" and "enemy association." (This had inspired Horatio Bottomley to write an article entitled "Hang Hamilton!")

And that, during 1924 and 1925, Gerald had spent several months in various French and Italian prisons, charged with swindling a Milanese jeweler out of a pearl necklace.

But now Gerald betrays himself into admitting that he has a double standard. While condemning *The Times* for employing a notorious traitor and thief, he maintains that he was really neither the one nor the other. Gerald wasn't a traitor, because he wasn't British—well, technically, perhaps, but not in his heart, which was Irish through and through. Call him an Irish rebel, if you like, and a potential martyr to the cause of Irish freedom. He had proved his loyalty to Ireland by corresponding with Roger Casement, when Casement was in Berlin trying to get German help for a rising against the British. (Gerald must have expressed himself with extreme caution, for no evidence of his participation in this plot had ever been produced against him.)

As for the pearl necklace—that accusation was really just another technicality. If the jeweler hadn't sent in his bill so much earlier than Gerald had expected him to, and if Gerald himself hadn't delayed so long in taking care of the matter ("My usual inclination towards a policy of *laisser aller*"), all the resulting unpleasantness could have been avoided. At worst, it was merely, as you might say, robbing Peter to pay Paul—and, anyhow, Gerald would never have become involved in the affair if he hadn't wanted to oblige a friend who was in financial difficulties . . . Gerald had the art of talking like this without showing any genuine indignation and without exactly defending himself. He was well aware of his own double standard and he couldn't help giggling in the midst of his solemn sincerities. Having giggled, he would skip to happier themes: the many royal and titled ladies and gentlemen he had known; the palaces, castles, and chateaux he had been a guest at; the exotic meals he had eaten and the now extinct wines he had drunk.

It seems to me that Christopher "recognized" Gerald Hamilton as Arthur Norris, his character-to-be, almost as soon as he set eyes on him. When William Bradshaw (the I-narrator of the novel) meets Mr. Norris on a train, their encounter seems remembered, not imagined, although its setting is fictitious. In these first sentences, Hamilton and Norris are still identical:

My first impression was that the stranger's eyes were of an unusually light blue . . . Startled and innocently naughty, they were the eyes of a schoolboy surprised in the act of breaking one of the rules . . . His smile had great charm. His hands were white, small, and beautifully manicured. He had a large blunt fleshy nose and a chin which seemed to have slipped sideways. It was like a broken concertina. Above his ripe red cheeks, his forehead was sculpturally white, like marble. A queerly cut fringe of dark grey hair lay across it, compact, thick, and heavy. After a moment's examination, I realized, with extreme interest, that he was wearing a wig.

From Christopher's point of view, Gerald was enchantingly "period." He introduced Wystan, Stephen, and other friends to him, and soon they were all treating him like an absurd but nostalgic artwork which has been rediscovered by a later generation. Gerald vastly enjoyed this new aspect of himself and began to play up to it. No doubt he realized that these naïve young men who marveled at his wig, his courtly mannerisms, and his police record were unconsciously becoming his accomplices. They were making him acceptable in circles which he had never entered before—the circles of modern bohemia, which would welcome him *because* of his shady past, not in spite of it. Not all bohemians are poor. Gerald could look forward to establishing fresh contacts which might be advantageous.

(This reminds me of a charming young man who was briefly welcomed into those same circles because he admitted frankly to being a cat burglar and seemed therefore "pure in heart," according to the Lane-Layard creed. The homes of some of his admirers were subsequently burgled, but nothing was proved against him.)

Gerald therefore didn't really mind when he found that his new friends were referring to him as "a most incredible old crook"; although he would always protest, for form's sake. On one occasion, a fellow Hamilton connoisseur remarked to Christopher, "It seems that Gerald has had a moral lapse"; to which Christopher replied, "Gerald having a moral lapse is like someone falling off a footstool at the bottom of the Grand Canyon." Christopher was pleased with this *mot* and repeated it to Gerald, who giggled, wriggled, and exclaimed, *"Really!"*

Aside from Gerald's temperamental extravagance, which drove him to run up bills he knew he couldn't possibly pay, his wrongdoing seems to have been almost entirely related to his role as a go-between. If you wanted to sell a stolen painting to a collector who didn't mind enjoying it in private, to smuggle arms into a foreign country, to steal a contract away from a rival firm, to be decorated with a medal of honor which you had done nothing to deserve, to get your criminal dossier extracted from the archives, then Gerald was delighted to try to help you, and he quite often succeeded. All such transactions involved bribery in one form or another. And then there were Gerald's operational expenses. And certain unforeseen obstacles which arose—probably with Gerald's assistance—and had to be overcome, at considerable cost. All in all, a great deal of money would pass from hand to hand. The hands in the middle were Gerald's, and they were sticky . . . Of course, in so-called legitimate business, there is a phrase to describe and justify what Gerald did; it is called taking a commission. And if, in order to practice his trade, Gerald had to hobnob with buyable chiefs of police, bloodthirsty bishops, stool pigeons, double agents, blackmailers, hatchet men, secretaries and mistresses of politicians, millionairesses even more ruthless than the husbands they had survived— well, that is what's called being a man of the world.

Like all deeply dishonest people, he made the relatively honest look hypocritical and cowardly. Only a saint could have remained in contact with him and not been contaminated. And, by associating with him, you incurred some responsibility, even if it was only one tenth of one percent, for the really vile things which many of *his* associates had undoubtedly done. I remember a man, he was connected with French counterespionage, whom Christopher met through Gerald; he had the most evil face I have ever seen in my life.

Gerald didn't look evil, but, beneath his amiable surface, he was an icy cynic. He took it for granted that everybody would grab and cheat if he dared. His cynicism made him astonishingly hostile toward people of whom he was taking some advantage; at unguarded moments, he would speak of them with brutal contempt. In Christopher's case, Gerald's cynicism was justified. He would certainly have let Gerald tempt him into serious lawbreaking if he hadn't been so cautious by nature.

Looking back on Gerald's career, I find his misdeeds tiresome rather than amusing. His dishonesty was tiresome because it was so persistent; he was like a greedy animal which you can't leave alone in the kitchen, even for an instant. And yet, what did all his intrigues obtain for him? He used to boast coyly of his coups, to hint at having netted "a cool thou" or "a positively glacial sum"; but when you pressed him for details, he became evasive. Probably he was ashamed of the self-indulgence with which he squandered whatever money he had grabbed. Throughout his life, he was pestered by creditors. The strange truth is that he was an amateur, hopelessly unbusinesslike, romantic, and unmodern in his methods. Crime, as he practiced it, doesn't pay. It is as demanding and unrewarding as witchcraft.

Nevertheless, despite the anxieties amidst which he lived, Gerald genuinely enjoyed himself. And he shared his enjoyment with his friends. When the weather was dull and life was gloomy, he cheered you up by the charm of his absurdity. He would dress for some humdrum gathering as if for a brilliant social event and thus almost manage to turn it into one. He could make you feel you were at a banquet when, in fact, you were supping off scrambled eggs and *vin ordinaire*. He laughed at your jokes, he flattered you, he was sincerely delighted when you were pleased. He was therefore liked by many people who thoroughly disapproved of him. Others, including Frl. Thurau, adored him without any reservations. He referred to her as La Divine Thurau.

Gerald had an Irish genius for embracing causes with passion and taking sides furiously in a dispute. The passion and the fury were often temporary, and he felt no embarrassment in changing his convictions later. At one time or another, he was a pacifist, a crusader for Irish independence (no matter what that might cost in the blood of others), a near-Communist, a right-wing extremist, a critic of the Vatican's foreign policy, a devout Catholic. Not unnaturally, he was suspected of having ulterior motives; often, no doubt, he had. But it is difficult to find anything sinister in the hard work he did for the Fight the Famine Council and the Save the Children Fund, after the First World War. And he often wrote letters to the press, in favor of legalized abortion, prison reform, and the abolition of capital punishment, which were admirably outspoken and lucid.

Mr. Norris fails to reveal what was the most enduring bond between Gerald and Christopher, their homosexuality. When it came to breaking the laws which had been made against the existence of their tribe, Christopher was happy to be Gerald's fellow criminal.

FIVE

Edward and Wystan had read *The Memorial* in manuscript, shortly before or after the New Year. Both had praised it, each in his own peculiar language—to which Christopher was so accustomed that he never reflected how bizarre it would look on a book jacket:

> *Upward:* All the trumpets spoke and a man with gray ears wept in torrents of sulphur over Charlesworth, Lily and the attempted suicide of Edward Blake.
> *Auden:* You alone have had the courage and the reagents to bring out the Figure in that carpet. May I also utter a word of praise for Isherwood's weather.

Christopher didn't doubt the sincerity of their enthusiasm. Nevertheless, he was still worried. These were his closest friends. The relation between them and himself was essentially telepathic. Mightn't they have understood telepathically what it was that he had wanted to express in this book and thus overlooked the fact that he had failed to express it? And, if this was so, how would the book seem to untelepathic Jonathan Cape? Cape had published Christopher's first novel, *All the Conspirators,* in 1928. Now, in March 1931, he was making up his mind whether or not he should publish *The Memorial.* Christopher left for London on March 10, to be on the spot and get the news of Cape's decision with a minimum of delay.

During their separation, Christopher had made peace with Kathleen by default. She was a passive fortress and he had stopped attacking her. What was the use? She was impregnable, anyway. They had exchanged a few letters, in which their differences were never referred to.

The day after Christopher's arrival, Kathleen wrote in her diary: "We sat talking in my room till nearly one A.M. It was almost as it used to be long ago." But, a day or two later, she had become anxious:

> Fear the state of things is worse than ever and he looks so far from well, in a way he is glad to be back but is restless and not happy, and absorbed in Otto who is more a cause of misery than happiness.

It seems extraordinary to me, now, that Christopher would have so far exposed himself as to let her see that Otto was "a cause of misery" to him—thus admitting to a failure in his homosexual life and confirming her prejudice against it. Even in his late twenties, he still had a childlike urge to confide in her which he seemingly couldn't control.

On March 14, Jonathan Cape turned down *The Memorial,* firmly and politely: "I realize that there is a risk in letting you go, as you may make a connection elsewhere which will endure. It certainly should be published."

The rejection of your second novel—quite a common experience—is more painful than any number of rejections of your first; at least, Christopher found it so. As long as no publisher had accepted a book by him, he could regard all publishers as the Others, mere merchants whose literary judgment was worth nothing, except money. But Jonathan Cape couldn't be thus dismissed. He had shown himself to be a man of rare taste, a non-merchant and other than the Others, when he had accepted *All the Conspirators* after two publishers had rejected it. Christopher's self-confidence was shaken.

In the event of a refusal by Cape, Stephen Spender had advised Christopher to leave the novel with Curtis Brown, the literary agents, and let them try to place it elsewhere. He now met with a representative of Curtis Brown and was given an expensive lunch, from which he rose with his hopes irrationally raised.

Meanwhile, Stephen was loyally awaiting him in Berlin. Christopher wrote telling Stephen to "hold the fort a little longer." Holding the fort evidently included coping with some kind of trouble which Otto had got himself into. Kathleen records that Stephen wired back: "All well Otto." Christopher returned to Germany on March 21.

In June or early July, Christopher, Stephen, and Otto went to Sellin on Ruegen Island for a summer holiday. Here Wystan joined them, rather unwillingly. Unlike Christopher, who felt indecent until he was darkly sunburned, Wystan had no use for the beach and the sea. His white-skinned body, when exposed, became painfully pink. He preferred rainy weather. During much of the day, he shut himself up in his bedroom with the blinds pulled down, ignored the summer, and wrote. I suppose he was working on *The Orators*.

Stephen was writing too, though he spent much of his time out of doors, keeping Christopher and Otto company. He was recording their holiday with his camera. This had an automatic shutter release, so Stephen himself wasn't necessarily excluded from the record. In a recent letter to me, he recalls that:

with a masturbatory camera designed for narcissists I took—or it took—the most famous photograph in the history of the world, of US THREE.

Stephen, in the middle, has his arms around Wystan and Christopher and an expression on his face which suggests an off-duty Jesus relaxing with "these little ones." Christopher, compared with the others, is such a very little one that he looks as if he is standing in a hole.

Stephen also took pictures of Otto—some absurd, some animally beautiful: Otto in a loincloth, strumming on a guitar and pretending to be an Hawaiian boy; Otto caught unconsciously taking the pose of a Michelangelo nude on the Sistine Chapel ceiling. How delighted Otto would have been to know that in 1974 several of these pictures would be displayed, as part of a television documentary, before an estimated five million British viewers! And how delightedly—and wrongly—Stephen, Wystan, and Christopher would have assumed, on the basis of this single fact, that the England of the nineteen-seventies would be an earthly paradise of love and liberty.

All in all, this Ruegen visit wasn't a success. Wystan soon returned to England. Christopher and Otto squabbled, because Otto spent his evenings dancing with beach girls at the local casino and didn't come home until the small hours. On the last day, Christopher cut his toe on a sharp bit of tin while wading into the sea. The cut festered and he was a semi-cripple for several weeks after his return to Berlin.

Meanwhile, Stephen had been in Salzburg. When he wrote that he would like to rejoin Christopher and asked if there was a room free for him, Christopher replied:

> I think I could find you something cheaper two doors away. I think it is better if we don't all live right on top of each other, don't you? I believe that was partly the trouble at Ruegen. Anyhow I'm resolved not to live with Otto again for a long time. Because, these last days, when he's been in to see me for quite short periods, have been absolutely wonderful . . .

This is the first indication that Stephen has been getting on Christopher's nerves. Christopher only mentions Otto because he is embarrassed to have to admit that he doesn't want Stephen living in the same apartment with him. Stephen took the hint. Instead of returning to Berlin, he went back to London.

Curtis Brown had been unable to find a publisher for *The Memorial;* it had been rejected by three more of them, Davies, Secker, and Duckworth. Stephen now took the manuscript personally to John Lehmann, who was managing the Hogarth Press for Leonard and Virginia Woolf. Stephen had already praised *The Memorial* to Lehmann as one of the masterpieces of their generation. Stephen's extravagant enthusiasm could sometimes be a danger to its object, but Lehmann wasn't deterred. He read the manuscript, decided that he liked it very much, and promised Stephen to do everything he could to persuade the Woolfs that they must publish it. When Christopher heard this news, he felt ashamed of himself for having rebuffed Stephen and wrote to him warmly, thanking him for all his efforts on behalf of *The Memorial:* "If the Hogarth do take it, it will be entirely because of you."

Not long after this, Christopher reported to Stephen:

I had a letter from Curtis Brown to say that the Hogarth wants to read All the Conspirators before deciding about The Memorial. I'm afraid that'll be its death-blow, but am writing to my mother to forward a copy. If you are writing to Lehmann do implore him not to be put off by the Conspirators. Tell him I'll write my next book in *any* style they like—even that of Hatter's Castle.

(This was A. J. Cronin's first novel. Christopher hadn't read it yet; he despised it simply because it was a best-seller. When he did read it later, he was surprised to find that it moved him.)

> If the Hogarth (or Blackwell or the Universal Press or the Society for Promoting Christian Knowledge, for that matter) would only take my novel I feel I could put up with anything that's billed to happen to me this winter . . . There is always the possibility of the Prussian government being overthrown next Sunday by the Nazis and all foreigners expelled.

(Christopher liked to play the front-line alarmist for the benefit of stay-at-home civilians; he was apt to forget that Stephen had been in the front line too. He refers to a referendum which was to be held on August 2, to decide the fate of the Bruening administration. On this occasion, it was saved; but, in any case, there was no real danger of a Nazi takeover that year.)

> Jean talks of going to America in the winter. Hamilton has openly declared for Russia. Otto is a champion athlete.

(Jean never did go to America. She may have got the idea of doing so from an American whom she and Christopher had recently met, the original of Clive in *Goodbye to Berlin*. Like Clive, the American thrilled them by inviting them to come with him to the States and then dashed their hopes by leaving Berlin abruptly, without saying goodbye.

Gerald Hamilton, in *Mr. Norris and I,* writes that "I was in touch with the leading German Communists, who alone, as a political party, represented my point of view on social matters." That summer, he had been making speeches on his favorite reform projects at meetings sponsored by the Communists. The London *Times* heard of this and told him to resign from his job with them. So Gerald decided to look to the Left for a new paymaster.

He must have "declared for Russia" by making some sort of statement to the press.

I forget what kind of "champion athlete" Otto had become. Probably he had joined a local sports club and won a few races. His bursts of energy were always brief.)

In August, Christopher met Klaus Mann, Thomas Mann's eldest son; this was his first contact with a member of that family. Klaus and Christopher took to each other from the start. They were to become intimate friends who seldom saw each other, for Klaus was always on the move.

Like most other people who knew Klaus, Christopher supposed that it couldn't be easy for him, as a writer, to be his father's son. But Klaus was evidently able to accept Thomas, Nobel Prize and all; he didn't waste his life shivering enviously in that huge paternal shadow. Nor did he affect the grandeur and alienated gloom of so many European literary men. His manner was easy, lively, witty; yet he was capable of caring deeply about his friends and the causes he believed in, and of fighting on their behalf. Christopher found this combination lovable. At the same time, far down beneath Klaus's brightness, courage, apparent freedom from self-pity, there was an obstinate drive toward self-destruction. Christopher didn't become fully aware of it until shortly before Klaus's suicide in 1949.

On September 2, Stephen, who was still in London, phoned Kathleen to tell her that the Hogarth Press had accepted *The Memorial.* He must have wanted to let her have the pleasure of telegraphing the news to Christopher, which was truly considerate of him. Christopher was delighted, of course. But he soon managed to find grounds for renewed anxiety—in the devaluation of the British pound. Late in September, he wrote to Stephen:

I have heard nothing more of *The Memorial*. Can it be that they are backing out of it owing to this crisis? All things are possible. The pound was at 15 but is better today. I am living chiefly on what I earn by going for morning walks with a German-American boy who says Yep and No, Sir.

A few days after this, Christopher reports that the German-American boy, in the midst of some game, has

stuck a pointed stick into my eyelid about a millimetre from my eye. I am bathing the wound now and eating grapes supplied by Frl. Thurau, who really is the world's best landlady.

A standard tableau—played many times previously and often to be replayed: Christopher sensually enjoying his role of martyr-invalid.

Germany is pretty bloody. This Revolution-Next-Week atmosphere has stopped being quite such a joke and somehow the feeling that nothing really will happen only makes it worse. I think everybody everywhere is being ground slowly down by an enormous tool. I feel myself getting smaller and smaller . . . Gisa leaves tonight for Paris. She would like you to write to her and will send me or us both her address. It seems strange that that household has come to an end.

Thus Gisa Soloweitschik, like Natalia Landauer, made a fortunate exit from the Berlin scene before the coming of Hitler. She settled with her parents in France, where she married a Frenchman. Gisa and her husband were still there after the war. Stephen kept in touch with her, but Christopher failed to do so.

This job lasts till the end of October or possibly November. And then? Well, there is perhaps a vacancy in Hamilton's new "Anglo-American News Agency," which looks like being a pretty good hive of Bolshevik crooks . . . Did you say you had Mirsky's book on Lenin? I should be awfully grateful if you'd send it sometime.

I am depressed, but only up to a point. I spend most of the day laughing with Hamilton over his classic struggles with the bailiff.

The visits of the bailiff were due to Gerald's loss of his job with *The Times.* This had automatically put an end to his credit. His creditors were now trying to repossess the furniture and other valuables which he hadn't paid for—that is to say, almost everything in his flat. I can't remember if the "Anglo-American News Agency" ever actually came into being. Gerald obviously had to have a Communist-front organization of some sort, or at least a plan for one, before he could appeal to the Communist Party for financial help.

But the German Communists depended largely on Russian money, and here Gerald found himself up against hard-nosed professionals instead of the greedy, gullible amateurs he was used to. The Russians demanded results, and they were slow payers even after they had got them. According to Gerald, the German party officials often had to wait months for their salaries to come through. As Gerald's financial disappointment in the party grew, he became more and more critical of it. Through his eyes, Christopher began to see its seamy side—its private feuds, its inefficiency, its bewildered efforts to follow the changing tactics dictated by Moscow.

Christopher took it for granted that the Communists saw right through Gerald; that they valued him merely as a gentlemanly go-between whose appearance and fine manners would be helpful in their dealings with the gentlemen of the opposition. Still, Christopher couldn't help feeling sentimentally shocked that the Party of the Workers could thus forget its proletarian ethics and stoop to use this unclean instrument.

Amidst these doubts, Christopher was reading about Lenin with reverence and enthusiasm. Hence, he was capable of asking Stephen for the Mirsky book, alluding to "Bolshevik crooks," and decorating his signature with a hammer and sickle, all in the same letter. He was what party dialectitions used, in those days, to call "unclear."

That autumn, Jean got herself a theatrical job—a tiny one, but in a tremendous production: Max Reinhardt's *Tales of Hoffmann,* which opened on November 28. This was one of the last great spectacles of the pre-Hitler Berlin theater and, in a sense, Reinhardt's farewell to it. Christopher was to meet him and his family in their Californian exile, during the war.

Of all the opera's splendid stage pictures, the one most vivid in my memory is that of the Grand Canal in Venice, with a gondola traveling down it. In order to make the gondola appear to move, Reinhardt moved the set itself. The huge palace fronts swung slowly around as the gondola rounded a curve of the canal. The movement of the palaces caused a profound mechanical rumbling which was sometimes louder than the music but which nevertheless seemed part of the intended effect. It was magnificently sinister, like the tread of doom.

In the course of the ball scene at the Venetian palace of the courtesan Giulietta, several pairs of lovers were carried onto the stage. Each pair reclined on a litter, locked in each other's arms. These lovers were merely extras and few members of the audience can have paid any attention to their embraces, once they had made their entrance, for a dazzling corps de ballet was performing in the middle of the stage. But Christopher watched one pair of lovers intently, through opera glasses, until the end of the scene. Even so, he couldn't be sure if what Jean had told him was true—that she had sex with her partner in full view of the audience at every single performance.

The Memorial was published on February 17, 1932. There were a few really favorable notices. The best of them was in the *Granta*. I remember how one reviewer remarked that he had at first thought the novel contained a disproportionately large number of homosexual characters but had decided, on further reflection, that there *were* a lot more homosexuals about, nowadays.

That spring, Francis returned to Germany. Soon after their reunion, he told Christopher that he didn't want to stay cooped up in Berlin. He planned to take a house in the country, drink less, spend a lot of time out of doors, go to bed early, and be healthy. He urged Christopher to join him in this experiment. Christopher promised to think it over—he was inclined to say yes, for several reasons. Seeing Francis again, he felt a renewed affection for him; there was no special person to keep him in Berlin, now that his affair with Otto had at last cooled off; living with Francis would be far cheaper than the Nollendorfstrasse, since he would only have to pay for his food; also, he had started work on an autobiographical book (which would one day become *Lions and Shadows*) and he knew that the dullness of the country would make it easier for him to concentrate on it.

Francis had already engaged Erwin Hansen, Karl Giese's friend from the Institute, as his cook and housekeeper and told him to find someone to help with the housework. So Erwin hired a boy named Heinz. On March 13, shortly before Francis, Erwin, and Heinz were due to leave for the country, Christopher and Heinz met. Meeting Heinz was what finally decided Christopher to go with them.

It must surely have been Erwin who had arranged that they should live at Mohrin. Perhaps he had friends there. Perhaps his friends even owned the house which Francis was to rent. Only some such personal motives could explain his choice of that particular village out of so many almost identical others. Mohrin was northeast of Berlin, near what was then the Polish frontier. (Now it is inside Poland and is spelled Moryń.)

As a very young man, Christopher had read Turgenev and Chekhov and had yearned romantically for the steppe, the immense land ocean which stretches east, unbounded, to the Ural Mountains and then endlessly on across Siberia. At Mohrin, he was actually on the edge of that ocean. But the ocean seemed less inspiring, here, than it had seemed in London, ten years earlier. God, it was flat.

All the houses of all these villages had double windows, to keep out the cold of the long, terrible winters. Now the spring was beginning—a short poignant episode of awareness, between the numbness of the snow and the stupor of the summer heat. In the spring you might become fully conscious for a few weeks, look around you and decide to leave this village forever—or fall in love with someone you had known all your life and stay here with him until you died. The poplars had new leaves and the lilac was coming into bloom. The ice was cracking on the Mohrinersee, the dull little local lake; it would be stored in cellars to refrigerate food during the hot months ahead. Showers of rain followed each other. The snow had melted into mud. You could work at home and then walk around the lake, and then have a few drinks at the inn, and then come back home. Or you could omit the lake, or the inn. Or you could drink first and walk later. That was the extent of your choice. Whenever you stepped out of doors, after the first week, it was with the certainty that you would never meet anybody whose face you didn't recognize. This was a place where, to use a favorite expression of Frl. Thurau's, "the foxes say goodnight to each other."

As soon as Francis realized that Christopher and Heinz were going to bed together, he announced that Christopher must pay half of Heinz's wages. Christopher agreed to this with more amusement than indignation; it was the way Francis was. He said nothing to Heinz. But Erwin, who thought that Francis was being stingy and who was anyhow a bit of a mischief-maker, told Heinz what had happened. Heinz went outside the house and burst into tears. It was his declaration of love.

Christopher had no hesitation in falling in love with Heinz. It seemed most natural to him that they two should be drawn together. Heinz had found his elder brother; Christopher had found someone emotionally innocent, entirely vulnerable and uncritical, whom he could protect and cherish as his very own. He was deeply touched and not in the least apprehensive. He wasn't yet aware that he was letting himself in for a relationship which would be far more serious than any he had had in his life.

Heinz was a slim boy of about seventeen with large brown eyes. His nose had been broken with a brick wielded by one of his age mates when he was still a child; it had a funny but attractive dip in the middle. Heinz had some difficulty in breathing through it. This nose, together with his big protruding lips, round head, and close-curling hair, gave him a somewhat Negroid appearance. He was delighted when Christopher called him Nigger Boy, and he used to repeat the nickname to himself, chuckling. His face was young and good-natured, with a wide grin, when he was happy. When he wasn't, it became older and you saw the grim sullenness of the peasant. He hadn't at all the air of a city dweller. He only looked at ease dressed in working clothes, a thick magenta sweater and a cap with a shiny peak, which he wore on one side of his head; in his best suit, he seemed disguised and self-conscious.

Heinz's father was alive but Heinz seldom saw him. He had no brothers or sisters, no girlfriend, no particular boyfriends. He lived with his grandmother, an old lady who looked exactly as he would look in his seventies. The grandmother had a basement flat which she kept so hot that you began to sweat when you entered it. If anyone suggested opening a window, she would growl, "I don't heat for the street."

Francis soon got tired of Mohrin and began going off to Berlin for long weekends, taking Erwin with him. Thus Christopher found himself keeping house with Heinz. This was a kind of happiness which he had never experienced before; he now realized that he had always desired it. Unlike Otto, or any of the boys he had known from the bars, Heinz actually enjoyed work for work's sake. No lover, however literary, could have shared Christopher's work with him. But Heinz did the next best thing; while Christopher wrote, Heinz collaborated with him indirectly by sweeping the floors, tidying up the garden, cooking the meals. Whenever Christopher had written while Otto was nearby, he had been conscious of Otto's restlessness and boredom and had felt responsible for it. His effort to go on writing became an assertion of his will against Otto's, although Otto was probably unaware that he was interfering with Christopher's work; he merely wanted attention. As for Heinz, he was certainly quite unaware how much he was helping Christopher. This odd pair, enjoying these few days of privacy and occupation with pauses for eating and making love, were absurdly like the most ordinary happily married heterosexual couple.

Then Francis and Erwin would return, bringing with them one or more boys from the Berlin bars. By now, Francis and Heinz had taken a rooted dislike to each other. Francis found fault with Heinz at every opportunity; Heinz became sullen in his presence. Christopher retaliated by being unpleasant to Francis's boys. This didn't create any serious hostility between Francis and Christopher; each understood the other's motives too well. Francis had asked Christopher to come with him to Mohrin on the assumption that their life there would be a dialogue between two intimate friends, with Erwin and other employees kept in the background, on an inferior level. Christopher had violated what Francis regarded as an unspoken agreement by treating Heinz as an intimate. Francis felt betrayed, and Christopher didn't blame him.

As the weeks passed, Francis and his household caused a scandal in the village, merely by being themselves. Someone denounced them to the police. Erwin the diplomatist prevented an official inquiry from being made. But it became obvious that they would all have to leave before long.

Meanwhile, Stephen Spender arrived in Berlin and came out to pay them a short visit. Christopher had tried hard to discourage him from doing this, but Stephen had seemed unconscious of Christopher's attitude. He hated having Stephen and Stephen's camera invade the scene of his love affair with Heinz. Clicking that camera, Stephen seemed to mock and expose you, even while he flattered you by his piercing curiosity. Jealously, almost superstitiously, Christopher feared that Stephen would somehow alter his image in Heinz's eyes and make Heinz unable to go on loving him. (It was Stephen, not Christopher, who ought to have said, "I am a camera," in those days. Now we survivors can feel nothing but gratitude to him for his tireless clicking. He saved so many bits of our youth for us.)

Stephen soon left Mohrin, however, and there was no open quarrel. When he had gone, Christopher felt immediate relief from his own fears and aversion. He even regretted the loss of Stephen's lively company and wrote to him in the normal tone of friendship, describing the humors and horrors of country life. In view of Christopher's ambivalent attitude, these letters now ring shockingly false.

Early in July, they were together again, back at Sellin on Ruegen Island, with Heinz and with Stephen's younger brother, Humphrey. During this holiday, there was less tension between them—largely because of Humphrey's presence. Humphrey was a charming, easygoing, friendly young man. Like Stephen, he was a photographer—soon to become professional—but he was definitely not a camera. Christopher never thought of him as a menace to his relationship with Heinz. Humphrey would never invade anybody's privacy.

He did, however, once ask Christopher an unusual personal question; it was while the two of them were out walking alone together. Humphrey said suddenly, "You speak German so well—tell me, why don't you ever use the subjunctive mood?" Christopher had to admit that he didn't know how to. In the days when he had studied German, he had left the subjunctive to be dealt with later, since it wasn't absolutely essential and he was in a hurry. By this time, he could hop through the language without its aid, like an agile man with only one leg. But now Christopher set himself to master the subjunctive. Very soon, he had done so. Proud of this accomplishment, he began showing it off whenever he talked: "Had it not been for him, I should never have asked myself what I would do if they were to—" etc., etc. Humphrey was much amused.

SIX

On August 4, 1932, Christopher began another visit to
England. It was to be made memorable by some old
friends and by some new ones. His first few days there
were spent chiefly with Jean Ross—who had now left
Germany for good—or with Hector Wintle, his friend
since their schooldays at Repton and, for a short while,
his fellow medical student. (Hector is called Philip Lindsay in *All the Conspirators* and Philip Linsley in *Lions and
Shadows;* the slight alteration was made because some
libel-conscious lawyer feared that the repetition of the
original surname might annoy the novelist Philip Lindsay. As far as I know, Mr. Lindsay neither read Christopher nor cared what he wrote.)

Christopher had grown accustomed to thinking of
Hector as one of his least fortunate friends. For years, he
had had to pore over textbooks, squeeze through exami-
nations, and toil at St. Thomas's Hospital amidst the
squalor of moaning, messy patients. His heart had been
weak, ever since an early attack of rheumatic fever, and
he had been told that the twinges he felt in his fingers
were symptoms of progressive rheumatoid arthritis
which would probably cripple him. Hector was no tight-
lipped martyr. He complained unceasingly and most
amusingly of his bad health, his lack of money, and his

hatred of studying medicine. He was one of those rare beings who could make you thoroughly enjoy his misfortunes even while you were sympathizing with him. Christopher would listen to him by the hour and always feel the better for it; Hector's plight made him grateful for Uncle Henry's allowance and for his own irresponsible life. And Hector's perseverance was inspiring. He had spent all his spare time steadily writing novels or pursuing girls. The novels, so far, had always been rejected; Hector, himself, had seldom been. The novels were well written but a bit forbidding; Hector was accessible, charming, and full of suave, plump sex appeal.

Now, at last, he had finished with St. Thomas's and was about to embark on his maiden voyage as a ship's doctor. The ship—auspiciously named the *Hector*—was bound for China and Japan. For the first time in their long friendship, Christopher envied him. A few weeks from now, the *Hector* would actually, unbelievably, be entering Hong Kong harbor! Hector, with his own eyes, would behold that magic island—annexed to the empire of Somerset Maugham since its occupation by the characters of *The Painted Veil*. Hector himself, lounging at the rail in his white uniform, disdainfully regarding the junks and sampans with a frown of studied sophistication, would at that moment become an honorary Maugham character, a junior colleague of Dr. Macphail in *Rain* . . . Hector was entertained by Christopher's fantasies, but being a realist, he was far more excited by the prospect of the affairs he hoped to be having with the ship's female passengers.

On August 12, Christopher went to the Hogarth Press for his first encounter with John Lehmann. (If Leonard and Virginia Woolf were somewhere around, he didn't get to meet them, much to his disappointment.) In his autobiographical book, *The Whispering Gallery,* John writes warmly about his reaction to Christopher: "It was

96

impossible not to be drawn to him"; and humorously about Christopher's supposed reaction to himself:

> The sense of alarm that seemed to hang in the air when his smile was switched off, a suspicion he seemed to radiate that one might after all be in league with the "enemy" . . .

John's intuition was correct. Christopher *was* suspicious of and on his guard against this tall handsome young personage with his pale narrowed quizzing eyes, measured voice which might have belonged to a Foreign Office expert, and extremely becoming, prematurely gray hair—a hereditary characteristic. Seated behind his desk, John seemed the incarnation of authority—benevolent authority, but authority, nonetheless. What Christopher didn't, couldn't have realized until they knew each other better was that this personage contained two beings whose deepest interests were in conflict: an editor and a poet. John the Editor was also in conflict with the policy of the Hogarth Press. For he was destined to become the great literary obstetrician of his own age, to bring the writing of the thirties to birth and introduce it to the world. The Woolfs belonged to the previous generation, and their press, despite its appearance of chic modernity, tended to represent the writing of the twenties and the teens, even the tens . . . Meanwhile, John the Poet simply wanted to write his poems, leading a life which would leave him free to do so and taking no more than a colleague's friendly interest in the work of his contemporaries. He hated to waste precious time publishing books— even books by those he most admired—and he had no interest in exercising authority, however benevolent. The worst enemies of John the Poet were his friends, because they selfishly clamored to be published by him.

Through John, Christopher got to know his sisters, Rosamond, Beatrix, and (slightly) Helen. Rosamond, like John, was prematurely gray; this gave her the glamour of an eighteenth-century lady with powdered hair. Kathleen later described Rosamond in her diary as "disturbingly beautiful." I find the description odd. To Christopher, it seemed that Rosamond wore her beauty modestly and with humor, as though she were embarrassed at being overdressed. She was equally modest and humorous about the enormous success of her novel *Dusty Answer,* which had been published in 1927. A famous French writer had said to her, "Thank you, madame, for existing"; Rosamond laughed as she quoted this, and added apologetically that the French version was far superior to her English original. Christopher hadn't cared much for *Dusty Answer,* but he could conscientiously say, "Thank you, madame," for her *Invitation to the Waltz,* which had appeared that year. Since praise of one's latest novel is always the sweetest, their friendship got off to a good start. But Rosamond remained within the world of her marriage and her country home. It was Beatrix who was to form a much closer friendship with Christopher when she entered his Berlin world that autumn.

In the middle of August, Edward Upward came to spend a weekend with Christopher at Kathleen's house. Christopher had seen him in Berlin at the beginning of April, on his way back from a tour in Soviet Russia. Edward hadn't returned from his trip an uncritical raving Russophile; he was too British for that. But Christopher knew that he had been profoundly moved. What he had glimpsed in Russia lay much deeper than any visual impressions of Lenin's tomb and the Red Square and the parades. It was the implication of the revolution itself for the rest of the world, including England. Instead of dwelling on the huge triumphant events of 1917, Edward's imagination had been stirred by the drama of a revolution's tiny hidden beginnings. This was what he had already conveyed in his extraordinary short story called "Sunday."

"Sunday" is the monologue of a downtrodden office employee—actually Edward, during a schoolmastering job at Scarborough—who, as he talks to himself about his fears of his employers and the system they represent, gradually gathers courage and enters into a new affirmative, aggressive mood:

> It is mad to be content to hate every external danger, to be an ostrich, to accept any explanation which minimises the importance of material gains or losses, to fail to try to find a real solution . . . Don't flatter yourself that history will die or hibernate with you; history will be as vigorous as ever but it will have gone to live elsewhere . . . with people who are not content to suppress misery in their minds but are going to destroy the more obvious material causes of misery in the world . . .

What made "Sunday" so intensely exciting to Christopher was Edward's declaration that "history"—the force of revolutionary change—is at work everywhere, even in the dullest, stuffiest, most reactionary of settings, such as this seaside resort. Edward's message was: "Politics begin at home." You don't have to hover nervously on the outskirts of some publicized foreign battleground, like Berlin. Just ask the way to a certain café in your own town. Behind it, you will find a small club where Communist meetings are held. Go inside. That is the first step which the downtrodden employee, the discontented schoolmaster, must take, if he wants to become one of those with whom history has gone to live:

> At first he may be regarded with suspicion, even taken for a police spy. And quite naturally. He will have to prove himself, to prove that he isn't a mere neurotic, an untrustworthy freak. It will take time. But it is the only hope. He will at least have made a start.

Christopher was thrilled by the austerity of Edward's tone. He was also chilled—more so than he would admit to himself. Did he already know that he would never take the street to that café?

What he did know was that the bond between Edward and himself was as strong as it had ever been. He had only to read "Sunday" to realize that. Edward might be forced, by the logic of his convictions, to condemn certain writers whose style he had admired, on the ground that their ideas derived from a decayed social class. But the effort to find one's own appropriate style, to sharpen the instrument of one's language—that Edward could never condemn. To do so would be against his nature. And no Communist comrade would ever come as close to him as Christopher came in their discussions of the problems of style; for, at heart, the party-liner must dismiss such problems as secondary, and the study of them, if persisted in, as ultimately escapist. Edward would never be able to feel that. The style of "Sunday" proved it. "Sunday" was as essentially Upward as anything he had ever written.

Christopher also knew—but I cannot say how consciously, at that time—that his ambiguous position as an outsider, a non-joiner, was valuable to Edward; it was something which Edward would have to reckon with, for the rest of his life. He might be forced to condemn Christopher but he could never absolutely disown him. And their relationship, embarrassing though it might sometimes be to Edward, was going to help Edward see his own beliefs in a truer perspective.

Olive Mangeot (Madame Cheuret in *Lions and Shadows*) had become a Communist, largely through Edward's influence. She was now separated from her husband, André, and lived with her elder, nearly grown-up son, Fowke. Her younger son, Sylvain, continued to live with André. Olive's transformation from an apolitical bohemian to a seller of the *Daily Worker* and an active member of various left-wing groups had produced no noticeable change in her personality. She was still her easygoing, relaxed yet energetic self. It was said that her method of weaning "the unclear" away from Trotskyism was positively soothing. On the rare occasions when Olive couldn't clarify the muddled minds of "the trotters," she applied what she called "Mother's painless purge," with the result that they found themselves separated from the group, feeling bewildered perhaps but without any hard feelings toward her.

From this time onward, Christopher saw Olive very often, whenever he was in England. She provided a club for him and his friends to which he brought nearly all his new acquaintances. Kathleen was rightly jealous of Olive's influence over Christopher, but she didn't really understand its nature. Olive was, in a sense, a mother figure in Christopher's life and, as such, a rival to Kathleen. But she was totally undemanding and unpossessive and she never tried to influence him in any direction. They simply loved each other and were profoundly at ease together. Olive, he knew, would never disown him, no matter what he did. He had put her doubly into *The Memorial*—in the characters of Margaret Lanwin (Olive as she then was) and of Mary Scriven (Olive as she might be in later life).

In September, Wystan came to London for a few days. It must have been during this visit that he took Christopher to meet Gerald Heard and his friend, Chris Wood.

Gerald Heard was then a prominent figure in the British intellectual world. He knew most of the leading scientists and philosophers personally and he gave BBC radio talks explaining the latest findings of science in popular language. He was interested, agnostically, in the investigations of the Society for Psychical Research but wasn't prepared to say that they had found definite evidence of survival after death. He had written several books on evolution and prehistory and one which was called *Nar-*

cissus: An Anatomy of Clothes. Gerald himself obviously gave thought to what he wore, and would sometimes dress in a style which was slyly exotic. He was a slim, clean-shaven man in his early forties, with a melodious, faintly Irish accent. Christopher had never met anybody quite like him. He was witty, playful, flattering, talkative as a magpie, well informed as an encyclopedia, and, at the same time, life-weary, meditative, deeply concerned, and in earnest. Christopher's instinct told him at once that Gerald wouldn't be impressed by talk about Communism; here was a man to whom political systems and theories were irrelevant and of minor importance.

Chris Wood was about ten years younger than Gerald; handsome, shy but friendly, rich. He dressed simply, in clothes which were of good material but often shabby. He insisted on cycling about London, despite the ever increasing traffic. He could be capriciously extravagant, buying musical boxes and watches of exquisite design; then tiring of them and giving them away to his friends. He had recently bought a telescope—no doubt because Gerald talked so much about astronomy—but he only used it, now and then, to look into other people's windows and try to read letters lying on their desks. He played the piano well but with an obstinate determination to remain an amateur. He also wrote short stories which showed considerable talent but shook his head firmly when Christopher told him he should publish them. He had a pilot's license and had flown as far as Berlin. Gerald often went flying with him. Chris praised Gerald's fearlessness on these and other occasions. He told how Gerald had climbed to the top of a high building under construction, while it was still a skeleton of girders, in order to interview the steeple jacks about the dangers of their profession.

Chris and Gerald had one of the flats in a new luxury block just off Oxford Street. (Richard remembers that Christopher described it to him, with envious irony, as "the last thing in tasteful modernity—they have a cat which tones in perfectly with the furnishings.") Its elegance seemed to inspire a certain guilt in both of them. Chris expressed this by behaving as though he were staying in a hotel suite for which he felt no responsibility and which he might vacate in a day or two. Gerald disclaimed his responsibility in a subtler manner, by giving you to understand that he wasn't sharing the place with Chris but merely visiting it for a while as Chris's guest. When you came to see Chris, Gerald didn't welcome you like a co-host; he remained somewhere out of sight. Later he might pop his head unexpectedly around the door into the living room with an amused gleam in his eye, murmur something polite, and disappear again.

Since Wystan was primarily Gerald's friend, the two of them would withdraw to Gerald's room for abstruse scientific conversation, leaving Chris and Christopher alone together. Thus they quickly became intimate. It may even have been at their first meeting that Chris coyly asked Christopher if he had been at the Hirschfeld Institute on such and such a date. Christopher couldn't be sure but thought it was probable. Chris then told him that this was the day on which he had visited the Institute and had very briefly glimpsed, going up the staircase, the most attractive young man he had ever seen in his life. Chris implied that this young man might have been Christopher. He also implied that Christopher, as Chris now saw him, was sadly inferior to that glimpse. Therefore, the attractive young man was either an untraceable stranger whom Chris could never hope to meet again; or he was Christopher, in which case he didn't exist . . . Chris cherished frustrations of this sort. He would gloat over the impossibility of finding the delicious marmalade which he had had for breakfast when he was six. The young man on the staircase was to become a private joke between Chris and Christopher for many years.

What struck you, when you saw Gerald and Chris together, was a kind of family resemblance which was psychological rather than physical. It was expressed in certain gestures and intonations—carefully unemphatic, fastidiously understated. They stood side by side and looked at you like a pair of smiling conspirators. William Plomer somehow caught the effect they produced—on Christopher, at any rate—when he said, "I like their dry eyes and voices."

Christopher had met William Plomer through Stephen Spender, who had previously introduced him to some of Plomer's poems and his stories about South Africa and Japan. Christopher admired the work and soon he began to admire Plomer himself even more. He was a big man with big round glasses and the look of a benign muscular owl. His descriptions of people were witty and exact; once, he called someone "an art lout." He seemed to take everything lightly. Then, beneath the malice and fun, you became aware of an extraordinary strength—a strength which lent itself to others; it was hard to feel depressed or sorry for yourself in his presence. You also became aware that his fun was that of a person who was capable of intense private suffering. Therefore, it would never seem trivial under any circumstances. He would have been wonderful in a lifeboat with the survivors of a shipwreck. Ten years later, it would be said of him that he was an ideal companion in an air raid.

On September 14, Christopher wrote a postcard to Stephen—who must have been out of town for a day or two:

Yesterday evening, Plomer and I visited an opium-den. Today he is taking me to see E. M. Forster. I shall spend the entire morning making-up.

I have only the dimmest memory of the alleged opium den. I think it was a pub somewhere in the dockland area, frequented by local Chinese and visiting Asian seamen. Plomer liked to keep the outskirts of his life hidden in an intriguing fog of mystery; now and then he would guide you through the fog to one of his haunts, with the casualness of a habitué. No doubt, opium was obtainable there, but I am sure that he and Christopher didn't smoke any . . . By "making-up" I suppose Christopher merely meant that he would try in every way to look and be at his best for this tremendous encounter.

It *was* tremendous for Christopher. Forster was the only living writer whom he would have described as his master. In other people's books he found examples of style which he wanted to imitate and learn from. In Forster he found a key to the whole art of writing. The Zen masters of archery—of whom, in those days, Christopher had never heard—start by teaching you the mental attitude with which you must pick up the bow. A Forster novel taught Christopher the mental attitude with which he must pick up the pen.

Plomer had been able to arrange this meeting because Forster had read *The Memorial*—at his suggestion, probably—and had liked it, at least well enough to be curious about its author. (Thenceforward, Christopher was fond of saying, "My literary career is over—I don't give a damn for the Nobel Prize or the Order of Merit—*I've been praised by Forster!*" Nevertheless, Christopher's confidence in his own talent easily survived the several later occasions when Forster definitely didn't like one of his other books or when he praised books by writers whom Christopher found worthless.)

Forster must have been favorably impressed by Christopher; otherwise, he wouldn't have gone on seeing him. And Christopher made a good disciple; like most arrogant people, he loved to bow down unconditionally from time to time. No doubt he gazed at Forster with devoted eyes and set himself to entertain him with tales of Berlin and the boy world, judiciously spiced with expressions of social concern—for he must have been aware from the start that he had to deal with a moralist.

Forster never changed much in appearance until he

became stooped and feeble in his late eighties. He was then fifty-three but he always looked younger than his age. And he never ceased to be babylike. His light blue eyes behind his spectacles were like those of a baby who remembers his previous incarnation and is more amused than dismayed to find himself reborn in new surroundings. He had a baby's vulnerability, which is also the invulnerability of a creature whom one dare not harm. He seemed to be swaddled, babylike, in his ill-fitting suit rather than wearing it. A baby with a mustache? Well, if a baby *could* have a mustache, it would surely be like his was, wispy and soft . . . Nevertheless, behind that charming, unalarming exterior, was the moralist; and those baby eyes looked very deep into you. When they disapproved, they could be stern. They made Christopher feel false and tricky and embarrassed. He reacted to his embarrassment by trying to keep Forster amused. Thirty-eight years later, a friend who was present at the last meeting between them made the comment: "Mr. Forster laughs at you as if you were the village idiot."

I suppose that this first meeting took place in Forster's flat, and that, on the wall of its living room, there hung Eric Kennington's pastel portrait of T. E. Lawrence's bodyguard, quarrelsome little Mahmas, with his fierce eyes and naked dagger. This was the original of one of the illustrations to the privately printed edition of *Seven Pillars of Wisdom.* Lawrence had given copies of the book away to his friends, including Forster. Christopher left the flat clasping this magic volume, which Forster had lent him.

Toward the end of Christopher's visit to London, his long-impending showdown with Stephen Spender took place. Stephen gives an account of this in *World within World.* He writes that Christopher showed irritation with him so clearly, when they were together at a party, that he went to visit Christopher next day and suggested that they should see nothing, or very little, of each other when they returned to Berlin. Christopher replied in "accents of ironic correctitude" that he wasn't aware of any strain between them. At this point, I have a memory of my own. Stephen, annoyed by Christopher's evasiveness, exclaimed, "If we're going to part, at least let's part like men." To which Christopher replied, with a bitchy smile, "But, Stephen, we *aren't* men." I can only assume that Stephen's challenge caught him unprepared and that he was playing for time to prepare a self-justifying case. Later that day, he wrote Stephen a letter. Stephen paraphrases it as follows:

> If I returned to Berlin he would not do so, that my life was poison to him, that I lived on publicity, that I was intolerably indiscreet, etc.

Stephen thinks that Christopher was annoyed because he had reached London before Christopher and had told their mutual friends all Christopher's favorite stories, including several which he didn't want to have broadcast indiscriminately. This is true, no doubt. But Christopher's deeper motive in quarreling with Stephen was to get him out of Berlin altogether. I don't think he consciously knew this at the time. It is obvious to me now. Christopher regarded Berlin as his territory. He was actually becoming afraid that Stephen would scoop him by writing Berlin stories of his own and rushing them into print!

Stephen and Christopher met again and made up their quarrel even before Christopher returned to Berlin. Now that Christopher knew that Stephen wouldn't be coming back there, he was eager for a truce. He needed Stephen's friendship fully as much as Stephen needed his. Christopher tended to make friends with his moral superiors. It was only with Stephen that he had faults in common—which was relaxing and created a special kind of intimacy, when it didn't provoke competition.

From the middle of August onward, Christopher had begun work on what was to be the very first draft of his fiction about Berlin. This was a short story or the outline for a novel; its subject matter was Jean's adventures combined with Christopher's encounters with the Nowaks. It was as crude as his first drafts always were. But it accomplished the enormous feat of making this shapeless blob of potential material emerge "out of the everywhere into here."

He dictated the draft to Richard. This was a supreme act of intimacy. It is immeasurably more embarrassing for a writer to invent crudely in someone else's presence than to confide to him the most shameful personal revelations. He could have done it with no one else he knew. I think Richard himself valued this intimacy. He patiently wrote the whole thing out in longhand, only regretting that he couldn't typewrite, because it made the dictation slower. They worked mostly in the mornings and had finished in about four weeks.

Their collaboration brought a feeling of subdued excitement into the household. Something—no matter exactly what—was going on upstairs, behind Christopher's closed door. Elizabeth the cook was aware of it. Nanny the house parlormaid was part of it. She, who had been nurse to both brothers in succession, now rejoiced that she was once more allowed to join in their games; she brought them cups of tea and answered the telephone, telling callers that they couldn't be disturbed. As for Kathleen, what mattered to her was that Christopher was functioning as a writer *under her roof;* this was a solid respectable fact which she could report to her friends. Kathleen felt a need—though she would never have acknowledged it—to reassure herself by looking at Christopher through the eyes of the outside world. In this connection, the few good reviews of *The Memorial* were like references and Christopher's newly acquired literary colleagues were like sponsors who guaranteed his competence. Thanks to them, Christopher the Writer had now begun to seem real to Kathleen; before them, he had never quite existed. (Wystan, Edward, and Stephen didn't and would never count as Christopher's colleagues, from Kathleen's point of view; they were merely school friends.)

Christopher found Kathleen's attitude ridiculous; but he himself was enjoying his enhanced status. It was fun to be both the self-exiled mysterious "Man from Berlin" and the socially welcome novelist whose next book was "awaited," even if not very anxiously, in Bloomsbury circles. However, a Man from Berlin should be talked about rather than seen—the mystery is solved by overexposure. And a next book is best awaited in its author's absence. Christopher left England again on September 30.

SEVEN

From Forster, October 12, 1932:

> Dear Isherwood—we do drop "Mr.," don't we? I was
> very glad to have "All the Conspirators." I don't like
> it as much as "The Memorial," but that is not the point,
> and there are things in it I do like very much . . . I hope
> you found your friend better than the news suggested.
> It is an awful worry, that illness at this time of the year.
> I'm very sorry you've got this on you, and annoyed
> with Life generally for being so often *just* wrong.
> Again and again the wonderful chariot seems ready to
> move . . .

The people Forster approved of were those who were
capable of devotion to a friend and of suffering when he
was sick or in trouble. Forster took it for granted that
Christopher was such a person. Christopher tried hard to
live up to this image of himself. But Forster's faith in him
would often make him feel guilty of coldheartedness.
Edward Upward reported:

> Back today from lunch with Richard and Ma. I noted
> that she hadn't yet heard of Heinz and I said nothing
> to enlighten her. But even if I had I don't think she

would have protested—it's quite astonishing how you have educated that woman. I foresee a time when, like the son who was sent to Australia for stealing, you will be able to do nothing wrong.

Otto had had the power to make Christopher jealous and anxious. Heinz didn't yet have this power. While Christopher was in London, he had never worried that Heinz might leave him; so he had never felt the need to talk about Heinz to Kathleen. He was already closer to Heinz than he had ever been to Otto, but their relationship wasn't painful. This he was learning to be grateful for—as he told Stephen Spender:

In the old days I was obsessed with the idea of a *high tension!, extreme danger!* relationship, which gave off ten-foot sparks and electrocuted everyone in the neighborhood. Now I see that there's something to be said for decency and a little mutual consideration and pleasantness. Thanks to Heinz.

Christopher's tone is ironically apologetic. He is aware that his love life has ceased to be gossip-worthy. Christopher himself was a keen matchmaker for his friends; but he quickly lost interest if the match turned out to be harmonious.

On November 3, Christopher wrote to Stephen, who was now in Spain:

Here we are very wet and chilly. And this morning Berlin has woken up to find a general strike of trams, buses, and U-bahn. Nobody seems to know how long it will last. Probably till after the elections, I should think, on Sunday. Nazis and Communists are assisting each other on the strike pickets.

The Nazis had forced themselves into this uneasy temporary alliance because they couldn't let the Communists take credit for being the sole supporters of the striking transport workers, just before an election. The strike resulted in widespread public violence against strikebreakers and others. Christopher himself got a glimpse of it, which he describes in *Goodbye to Berlin:* a young man being attacked on the street by a gang of Nazis returning from a political rally. The Nazis were carrying rolled banners with spikes on their ends. They stabbed the young man in the face and left him with one eye probably blinded. Half a dozen policemen stood a few yards away, ignoring the incident.

Christopher goes on to tell Stephen that Gerald Hamilton has been to Coburg to be present at the wedding of the eldest son of the Crown Prince of Sweden and Princess Sybilla of Coburg. During the marriage sermon the preacher said: "A people which has deprived its from-God-appointed rulers of employment must not wonder if the Heavenly Powers condemn its working classes to unemployment also." This was a graceful reference to the various deposed royal persons who were in the congregation. One of these was the exiled Tsar Ferdinand of Bulgaria, with whom Gerald was staying. The tsar was fond of Gerald and bestowed various decorations on him, from time to time, which he later sold . . . Gerald, who seemed able to change worlds without the least discomfort, had descended from these aristocratic heights to Berlin and his proletarian boyfriend, an actor who was just then appearing in Gorki's *The Lower Depths.* Christopher describes the boyfriend as being "more Communist than Lenin." He used to reprove Gerald for counterrevolutionary laxity and self-indulgence.

Christopher's letter concludes:

Heinz is spotty and his moustache is quite luxuriant. To annoy me he refuses to shave. We see each other three times a week and it is always very nice. My novel creeps on and on. Otto is going to have another child. And the Pound. And this strike. And the rain. And no fire. Never mind, this afternoon I shall go to the cinema.

In the elections of November 6, the Nazis lost two million votes and thirty-four seats in the Reichstag, while the Communists gained three quarters of a million votes and eleven seats. Many leftists, including some expert political observers, believed that Hitler would never recover from this setback and had ceased to be a menace. Christopher, wild with joy, wrote to his friends that Berlin was Red. It was—in the sense that the Communists had a majority there of 100,000. But the fact remained that the Nazis were still the largest party in the country.

About this time, Stephen must have written to tell Christopher that he wasn't going to dedicate his book of poems to him, as originally intended. This letter has been lost, but I suppose Stephen argued that, in view of their imperfectly patched-up quarrel, the dedication would be insincere. Christopher answered (November 14):

Of course I quite understand about the dedication. In fact, I'd half thought of writing and suggesting it to you myself.
This afternoon is sad brilliant autumn sunshine, the sort of afternoon we might have chosen for a walk in Grunewald, the sort of afternoon on which Virginia Woolf looks out of her window and suddenly decides to write a novel about the hopeless love of a Pekingese dog for a very beautiful maidenhair fern.

(Despite Christopher's admiration for *Jacob's Room, Mrs. Dalloway,* and *To the Lighthouse*—which was considerable, though not nearly as great as mine is, today—he sometimes used Virginia as an enemy image of the ivory-tower intellectual. For instance, after he and Stephen had been to see *Kameradschaft,* Pabst's film about the coal miners, in 1931, Christopher told Stephen that, when the tunnel caved in and the miners were trapped, he had thought: "That makes Virginia Woolf look pretty silly." Stephen replied that he had been thinking something similar, though not specifically about Virginia.)

Heinz and I wistfully looked up Malaga on the map and decided that "some day" we would travel—yes really—perhaps even as far as Munich.

(There is some mild bitchery here and in the next paragraph. Stephen is about to leave for Málaga—wandering through the warm lands of escape while Christopher remains shivering and penniless at his post on the Berlin battlefield.)

Today I am moving into the big front room. It is lighter for the winter months and, for some reason, easier to heat. Frl. Thurau is very reproachful because I insist on turning out all her potted plants. Their moist stink when the oven is alight is probably as near as I shall ever get to a tropical forest. I do envy you your winter in the sun. I imagine you bursting into blossoms of health, while here in Berlin I get uglier and more shrivelled every day. My hair is scurfy and drops out, my teeth are bad, my breath smells. However, I do see that it's absolutely necessary for me to stay on here at present. The last part of my novel requires a lot more research to document it.

Please understand, Stephen, that there is nothing for you to apologize for about our time in Berlin. I am an entirely impossible character; unstable, ill-natured, petty and selfish. I don't say this in a mealy-mouthed way. I have the virtues of my defects. But I can't imagine that I ever could or should be able to live intimately with an equal for long.

Christopher may have explained himself further; the next page of the letter is missing. The final page contains a few items of news. Frau Nowak is being sent back to the sanatorium again. Christopher hardly ever sees Otto because he has cut off Otto's money entirely—this may mean that he refuses to contribute to the abortion of Otto's illegitimate embryos. However, he has applied to Wilfrid Israel, who may be able to get Otto a job as errand boy to a publisher. Christopher has been translating a report on the work of the I.A.H, a Communist organization with which Gerald Hamilton was involved. Christopher tells Stephen that he thinks he will become a member of it—"it's the next nearest thing to being a Communist." Christopher never did join the I.A.H, much less the Communist Party. This was the only time in his life when he came anywhere near to doing so.

John Lehmann's sister Beatrix was now in Berlin and she and Christopher saw each other often. They were much alike in temperament, a natural elder sister and elder brother. Both thought of themselves, rightly or wrongly, as strong people weary of guarding the weak. Both were comedians who made each other laugh continually: Beatrix with her gallows humor, Christopher with his melodramatic clowning. Both, at that period, saw eye to eye politically. Both sincerely admired each other's work. Christopher was astonished by Beatrix's talent as a writer and he loved to watch her act. (A character actress with looks which enabled her to play romantic leads, she was equally capable of becoming Juliet or Juliet's nurse; there might, however, be occasional eerie glimpses of the one within the other.) Both Beatrix and Christopher were psychosomatic types, prone to sudden sicknesses. But here there was a difference between them. While Christopher stayed in bed, Beatrix would go on stage, blazing with fever or nearly voiceless with laryngitis, and soar to her greatest heights.

My last memory of Beatrix in Berlin is that she and Christopher spent New Year's Eve together at a French restaurant, eating Sylvester carp, the traditional New Year's Eve dish. They were so engrossed in their talk that they were unaware of the moment at which 1933 came in. Someone remarked that this would bring them bad luck in the year ahead.

In mid-January, Christopher wrote to Stephen, who had now returned from Spain to England:

> I have put off answering you because of the really terrifying reports of the revolution in Barcelona. Did you see much of it? I gathered that the posts and all other communications were suspended, that there was no light and that the streets were full of machine guns. So it seemed useless to write.

(This refers to the rising of Anarchists and Syndicalists which began early in January in Barcelona and spread to other cities. It was suppressed by government troops. Stephen hadn't referred to it in his last letter, being preoccupied with a personal problem. He had been trying to keep the peace between some intensely neurotic individuals, one of whom was an alcoholic. He later made their feuds and agonies well worthwhile by distilling from them his hilarious story, "The Burning Cactus.")

Beatrix Lehmann leaves on Monday for England, via Hamburg, where she is engaged to appear with some English players, in the title role of Candida. As for

Heinz, we get on very well indeed. At the moment, we've just parted for ever, but that is neither here nor there.

Frl. Thurau has a new lodger, a Norwegian film actor with incredibly beautiful blond hair. He plays a card game called Black Peter with Frl. Thurau and the two whores. The loser has some kind of indecent picture—a cunt or penis or bubs—drawn on his cheek with an eyebrow pencil. By the end of the evening they are all black-faced.

The political situation here seems very dull. I expect there is a great deal going on behind the scenes, but one is not aware of it. Papen visits Hindenburg, Hitler visits Papen, Hitler and Papen visit Schleicher, Hugenberg visits Hindenburg and finds he's out. And so forth. There is no longer that slightly exhilarating awareness of crisis in the gestures of beggars and tram-conductors.

Shortly after writing the above, Christopher got his copy of Stephen's poems. The book wasn't dedicated to anybody, but Stephen had inscribed it: "For Christopher in admiration and with love from the writer Jan 10 1933." (When the second edition appeared in 1934, it was dedicated to Christopher.)

Thanking Stephen, Christopher wrote:

I think the print and binding is perfect. I feel nearly as pleased with the book as if I'd written it myself—and keep taking it out of the shelf and turning over the pages. The blurb is portentous tripe. What idiot wrote it?

(This blurb had already been apologized for by Stephen in an earlier letter: "It seems to have been written out of pure malice and I'm afraid it will annoy Wystan." Here are some extracts:

If Auden is the satirist of this poetical renascence Spender is its lyric poet. In his work the experimentalism of the last two decades is beginning to find its reward . . . Technically, these poems appear to make a definite step forward in modern English poetry. Their passionate and obvious sincerity ranks them in a tradition which reaches back to the early Greek lyric poets.)

Christopher continued:

I still stick to my favorites: The Port. Children who were rough. Oh young men. After they have tired. And, above all, The Pylons. The Pylons is the best thing in the book, I think.

(I don't agree with the majority of Christopher's choices, now. He was charmed by Stephen's left-wing romanticism, with its accent on Comrades. I prefer the explosive egotistic artlessness of the "Marston" poems; as I read them, I can hear the young Stephen's voice, blurting them out. This book also contained: "I think continually of those who were truly great . . . ," which ends with what was to be one of Spender's most quoted lines: "And left the vivid air signed with their honour." I find that I still want to boast of the fact that, when Stephen showed Christopher his original draft of this poem, it ended: "And left the air signed with their vivid honour." It was Christopher who urged the transposition of "vivid.")

Here it is very cold and snowing. I am writing with a rug round my knees. Uncle has sent my allowance. So London will not see me for three more months, at least. Heinz cooked a schnitzel here last night. God knows what he did to it. He made it smell like an Airedale dog.

At the end of January, John Lehmann came to Berlin to see Christopher. This was his second visit. His first had been a brief one, during October 1932. Lehmann had now, after much self-searching, left the Hogarth Press and gone to live in Vienna, in order that John the Poet could function without obligations and restraints. It was with John the Poet that Christopher became friends. When they were together, Christopher felt inspired to improvise sex fantasies of indefinite length—episode leading into episode, Arabian Nights style, sometimes for hours at a stretch. His affection for John the Poet became so firmly established that, when John the Editor later reappeared, Christopher was able to work for him, admire his ability, and feel awed by his energy, while still finding his personality comic. John the Poet was always there in the background, sharing Christopher's amusement.

On January 30, President Hindenburg appointed Hitler to be the new Chancellor of Germany. A huge torchlight procession of singing Nazis celebrated this triumph of backstairs intrigue and manipulation of the gaga old President. Christopher wrote to Stephen:

> As you will have seen, we are having a new government, with Charlie Chaplin and Father Christmas in the ministry. All words fail.

By "Father Christmas," Christopher may have meant either Hindenburg himself or Alfred Hugenberg, the Nationalist Party leader, Hitler's temporary ally. Hugenberg was then nearly seventy, so he qualified for the role . . . Christopher, like other optimistic ill-wishers, kept repeating that this appointment was a blessing in disguise; Hitler would now have to cope with the economic mess, he would reveal himself as an incompetent windbag, he would be forced to resign, and the Nazis would be forever discredited.

I don't blame Christopher the amateur observer for his lack of foresight. I do condemn Christopher the novelist for not having taken a psychological interest, long before this, in the members of the Nazi high command. Even as late as 1932, it would have been possible for him to meet them personally. Goebbels, the party propagandist, was obliged to make himself available to the foreign press. And it wasn't too difficult to arrange interviews with Goering or even Hitler. Christopher wasn't Jewish, he belonged to the Nazis' favorite foreign race, he spoke German fluently, he was a writer and could easily have been accepted as a freelance journalist whom they might hope to convert to their philosophy . . . What inhibited him? His principles? His inertia? Neither is an excuse. He missed what would surely have been one of the most memorable experiences of his Berlin life.

On February 27, the Nazis caused the Reichstag building to be set on fire. Then, accusing the Communists of having done it as a signal for an uprising, they declared a state of emergency and began making mass arrests. "Charlie Chaplin" had ceased to be funny.

Stephen wrote (March 1):

> The news from Germany is awful. [A big deletion.] No, perhaps I had better not say anything that might conceivably get you into trouble. Or is this a ridiculous fear?

Stephen was back in London, suffering from a tapeworm which he had picked up in Spain. The problem, in removing a tapeworm, is to get rid of its head, which hooks itself to the lining of the alimentary canal and hangs on, even when the entire chain of segments attached to it has been evacuated. Sometimes the head can't be found in the stool so the doctor doesn't know if it has been lost or is still inside the patient. Christopher bought a particularly repulsive postcard photograph of the head of Goebbels and sent it to Stephen, inscribed: "Can *this* be it?!!!"

I have been in bed four days receiving purgatives of the most powerful kind and practically starving. So please excuse my writing as I am weak and trembling with joy at your letter.

(Christopher's joy-inspiring letter must have been written in answer to one of Stephen's which has been lost. Stephen had evidently expressed fears that a certain person, a member of the "Burning Cactus" group who had been with him in Spain and had now come to Berlin, was making mischief and trying to revive the quarrel between him and Christopher. Stephen, in his tapeworm-weakened, hyper-emotional state, is trembling with joy because Christopher's letter has assured him that this isn't so.)

I had kept worrying during the last few days lest we might have another estrangement. When I was first in Barcelona I was awfully upset about our quarrel and I could not get out of my head the letter you wrote me in London . . . I did not feel bitter or anything but I had waves of being very upset and then at other times I had waves of feeling just the same and I used to wait for those times to write to you.

As far as our friendship is concerned, it is not exactly that I want to be with you or see you very much. Of course, whatever happens, I shall go on living just in the same way and I shall go on with my work, but if

I felt you had abandoned the irritating, continual effort
to love me and forgive me I would be very disappointed: in fact much more than that. You and F. are
the people I most like. For F. everything's simple and
there is no conflict. With you it is different, but in spite
of everything you are always fighting and there is
something very clear in my picture of you.

Love to Heinz whom I am glad you are always with.
I am writing 3 stories and lots of poems. I am 24!

In the elections of March 5, the Nazis failed to win a clear
majority, despite their campaign of propaganda and in-
timidation. But their failure had no practical significance.
For, on March 23, the Reichstag was bullied into passing
the so-called Enabling Act, which made Hitler master of
Germany. In a mad, meaningless way, his successive steps
toward absolute power had all been legal.

After the elections, the weather turned suddenly mild
and warm; the porter's wife at Nollendorfstrasse 17
called it "Hitler's weather." The street itself, like all
others, was hung with black-white-red swastika flags; it
was unwise not to display them. Uniformed Nazis strode
along the sidewalks with stern official expressions on
their faces; it was advisable to step aside for them. They
also came into the cafés and restaurants, rattling collecting boxes for the party; it was necessary to give them
something. On the Nollendorfplatz and in other squares
and public places, there were radio loudspeakers blaring
forth speeches by Goering and Goebbels. "Germany is
awake," they said. People sat in front of the cafés listening to them—cowlike, vaguely curious, complacent, ac-
cepting what had happened but not the responsibility for
it. Many of them hadn't even voted—how could they be
responsible? The city was full of rumors about what went
on behind the scenes, in the Storm Troop barracks,
where the political prisoners had been taken. It was said
that some were made to spit on Lenin's picture, swallow

castor oil, eat old socks; that some were tortured; that many were already dead. The government denied all this, furiously. Even to repeat such rumors was treason. New ways of committing treason kept being announced in the press.

Some foreign journalists—those who were openly critical of the Nazi government—used to dine together, most evenings, at a small Italian restaurant. Among them was Norman Ebbutt of the London *Times*. Everybody else in the restaurant, including at least one police spy, watched them and tried to overhear what they were saying. If a German went up to their table and talked to them, he was pretty sure to be questioned by the police later.

One day, a young man came to see Christopher at the Nollendorfstrasse. He knew an escaped eyewitness who could describe conditions in the barracks and give the names of prisoners there; he wanted this to be published outside the country. Christopher had got to know Ebbutt, so he went to him with the information. Ebbutt had already made himself unpopular with the authorities by his revelations; even his own editor was worried about his frankness. The Nazis finally expelled him.

Most of Christopher's Jewish friends had left Germany or were about to leave. Dr. Hirschfeld had been away on a world tour since 1930. The tour had ended in France, where he remained, knowing that it would be fatal for him to return. Karl Giese had joined him there. Christopher must have made some effort to contact Wilfrid Israel—halfhearted, no doubt. Aside from any cowardice he may have felt, he was aware that he might compromise Wilfrid even further—if that were possible; "foreigner" was already becoming a dirty word, and Christopher was a foreigner who must certainly be listed in the police archives as a member of the Hirschfeld Homosexuals and the Hamilton Reds. (Gerald Hamilton himself had already been closely cross-examined by the political police and had hastened to leave the country.)

When the Nazis held their first boycott of Jewish businesses on April 1, Christopher went to see what was happening to the Israels' department store. Nothing much, it appeared. Two or three uniformed Storm Troopers were posted at each of the entrances. Their manner wasn't at all aggressive; they merely reminded each would-be shopper that this was a Jewish store. (In the small provincial towns, where everybody knew everybody and personal hates were fierce, there were window smashings, and shoppers were forcibly disgraced by being marked with rubber ink stamps on their foreheads and cheeks.) Quite a number of people did go into Israel's while Christopher was there, including Christopher himself. When he came out again, having made some token purchase, he recognized one of the boys at the entrance. They knew each other from the Cosy Corner. During the past year, politics had increasingly divided the bar boys. They had joined one or other of the street gangs which were encouraged, though not always officially recognized, by the Nazis or the Communists or the Nationalists. Now the non-Nazis were in danger, but many of them changed sides and were accepted. If you did get beaten up, it was more likely to be because you had a private enemy; this was a great opportunity to settle old scores.

Boy bars of every sort were being raided, now, and many were shut down. Christopher had lost touch with Karl Giese's friends. No doubt the prudent ones were scared and lying low, while the silly ones fluttered around town exclaiming how sexy the Storm Troopers looked in their uniforms. He knew only one pair of homosexual lovers who declared proudly that they were Nazis. Misled by their own erotic vision of a New Sparta, they fondly supposed that Germany was entering an era of military man-love, with all women excluded. They were aware, of course, that Christopher thought them crazy, but they dismissed him with a shrug. How could *he* understand? This wasn't his homeland . . . No, indeed it wasn't. Christopher had realized that for some time already. But this tragic pair of self-deceivers didn't realize—and wouldn't, until it was too late—that this wasn't their homeland, either.

On April 5, Christopher went to London, taking with him books, papers, and other belongings which he wanted to store in Kathleen's house before he left Germany for good.

Francis had written inviting Christopher and Heinz to join him in Greece, where he was about to have a house built for himself. He had also invited Erwin Hansen and Erwin had agreed to come. Christopher still hesitated. Partly because he remembered what life with Francis had been like at Mohrin, but more importantly because he was unwilling to opt for one particular place. The mere idea of travel excited him so much, at this time in his life, that he loved to enjoy it in the abstract, as an embarrassment of possibilities. This enjoyment had ceased to be mere daydreaming; for Christopher had just inherited a small legacy from his godmother, Aggie Trevor (see *Kathleen and Frank*). He could now afford to spend a summer anywhere in Europe or take a short trip farther still. According to a letter from Forster, Christopher was even considering Brazil.

During his stay in London, Christopher again dictated to Richard. This must have been a revised and longer version of the other manuscript. Kathleen's diary notes that he finished the first part of it a few days before he left, and showed it to Edward Upward. She mentions visits to the house by Bubi (who was then working on a Dutch freighter which smuggled Jewish refugees into England, one on each voyage), by Gerald Hamilton ("He wears a wig and has had an extremely adventurous life!"), and by Forster (whose name Kathleen underlines, evidently as a mark of her special respect).

It was at this time that Forster showed Christopher the

typescript of *Maurice*. Christopher felt greatly honored, of course, by being allowed to read it. Its antique locutions bothered him, here and there. When Alec speaks of sex with Maurice as "sharing," he grimaced and wriggled his toes with embarrassment. And yet the wonder of the novel was that it had been written when it had been written; the wonder was Forster himself, imprisoned within the jungle of pre-war prejudice, putting these unthinkable thoughts into words. Perhaps listening from time to time, to give himself courage, to the faraway chop-chop of those pioneer heroes, Edward Carpenter and George Merrill, boldly enlarging *their* clearing in the jungle. Carpenter and Merrill had been *Maurice*'s godparents. Merrill, as Forster was later to disclose, had psychophysically inspired him to write it by touching him gently just above the buttocks. (Forster—how characteristically!—comments, "I believe he touched most people's.")

Did Christopher think *Maurice* as good as Forster's other novels? He would have said—and I still agree with him—that it was both inferior and superior to them: inferior as an artwork, superior because of its purer passion, its franker declaration of its author's faith. This moved Christopher tremendously on that first reading.

At their meeting in 1932, the Master had praised the Pupil. This time, the Pupil was being asked by the Master, quite humbly, how *Maurice* appeared to a member of the thirties generation. "Does it date?" Forster was asking. To which Christopher, I am proud to say, replied, "Why *shouldn't* it date?" This was wise and true as well as encouraging, and it cheered Forster greatly. He told Christopher so in a subsequent letter.

My memory sees them sitting together, facing each other. Christopher sits gazing at this master of their art, this great prophet of their tribe, who declares that there can be real love, love without limits or excuse, between two men. Here he is, humble in his greatness, unsure of his own genius. Christopher stammers some words of praise and devotion, his eyes brimming with tears. And Forster—amused and touched, but more touched than amused—leans forward and kisses him on the cheek. (Nevertheless, he continued to call Christopher "Isherwood" for two more years.)

Almost every time they met, after this, they discussed the problem: how should *Maurice* end? That the ending should be a happy one was taken for granted; Forster had written the novel in order to affirm that such an ending is possible for homosexuals. But the choice of a final scene remained open. Should it be a glimpse of Maurice and Alec enjoying a life of freedom, outside the bounds of society? Should it be Maurice's good-humored parting from his faithless former lover, Clive: "Why don't you stop being shocked and attend to your own happiness?" Christopher wasn't satisfied with either ending. (The second was the one finally adopted.) He made his own suggestions—as did several of Forster's other friends. He loved this continuing discussion, simply as a game.

When Christopher returned to Berlin on April 30, he was anxious to get out of Germany again, as quickly as possible. Since an itinerary of the journey to Greece had already been planned for Erwin by Francis, he accepted this as the way of least effort and decided to go there too —at any rate, for a start. While still in London, he had heard that the Berlin police had arrested three Englishmen, all of them English teachers. (Kathleen's diary doesn't tell what the charge against them was; I suspect that it was homosexuality.) Also, Frl. Thurau had written that the police had called to question her about him, saying that this was merely a routine checkup. Christopher's common sense assured him that there was no need to be seriously afraid. Even if the worst came to the worst, he wouldn't fall into the hands of the Nazi Storm Troopers; foreigners were dealt with by the police, who treated you with respect for your civil rights. They would merely inform him that he was an undesirable alien and expel him from a country which he was only too eager to leave.

Nevertheless, there was terror in the Berlin air—the terror felt by many people with good reason—and Christopher found himself affected by it. Perhaps he was also affected by his own fantasies. He had always posed a little to his friends in England as an embattled fighter against the Nazis and some of them had encouraged him jokingly to do so. "Don't get killed before I come," Edward Upward had written, "I'll see you unless you've been shot by Hitler." Now Christopher began to have mild hallucinations. He fancied that he heard heavy wagons drawing up before the house, in the middle of the night. He suddenly detected swastika patterns in the wallpaper. He convinced himself that everything in his room, whatever its superficial color, was basically brown, Nazi brown.

Christopher had much more cause to worry on behalf of his two intended traveling companions. German citizens now had to get individual permits to leave the country. It was possible, though unlikely, that Heinz would have difficulty. But Erwin Hansen might well be refused and perhaps arrested into the bargain, as a Communist and as an employee of the Hirschfeld Institute. Erwin smiled at Christopher's fears, saying that the Nazis were too busy to bother about small fry such as himself. (A dangerously optimistic notion, for the Terror was still badly organized and therefore unpredictable in its choice of victims.) Meanwhile, until he could start for Greece, Erwin insisted on continuing to live at the Institute, as its janitor.

On May 6, the Institute was raided by a party of about a hundred students. They arrived in trucks, early in the morning, playing a brass band. Hearing the band, Erwin looked out of a window and—hoping to prevent some of the obviously impending damage—asked them politely to wait a moment while he came downstairs to unlock the doors. But the students preferred to enter like warriors; they smashed the doors down and rushed into the building. They spent the morning pouring ink over carpets and manuscripts and loading their trucks with books from the Institute's library, including many which had nothing to do with sex: historical works, art journals, etc. In the afternoon, a troop of S.A. men arrived and made a more careful search, evidently knowing what they were looking for. (It has been stated, since then, that some well-known members of the Nazi Party had previously been patients of Hirschfeld and that they were afraid that case histories revealing their homosexuality might be used against them. But, if this was so, they would surely have had the Institute's archives examined more discreetly. Christopher was later told that all the really important papers and books had been removed by friends of Hirschfeld and sent abroad, sometime before this.) A few days after the raid, the seized books and papers were publicly burned, along with a bust of Hirschfeld, on the square in front of the Opera House. Christopher, who was present in the crowd, said, "Shame!"; but not loudly.

The government then formally deprived Hirschfeld of his German citizenship. He was living in Nice and planning to reopen the Institute there. But he died before he could do so, on May 15, 1935. After his death, Karl Giese left France and went to Czechoslovakia. In 1936, he killed himself.

"I'm sure I don't know what makes you want to leave Berlin all of a sudden, like this," Frl. Thurau told Christopher sadly, with perfect sincerity. She, who had voted Communist—because of Christopher's urging—in the November 1932 elections, now called Hitler "Der Fuehrer" when she talked to the porter's wife. After all, like millions of others, she had to go on living in Germany and making the best of it, no matter who was in power. She would remain what she essentially was, a sweet, muddled victim of her rulers—guilty only by association with them—no more and no less of a Nazi than she had been a Communist.

When John van Druten wrote *I Am a Camera,* he thought it dramatically necessary to make his hitherto sympathetic landlady character speak out against the Jews, in the last act. He wanted to show that she was becoming influenced by Nazi propaganda. He also wanted to give the Christopher character a chance to rebuke her severely, thereby demonstrating the awakening of his conscience. Christopher approved the logic of this, while finding the Christopher character's conscience somewhat nauseating; it was so pleased with its own earnestness, so preachy. And he squirmed when the Christopher character had his moment of nobility, fistfighting the Nazis. But to protest would have been ungrateful. He had put himself willingly and gladly into van Druten's hands. And he himself could never have made an acceptable Broadway play out of this material.

Nevertheless, he was concerned about Frl. Thurau. She might one day see *I Am a Camera.* (It was in fact translated and performed in Germany.) She might think that Christopher was accusing her of anti-Semitism through van Druten's mouth, and be deeply hurt. Even if she *had* attacked the Jews—she is never made to do so in the novels—it would have been utterly indecent for Christopher to have played her prosecutor. He therefore asked van Druten to change the landlady's name from Schroeder (as in the novels) to Schneider. Christopher tried to convince himself at the time that this minor adjustment would reassure Frl. Thurau that the landlady in the play wasn't intended to be a portrait of her, as Frl. Schroeder was . . . It is painfully clear to me now that this was one of those compromises which private guilt makes with the box office.

In February 1952, Christopher returned to Berlin on a short visit, for the first time since the war. With Heinz and Heinz's wife, he went to see Frl. Thurau. She was still living on the Nollendorfstrasse, but in a much smaller flat. There were smashed buildings along the familiar street and most of the house fronts were pitted by bomb fragments and eaten by decay. Christopher hadn't announced his arrival in advance, and now he felt suddenly afraid that the shock of seeing him might upset her. He asked Heinz and his wife to go upstairs ahead of him. Standing back in the shadows of the staircase, he listened to Heinz greeting Frl. Thurau and then starting to break the news . . . We've heard Christoph is back in England . . . He might be coming over here, they say . . . Very soon . . . Who knows, perhaps he's here already? . . . Frl. Thurau had guessed, by this time. When Christopher appeared, she uttered a tremendous scream, a scream worthy of *Tristan and Isolde,* equally appropriate for death or bliss. It must have been heard all over the building.

As was to be expected, she was now enthusiastically pro-American; the Nollendorfstrasse was in the American occupation sector. Her feelings toward the Russians were mixed. She spoke of their politics with conventional disapproval and of their sexual appetites with grudging respect. Immediately after the war's end, she had met many Russian soldiers. "Every time I went out on the street they'd be after me," she told Christopher, with a certain complacency. "So I used to screw up my eyes— like this—and make a hump on my back, and limp. You ought to have seen me, Herr Issyvoo. Then even those Russians didn't want me any more. I looked like a regular old hag!" She looked better now, in her seventies, than she had in her fifties—despite all she had been through. Christopher asked her about the bombing. "Oh, the last year was terrible! We were in the cellar nearly all the time. We used to hold each other in our arms and say at least we'd all die together. I can tell you, Herr Issyvoo, we prayed so much we got quite religious!"

When they said goodbye, Frl. Thurau gave him the

brass dolphin clockstand, holding a clock on its tail, which is described in *Goodbye to Berlin* and about which "Isherwood" asks himself: "What becomes of such things? How could they ever be destroyed?" A prophetic comment—for a bomb blast had hurled it across the room and only slightly scratched its green marble base. It stands ticking away on my desk, as good as new, while I write these words.

EIGHT

Christopher had told Stephen in a letter:

> If we do go to Greece, I shall write a book as much like
> *Hindoo Holiday* as possible. This will pay for everything
> for the next ten years.

Joe Ackerley's *Hindoo Holiday* had been published in
1932. He was a close friend of Forster and of Plomer, but
I don't think Christopher had met him yet. Christopher
had admired *Hindoo Holiday* and wasn't intending to
sneer at it. All he meant by his remark to Stephen was
that he wanted to write a light, funny, salable travelogue.

Now, on the point of departure, Christopher started a
diary, in the hope that it would provide him with material
for this projected book.

May 13, 1933. It is a quarter past midnight and I have
just finished packing. In eight hours I am going to
leave Berlin, perhaps for ever. The paper says there
has been an earthquake in Greece. I am not exactly
tired, I feel only as if I were convalescent from a severe
illness. For days I have worried, worried whether
Heinz would get his passport, whether Erwin would
be arrested, whether they will remember to call us in

the hotel in Belgrade to catch the Athens train. I have already made the journey several times in my head, composed funny postcards to all my friends. And now the day which seemed too good, too bad to be true, the day when I should leave Germany, has arrived, and I only know about the Future that, however often and however variously I have imagined it to myself, the reality will be quite quite different.

That last long pompously false sentence is produced by Christopher's feeling that he ought to make some statement befitting the importance of the situation. It is false because it is out of character. I don't believe he ever imagined the day on which he would leave Germany; that suggests a calm foresight of which he was incapable. He was a worrier, not a foreseer. That part of his will over which he had no conscious control—he would have called it "circumstances"—swept him blindly into the future, often kicking, sometimes screaming.

When Edward Upward heard what Christopher's destination was, he had written:

Tell me the details and whether it is possible to live on an island for nothing and for ever. If it is I'll come.
But even as I say so my foredoomed function comes down on me like an iron extinguisher from the ceiling. I've got to stay here. Otherwise the guns will never fire again. They haven't fired yet this term. I've written a lot of *The Border Line* in my head but not one word on paper.
Three nights a week go regularly to party work—worthless to the party but it will be very valuable some day to my writing. And on an average one afternoon a week goes to the party too. It would be very easy for me not to have any spare time at all.

(Edward was then teaching at Dulwich and going to Communist Party meetings. *The Border Line,* on which he was working, was to become his first novel. It was published in 1938, as *Journey to the Border.*)

Does this sound like a voice from the sewer? Every day I develop more and more into my opposite. Holidays reverse the process, hence the awful birth pangs at the beginning of each term.

I see now, suddenly, what it was that seemed so obscurely tremendous about your original remark about our functions: you go to Greece because it's your opposite and I am here because this is mine. If we'd never met at Cambridge the roles would have been reversed and we should both have been very unhappy.

Edward meant that he was designed by nature to be a romantically footloose traveler and that Christopher was designed to be a humdrum stay-at-home, devoted to some daily duty. Their encounter had had the effect of changing each other's life roles and of helping each to find his proper subject matter as a writer. I think this was more or less true.

Heinz came round to pick Christopher up at six. Heinz hadn't been to bed at all because he had been afraid he would oversleep. They met Erwin on the platform of the Anhalter Station. He rolled up to them red-eyed, having drunk a bottle and a half of cognac, and greeted them with the Communist clenched fist, in defiance of the onlookers.

The train took them southward to the Czechoslovak border, by way of the valley of the Elbe, where they saw a hammer and sickle daubed in red paint on a cliff face above the river; the Nazis had much landscape cleaning of this kind still to do. At the border, Christopher watched tensely as the German officials examined the passports of Erwin and Heinz and at length admitted that they were in order. His own British passport had been returned to him after the merest glance.

When filling out the passport application, Heinz had asked how he should describe his profession. Christopher had told him to write *Hausdiener* (domestic servant). I suppose Christopher felt that Heinz ought to proclaim himself an unashamed proletarian, instead of hiding behind some bourgeois label such as student or *Privat* (of independent means). Anyhow, this proved to have been a fatally silly piece of advice.

They reached Prague that afternoon. The hotel was full of refugees from Germany. The wearing of Nazi badges was forbidden by the police. Compared with Berlin, the city seemed ancient, picturesquely untidy, loud with tram clatter and taxi tooting, rather French. I have never forgotten the dark little fourteenth-century synagogue, full of candle smoke, where you felt you could smell the Middle Ages.

Next day, they took the train on to Vienna. Erwin had some friends there, members of the League for Sexual Reform, a Hirschfeld-inspired organization. They wanted, of course, to hear all about the closing of the Institute. Erwin, not unnaturally, presented himself as the central martyr in the drama. This irritated Christopher:

> I get bored with Erwin when he starts being the heroic exile. We all know that the Nazis are behaving like swine, but why such a *fuss*. Fussing is for emigrés, not for Communists.

Christopher was charmed by Vienna—by the soft-spoken language of the Viennese, by the many fountains, by the Prater with its big wheel. He thought he would like to live there. John Lehmann, whom they saw on the sixteenth, encouraged him to do so. On the seventeenth, they moved on to Budapest. In a restaurant overlooking the Danube, they ate goulash, drank Tokay, and had a fiddle played within a millimeter of their ears, gypsy-style. After which they embarked on a river steamer for Belgrade.

As they steamed down the wide brown river, Christopher kept repeating to himself that they were entering the Balkans—a romantically dangerous region of blood feuds and (so he had been told) male marriages celebrated by priests. Arriving late the next evening in Belgrade, they found a café where

a dark girl with a mustache kept up a harsh, extremely dramatic shouting to the accompaniment of the tambourine. We drank wine and coffee out of dolls' coffee cups.

Early in the morning of May 19, they caught the Athens train:

The country was like England, with very beautiful trees. I'd expected palms. Beyond Skopje the brown mountains, the straw hats, the jet-eyed children with their heads bound in crimson rags. Soldiers with fixed bayonets along the line. Rain, heavy and cold. As it got dark, the empty train rushed through the deserted country, guarded by solitary armed men, towards the frontier.

May 20. We arrived at noon. Francis was on the platform to meet us, with a boy named Tasso. "Hullo, lovey," he said, "I never expected you'd come." He has syphilis again. We sat for hours and hours in a café while the rain swilled down the streets. We couldn't drink the turpentine wine nor eat the potatoes like soap, but there were strawberries. Everybody has a string of yellow beads to play with. Tasso has one fingernail, on the little finger of the left hand, which he has allowed to grow enormously long. This, says Francis, is fashionable. Tasso is very gay and makes little paper boats. Afterwards Heinz and I went back to our hotel. Tomorrow the island.

The island on which Francis was building his house is called St. Nicholas. It lies in the strait between the island of Euboea and the coast of the mainland, close to the shore, just north of the city of Chalkis. It is about a kilometer long.

Francis had rented St. Nicholas from the inhabitants of the nearest mainland village, who were its part owners. He had a lease on it for ten years at the rate of three pounds a year. Later, he hoped to persuade the villagers to sell it to him. Francis had decided to live on St. Nicholas because there was a tumulus just behind the beach opposite the island which was said to contain the remnants of one or more prehistoric villages. Its surface was littered with bits of pottery. Francis was already trying to get an authorization from the British School in Athens to excavate the tumulus. (As far as I know, he never did get this authorization. His name was becoming increasingly disreputable in official circles.)

The description of life on St. Nicholas in *Down There on a Visit* is taken directly from Christopher's diary. But the Englishman called Geoffrey is largely fictitious and the visit of Maria Constantinescu never happened. Waldemar, the boy who arrives from Germany with "Isherwood," isn't in the least a portrait of Heinz; he is a mere second edition of the character of Otto Nowak. "Isherwood" treats Waldemar very much as he treats Otto in *Goodbye to Berlin*, with condescending amusement and without any suggestion that they are seriously involved.

Christopher didn't fully realize, at first, what a great

nervous strain he was under, what an effort he was making to endure this place. St. Nicholas was like nothing he had ever experienced before. He was accustomed to say that he loved sunshine, and so he did, at some northern resort with comfortable lodgings into which he could retreat when he had had enough. But now here he was, transplanted from Frl. Schroeder's dark flat to a tent in the midst of this blazing sun-smitten outdoors—so beautiful with its encircling sea and mountains, so nearly uninhabitable with its heat, dirt, bad food and worse water, stinging flies and yelling Greeks. How could he ever have imagined he could work on his novel here?

Francis, on the other hand, seemed far more at home than he had been in Germany. He still drank a great deal, but he got up early and was busy all day long. He was never bored. He flew often into rages—with Erwin or with his boy employees, or with the men who were building the house—but these cost him no loss of energy and were immediately forgotten. Once, when Francis was screaming at someone in Christopher's presence, Christopher was suddenly possessed by the hysteria of the scene. He had a cigarette in his mouth and, involuntarily, he inhaled its smoke. This was the first time he had ever inhaled—he didn't know he knew how to—although he had been a smoker for ten years. The lift of the intoxication made him feel as though he were levitating; for an instant, he almost lost consciousness. After this, he began to inhale regularly and thus became a nicotine addict for the next thirty years.

Christopher got very little work done on his novel during their stay. The writing he did was mostly in his diary, where he describes his inability to write, with gloomy relish. If the sun shines, he is too lazy. If it rains, he is too depressed. Or else he is disturbed by the noise made by the boys and the domestic animals and the gramophone. Or he is suffering from diarrhea or worried by rectal bleeding.

I have utterly no inducements to stop staring at my shoes. Eat an orange? I have already exceeded my ration. Turkish delight? There isn't any. A glass of bottled water? Well, it's all I have. But I can't open the bottle. The boys have started playing that gramophone. I have finished my only detective novel: The Greek Coffin Mystery. All those energetic Americans. They are an example to me. I must pull myself together. I must write. If I don't, I'm lost.

The chief effect of Christopher's effort to write was to make him hostile to the non-writers—that is, to everybody else on the island. They were all making his task harder for him, simply by being there—all, with the possible exception of Heinz.

Heinz had become very much at home on St. Nicholas. After the first few days, he had stopped complaining about the food. Christopher notes sourly that Heinz was "quite uncanny" at being able to get along with the boys and the workmen. They had "interminable" conversations by means of pocket dictionaries, and soon they were exchanging Greek and German words. Heinz had private jokes with each one of them. He knew instinctively when to pinch their cheeks. They shook their fingers in each other's faces, laughing and exclaiming: "Ah na *na,* ah na *na!*" over and over again. From time to time, they would utter whoops of joy.

Nevertheless, Heinz and Christopher shared a tent; at least a fragment of their daily life was lived apart from the others. And when Christopher was in a mood to make the best of the situation, he would dwell on this aspect of it:

Bathed early for the first time. A perfect deep blue morning. Our tent is very nice, with the looking glass and the suitcase on a wooden box and the table for my typewriter, with the wire gadget Heinz has made for holding papers. We have our own oranges and marmalade. I should like to live with Heinz in this tent always.

Heinz is my one support. He makes everything tolerable. When he swims he says "Zack!" "Zack!" like the crocodile in Peter Pan.

Occasionally they spent a whole day alone together, rowing and sailing, or scrambling up the nearest of the coastal mountains. Three times, Christopher took a holiday from the island and went by train with Heinz to Athens. There they saw the sights, including what Heinz persisted in calling the "Micropolis," and enjoyed the food at a French restaurant and the comfort of a good hotel. It was a treat to make love without the interruptions common on St. Nicholas, where one of the boys or the builders was apt to stick his head into the tent at any moment.

July 8. I've had enough of this.

I'm tired of writing this discreet literary little journal, with one eye on the landscape and the other on the Hogarth Press. Let's be frank.

(Idea for a novel or story: a diary which begins very literary, chatty, amusing. In the middle, the diarist makes an admission which changes the whole significance of what he has been describing.)

I am potentially jealous of everybody on the island —of everybody to whom Heinz makes himself in the slightest degree agreeable.

Christopher admits that he has been jealous of Erwin (who very possibly *had* been to bed with Heinz in Berlin, before Christopher met him), of Tasso (who was quite capable of going to bed with any human being and with many sorts of animal), and of Mitso, Francis's chauffeur, as he was grandly called. Mitso was a good-looking young man. He had a wife and children in the nearby mainland village, but sometimes he spent nights on the island with the most attractive of the builders—so it was probable that he fancied Heinz as well. Christopher had once vented his jealousy of Mitso by making a hypocritical scene with him about a rabbit he had caught and put in a wooden packing case. (The boys were often horribly cruel to animals, but this rabbit seemed quite happy, munching grass.)

> I took the case and smashed it, letting the rabbit out, shouting in German (for Erwin's benefit), "Next time you torture animals don't let me see it!" I then threw the packing case at Mitso. This caused a great sensation among the builders. They couldn't understand it.

Christopher continues to describe the situation on July 8 as follows:

> Today, Heinz announced his intention of going rabbit-shooting with Mitso. At supper, realizing that I was cross about the proposed shooting-expedition, he was awkward, embarrassed, inclined to be sulky. Several times he snatched my spoon because he wanted to use it himself.
>
> "You seem to be in such a hurry, this evening," I said. "I'm not in a bit of a hurry," said Heinz, and added, with the perception of cruelty, "I wasn't thinking about the shooting at all. It's you who were thinking about it, and hoping I shouldn't go."
>
> Now he's with Mitso, and I know that, either to-night when he comes back or tomorrow morning, I shall have to crawl, pocket my pride, overlook his stupid clownish rudeness, because I simply daren't bring things to an issue. The discovery of my jealousy would put a weapon into his hands. I wonder if he dislikes me already, finds my demands upon his time boring and wearisome. And if I am jealous here, what shall I be in a big city where there will be men and

women who will really want to take him away from me?

There is only one protection for me. The only happiness, or indeed sanity, is in a core of detachment. I am eaten up with jealousy and devoured by boredom. I wait in vain to hear Heinz's whistling drawing nearer or the sound of him spitting out the mucus from his squashed nose.

This sounds like the prelude to a crisis. But—such is the power of inertia—Christopher and Heinz remained on St. Nicholas for nearly two more months.

During that period, one of the boys stole money and fled to Athens; another boy raped a duck. An effort was made to kill the rats which swarmed over the inhabited part of the island; they ate all the poison, but there wasn't enough of it. One evening, a boatful of fishermen landed uninvited and began cooking their fish. They shouted for wine. There was nothing to do but give it to them and join in a party lasting till dawn. Francis and Erwin spent most evenings drinking out of doors at a small kitchen table. They would sit there through the downpour of a thunderstorm, covering their drinks with their hands but not caring that they themselves were soaked to the skin.

Meanwhile, despite delays caused by saint's days and orgies and the damage done when the builders carelessly used too much dynamite in blasting for stone, the house got built, and was ready to be painted and have its floors paved. Set in the wall over the front door, there was a fragment of an inscription from the tomb of Seti I at Luxor. Francis had found it lying on the ground there and had smuggled it out of Egypt. So now he was saying he could tell his visitors that his home was three thousand years old.

Christopher seldom was able to talk to Francis alone. He was either with Erwin or the boys, or he was arguing with the builders about the house. If he *was* alone, he was often too drunk to make sense. His manner with Christopher was always polite, even when they had a domestic argument. On one occasion, Christopher protested because the boy whose job it was to wash the plates after meals had sores on his hands, probably of syphilitic origin. Francis treated this exhibition of "fussiness" with good humor. Christopher said that he and Heinz would wash up themselves but that, if they did, they ought to be charged less for their board. To which Francis replied, through Erwin, that Christopher might stay on without paying anything, as his guest, but that there could be no question, on principle, of allowing him to pay *less*. Heinz wasn't included in this invitation; Francis was still hostile to him, regarding him as a servant who was living with the gentlefolk, under false pretenses.

August 14. Things are bad with Heinz. For days he's been sulky or prepared to sulk. The slightest word sets him off. To the workmen he's as pleasant as he knows how. I'm very patient, but patience is wrong, even cowardly. I've probably got into the position of being the sink down which his bad moods drain off. We all have such a sink but I don't want to be it. I must seriously face the idea of leaving him.

August 16. We started talking in the morning, a fatal trick. Heinz became sullen, as he always does when I talk personalities. Finally he said that it would be better if we parted and he returned to Berlin. I asked him to reconsider it till after lunch. After lunch I talked to him again and shed tears, and finally he said: Well, all right, I'll stay with you, but we'll go to Paris at once. Since then we haven't spoken to each other. My own feelings and his are both in such a muddle that it's better not. He is quite astonishingly muddle-headed, a confusion of resentments. I suppose we shall have to part, but it shan't be till I want to. I must leave him, as I left Otto, in my own time.

144

When someone told Christopher he was a monster—it happened now and then—he would protest, and feel secretly flattered. The word sounds rather romantic. But here I am confronted by the reality of Christopher's monster behavior—his tears followed by cold calculation—and it shocks me, it hurts my self-esteem, even after all these years! The more reason for recording it.

From August 24 to August 28 they were in Athens, celebrating Christopher's birthday. His only comment is that the weekend was "nice" and that "I spent my birthday very pleasantly, chiefly in bed." This, however, was merely an armistice.

September 6. About lunchtime, in our tent, I deliberately raked the embers of a row which Heinz and I had three days ago, over the boat. It was so simple, like draughts. I moved. Heinz moved. I moved. Until Heinz had preposterously demanded that I should buy him a boat. "No, of course I won't." "You won't?" "No." "Then I shall go to Berlin." I shrugged my shoulders.

Our departure was semi-secret. I didn't want Erwin's attempts at reconciliation or the workmen's demonstrations. We were rowed away from the island just after sunset. We spent the night in the hotel at Chalkis.

I suppose Christopher did at least say goodbye to Francis, who would certainly never have attempted a reconciliation or even politely urged them to stay. He was lonely, amidst this crowd of employees and hangers-on. (He told Stephen Spender, who visited him in 1936, that not one of his boys had heard of Homer.) But his pride prevented him from admitting to his loneliness. All he probably said to Christopher was: "Have a nice journey, lovey."

If Christopher and Heinz didn't say goodbye to Erwin on this occasion, they were fated never to do so. Erwin returned to Germany several years later. Someone told me that he was arrested by the Nazis and died in a concentration camp, but I haven't been able to confirm this. I only know that he is dead now.

September 7. We came to Athens by the early train. I'd counted on cashing a check with a friend of Francis, but he wasn't in Athens. So it was only possible to raise enough money for Heinz's ticket to Berlin. He was to have left this evening. But we arrived too late at lunchtime to book a sleeping-berth for him. After lunch, Heinz said: "If you give me six thousand drachmas, I'll stay with you." I said: "Certainly not. I'm not going to buy you." So we went back to the travel bureau. All the sleeping-berths were booked. "It's a portent," I said.

So Heinz has said he'll come with me on the steamer to Marseille, starting from here on the 9th. He's sitting about with a face like death and won't speak. I shall have to get rid of him as soon as I'm in Paris.

Heinz sulked until they sailed and continued to sulk during the voyage, which took them through the Corinth canal and between the Lipari Islands and gigantic Stromboli, which they saw at dawn, smoking heavily. They were never alone together because they shared a cabin with four others. On deck, Heinz talked to a Swiss and Christopher to an Englishman, George Thomson, the translator of Greek classics.

Arriving at Marseilles on September 13, they wandered through the Old Port, down streets of stairs, and had their hats snatched by whores who were trying to entice them into the houses. When they advanced, the girls retreated; when they walked away, the girls advanced. At last, Christopher and Heinz gave up and walked away hatless. This adventure made them laugh together. Peace was instantly declared between them.

Instead of parting next day in Paris, they spent a couple of weeks in the suburb of Meudon:

> Once again, the French are preparing to say: Ils ne passeront pas. War is in the air. But we had our tiny room with the double bed and our ping-pong and meals, and were happy.

On September 30, Christopher took Heinz over to England. They stayed at Kathleen's house. The diary narrative breaks off here with the remark: "The atmosphere is chilly but polite."

The chill was largely of Christopher's creation. He had told Kathleen that he and Heinz had met for the first time in France, only a few days earlier. This was because he didn't want her to know that Heinz had been with him in Greece and that they had been together for a long while in Germany. But, having told this silly lie, he had let drop—with a carelessness which was part of his aggression toward her—several references to things Heinz had done while they were on St. Nicholas. Kathleen hadn't commented on this, but she was hurt that he had lied to her. She had realized instantly that Heinz was a working-class boy and she treated him as such—though with such a faint nuance of patronage that Heinz was unaware of it and thought her kind and liked her. Christopher detected every microscopic slight and raged inwardly.

Heinz's tourist permit to stay in England expired and he went back to Germany. I am sure that he did this unwillingly. He and Christopher were on the best of terms again and he had thoroughly enjoyed himself in London, where several of Christopher's friends had been charming to him; Beatrix Lehmann and Humphrey Spender in particular. I am not so sure how Christopher felt. The strain of having to live with Heinz under Kathleen's eye spoiled much of his pleasure. Also he wanted to be alone for a while, free from the necessary friction of their relationship, to get on with his writing. He hated letting Heinz return to Berlin. Hitler was making warlike moves; he had just withdrawn from the League of Nations. But even the pessimists agreed that he wasn't ready to risk actual war yet. So Christopher resolved to get some more money somehow and to find a way of bringing Heinz over to England for a much longer period, perhaps for keeps.

NINE

One morning in the middle of October, just after Heinz's departure, Christopher got a telephone call from Jean Ross. I have no verbatim record of what she said. The best I can do is to report it in the style of Sally Bowles —which will be anachronistic, for Jean was now beginning to shed her Sally Bowles persona. Her way of expressing herself already showed the influence of her new London friends—left-wingers who were humorous but dedicated, sexually permissive but politically dogmatic.

"Chris darling, I've just met this absolutely marvelous man. He's simply brilliant. I adore him . . . No, you swine —we most certainly do not! He's *old*—at least sixty, I should think. I mean, I adore his *mind* . . . You see, he's an Austrian, only he's a director in Hollywood. He's come here to direct a film . . . And, darling, this is what's so marvelous—*he wants you to write it!* . . . Well, no, as a matter of fact, he didn't know who you were. But he's got to find a writer at once, and I've told him about you, how you're an absolute genius only a bit unrecognized, so far. He seems really quite interested. He wants to read something you've written . . . Yes, I know you're terribly busy with your novel but, after all, it can wait, can't it— I mean, you can just dash this thing off and then you'll be filthy rich . . . But, *Chris,* I *promised* him you would!

Look, won't you at least send him a copy of your last novel—I never *can* remember its name . . . Yes, of course I've got one—I treasure it—only I lent it to someone and I've forgotten who . . . You won't? You old brute! Well, I'll tell you what—let's make a bargain, shall we? If I buy a copy myself, and you get this job—will you give me half your first week's salary?"

"It's a deal!" Christopher told her, laughing. He had long since lost faith in Jean's many moneymaking schemes. He dismissed this conversation from his mind.

Two days later, Jean called him again, breathless: "Darling—I bought your book and I gave it to him and" —here her voice became hushed with amazement—"he thinks it's *good!*"

What had actually happened was that the director, Berthold Viertel, leafed casually through *The Memorial* until he came to the scene in which Edward Blake tries unsuccessfully to kill himself. (A friend had once described his own suicide attempt to Christopher. This scene was based upon it.) Having read it, Viertel declared: "This I find clearly genial"—pronouncing the word as English but meaning it as the German *genial*, "gifted with genius." And that was that. Viertel read no further. Christopher, already as good as hired sight unseen, was invited to come for an interview.

(After performing this momentous act of introduction, with all its short- and long-term consequences for Christopher, Jean seems to have disappeared temporarily from his life. Perhaps she went abroad somewhere. I can't remember if Christopher kept his promise to give her half of his first week's salary. I am pretty sure that she would have held him to it. I hope she did.)

Berthold Viertel appears as Friedrich Bergmann in the novelette called *Prater Violet,* which was published twelve years later:

The gray bushy head, magnificent and massive as sculptured granite . . . the big firm chin, the grim compressed line of the mouth, the harsh furrows cutting down from the imperious nose . . . the head of a Roman emperor . . . but the eyes were the dark mocking eyes of his slave.

I couldn't help smiling as we shook hands, because our introduction seemed so superfluous. There are meetings which are like recognitions—this was one of them. Of course we knew each other. The name, the voice, the features were inessential, I knew that face. It was the face of a political situation, an epoch. The face of Central Europe.

This passage really only refers to Christopher's sense of recognition, not Viertel's. Yet, under the circumstances, Viertel's sense of recognition must have been much stronger and more exciting than Christopher's. While Christopher merely recognized in Viertel "the face of Central Europe," Viertel recognized in Christopher—from that very first moment, I believe—the exceedingly odd kind of individual his temperament required as a working companion.

The film which Viertel had agreed to direct was to be based on a novel by the Austrian writer Ernst Lothar, called *Kleine Freundin,* Little Friend. It is about a small girl whose parents are becoming estranged; this makes her so unhappy that she tries to kill herself. (Which may explain why the suicide scene in *The Memorial* caught Viertel's attention.) The girl's suicide attempt is unsuccessful but it reunites the parents, the girl, and her puppy. This old-fashioned sentimental theme had been modernized but not at all desentimentalized by the introduction of Freudian symbols and dreams. (In *Prater Violet,* the film which is being produced is an unashamedly corny musical comedy set in pre-1914 Vienna. Christopher persuaded John van Druten, who was a master of pastiche and parody, to invent its plot for him.)

Since *Little Friend* features a nymphet, the studio (Gaumont-British) had typecast Margaret Kennedy, authoress of *The Constant Nymph,* as its scriptwriter. My impression is that Miss Kennedy wrote an entire screenplay on her own; her name appears, above Christopher's, on the credit list of the film. Christopher never met her. Viertel did meet her, but there seems to have been no true marriage of their minds; he later described her as "a crocodile who wept once in her life a real tear"—i.e., *The Constant Nymph.* Fortunately for both of them, Miss Kennedy was obliged to withdraw from their collaboration almost at once, because she had to devote herself to the production of her own play *Escape Me Never!* (It became a hit early in 1934, starring Elisabeth Bergner.) So Viertel had had to get himself another writer.

Crocodile or no crocodile, a successful self-assured professional would never have suited Viertel as a working companion. He needed an amateur, an innocent, a disciple, a victim. He needed someone he could teach—"I am an old Jewish Socrates"—someone with whom he could share the guilt of creating this film, someone to whom he could truthfully say, as he said to Christopher: "I feel absolutely no shame before you; we are like two married men who meet in a whorehouse."

Christopher was an amateur, in both senses of the word. A lover of movies since childhood, he was also eager to learn the craft of film writing and prepared to begin at the beginning. Why shouldn't he play the humble novice? It caused him no pain to do so, for his arrogance as a novelist was wrapped protectively around his ego. Viertel was subtle enough to understand this. He addressed the Novelist as "Master," in the humorous tone of a fellow artist whose embarrassment mocks his sincere admiration. Meanwhile, he trained the Filmwriter with the impatient patience of a craftsman who has to make the best of a slow-witted apprentice.

Viertel chose to regard Christopher as an innocent, and used to call him Alyosha Karamazov. Viertel fancied himself as a wise old Lucifer, and this role demanded its opposite, the young unfallen angel who still had illusions about Heaven. Lucifer benevolently despises this angel but sentimentally envies him . . . Christopher wasn't an innocent but he could be infantile, which was the next best thing. He could take the pressure off crises in their film work by displaying such babylike dismay that he made Viertel laugh at him and cheer up and get a new idea.

As a disciple, Christopher attended closely to the way Viertel talked, trying to memorize his vocabulary and mannerisms. This was part of Christopher's instinctive functioning as a writer. He often caught himself studying someone without having been conscious that he or she was a model for a prospective fiction character. No doubt, Christopher's show of attention flattered Viertel and deceived him; the truth was that Socrates's opinions were of minor interest to his disciple. Christopher saw Viertel as the kind of intellectual who takes his intellectualism too seriously and thus becomes the captive of his own opinions. He could be dazzlingly witty, grotesquely comic, but never silly, never frivolous. Comparing him with Forster and Auden and Upward, and seeing the vast difference between Viertel and them, Christopher said to himself that only those who are capable of silliness can be called truly intelligent.

When I say that Viertel needed a victim, I mean a willing victim and a victim who could thrive on victimization. My theory is that Viertel's ideal victim could only have been a male homosexual—and not just any male homosexual but one who, like Christopher, was able to enjoy both the *yang* and the *yin* role in sex. If the relationship between Viertel and himself had been sexual, however, their collaboration wouldn't have worked; sex would have been a complication. If the victim had been a woman, Viertel would have regarded her sexually, to some extent, even if they hadn't been lovers. If the victim had been a heterosexual man, he would probably have hated submitting to Viertel's will, regarding it as a humiliation and a threat to his masculinity. But Christopher didn't think of submission in those terms; it was simply the *yin* role, which he enjoyed playing precisely because he knew himself equally able to play *yang*.

Therefore, Christopher suffered relatively little emotional wear and tear during those weeks of work on *Little Friend*. I am not claiming that he always kept his awareness of the *yang-yin* balance; indeed, I am going to describe some occasions when he lost it. But he managed pretty well.

From Viertel's point of view, one of Christopher's greatest assets was that he spoke Viertel's native language with sufficient fluency. Viertel's English was fluent, too, but he needed the release of being able to slip back into German when he was tired. And he loved making satirical asides to Christopher in public which no one else present was likely to understand. Best of all, Christopher was able to read his German poems. He had published two volumes of them, as well as a novel. Viertel thought of himself as a poet, first and foremost, and it was depressing for him to find himself almost without an audience in England, the land of poets. Once, when a friend told Christopher, in Viertel's presence, that a critic had referred to him as one of the most brilliant younger English novelists, Viertel exclaimed to Christopher demandingly, like a child: "And now tell him about *me!*"

Viertel's public persona was that of a Roman emperor; but, in the intimacy of their working hours, Christopher saw him as

> an old clown, shock-headed, in his gaudy silk dressing-gown; tragi-comic, like all clowns, when you see them resting backstage after the show.

Although he looked much older than his age, forty-eight —and had done so even as a young man, to judge from photographs—he was inspiringly vigorous and could work all day and half the night, if necessary. Nevertheless, he was a semi-invalid with a diabetic condition which caused him to eat ravenously and to suffer acute hunger pangs if he was kept waiting for meals. For the same reason, he was subject to storms of rage and black frosts of despair, from which, however, he could recover within seconds. He seemed to carry his own psychological "weather" around with him. In his company you were so powerfully aware of it that you scarcely noticed if the day was cold or warm, wet or fine.

He was chronically lonely for his family—his wife, Salka, and their sons, Hans, Peter, and Thomas. He talked about them continually and showed Christopher their latest snapshots and letters. Salka, born of a Jewish family in Poland, had come to Vienna during the 1914–18 war, as a refugee. There she met Viertel. During the early years of their marriage, they had both achieved success, she as an actress, he as a writer and stage director. They had moved from Europe to California in 1928. Their sons, said Viertel, were already becoming Americanized and beginning to regard Salka and himself as foreigners.

Viertel described their white house with its green roof, standing amidst the subtropical vegetation of Santa Monica Canyon, three minutes' walk from the Pacific Ocean. 165 Mabery Road—the British-sounding address became wildly exotic when Christopher tried to relate it to his idea of a canyon, a gigantic romantic ravine. He began to yearn to see this place; Viertel took it for granted that he would be visiting them there before long. (Forty years later, I am standing on the balcony of my home, looking out over the familiar little suburban valley, now so full of my own memories. There, on the street below us, is the Viertels' former home. It is strange to think that I have lived in the canyon much longer than they did.)

Since his arrival in the States, Viertel had directed at

least eight films and several famous actors and actresses, including Paul Muni, Claudette Colbert, Charles Boyer, Tallulah Bankhead. Salka had appeared in the German-language versions of three American films. One of these was *Anna Christie,* in which she played Marthy. Garbo, who had made a successful debut as a talkie actress in the American version, played Anna again in German. She and Salka had become close friends. Garbo respected Salka's wide experience and would ask her advice about possible new roles. She also wanted Salka to supervise the writing of her screenplays and used her influence to get Salka a contract with her own studio, Metro-Gold-wyn-Mayer.

That winter, Garbo's *Queen Christina*—on which Salka shared the writing credit with S. N. Behrman—was being shown in London, to full houses. When it became time to send Christmas presents overseas, Christopher went with Viertel to an art-book shop in Charing Cross Road. As the shop assistant wrapped one of the books they had bought, he asked whom he should mail it to. Viertel—speaking slowly and distinctly, as if this were some unheard-of and almost unpronounceable name—replied, "Miss Greta Garbo." The young man laughed loudly, thinking that Viertel must be pulling his leg. It was unimaginable to him that anyone could actually be on gift-giving terms with that infinitely remote, two-dimensional deity.

"When you are with us in California, you will see her every day," Viertel told Christopher as they left the shop. "She comes to swim and ride horseback with our boys."

Those were long, long days of rapid talk and snail-slow work, in Viertel's stuffy Knightsbridge flat, which only Auden could have made smokier and untidier. For hours, Viertel would talk of anything, everything except *Little Friend*—of the Reichstag fire trial, then in progress (he imitated Dimitrov defying Goering); of his productions for Die Truppe in Berlin during the 1920's (he recited speeches from the leading roles); of the poetry of Hoelderlin; of the awful future in store for the world; of the nature of Woman. It was then that the grimly grinning, sparkling-eyed Clown surpassed himself. I'm sure he couldn't have performed as brilliantly in the Viennese cafés of his youth. His envious colleagues would have interrupted him. Christopher never did. He only prompted.

At last, unwillingly, they would have to come back to their task. Viertel's attitude toward it varied continually. Sometimes he denounced it as prostitution, for which they would have to answer, in some future existence, to a Supreme Tribunal composed of Sophocles, Shakespeare, Ibsen, and Chekhov. Sometimes he saw Christopher and himself as heroic rebels against bourgeois culture: "We are breaking our heads off, fighting for Truth!" Sometimes he discovered a deep significance in the story, decided that it was even perhaps a kind of masterpiece. He philosophized over it, quoting Marx, Freud, Nietzsche, and his own elected Socrates, Karl Kraus (of whom Christopher, before meeting Viertel, had never heard). But such high moods of optimism didn't survive the daylight. No sooner had Christopher left him than Viertel's mind would be clouded in with doubts. And, when Christopher returned next morning, he would find that their latest draft of a scene had been unraveled by Viertel during the night, like Penelope's weaving.

Now and again, Viertel touched on a sensitive area. Once, he told a story about a famous actor who decided to watch two boys having sex with each other. Viertel made it clear that the actor himself wasn't homosexual, merely feeling bored and in the mood for any variety of freak show. The actor hired two homosexual youths. But, when they began to perform, one of them was unable to get an erection. Whereupon, the other advised him, in a stage whisper, to "pretend I'm Erich" . . . The point and joke of this story—as far as Christopher could guess—was that these preposterous little inverts were suggesting that one sex partner might be preferable to another; they were, in fact, behaving like heterosexuals. This was amusing because, as we know, all homosexuals are hot to go to bed with any male whomsoever. Ha, ha. "Pretend I'm Erich," Viertel said, imitating the boy's effeminate voice, and laughed heartily. Christopher laughed too, and felt ashamed of himself for doing so. Suppose Christopher had told a comparable story about the Jews—would Viertel have laughed? Either he would have found it completely pointless, or he would have flown into a rage, and rightly.

On another occasion, Viertel referred to Hitler's chief of staff, Ernst Roehm, and his notorious homosexuality. Viertel's comment was: "To such swine we will never belong!" His tone as well as his words implied that Roehm's swinishness consisted just as much in being a homosexual as in being a Nazi. Christopher should have challenged him on this, but he didn't. He kept silent. Worse still, he felt himself blushing as though he were guilty. Which he was—of cowardice.

Viertel also told him: "You are a typical mother's son, I think. You are very repressed sexually. But you must not be. The right woman will change all that." Could Viertel, with all his vaunted worldly wisdom, be so un-perceptive? No, that was impossible. Then he must be deliberately provoking Christopher, to make him confess what he was. This, Christopher vowed to himself with cold fury, he would never do.

Working on *Little Friend* certainly helped Christopher not to brood on personal problems; nevertheless, he missed Heinz more and more. And now, in the middle of December, with the end of the screenplay in sight, the studio asked Christopher to stay on its payroll throughout the shooting of the film. Officially, he was to be its dialogue director—which meant that he was to advise Viertel on the nuances of English intonation and to do emergency rewrites if necessary. Unofficially, he was to act as a go-between if Viertel and the studio were to get into an argument. Both sides realized already that this was more than likely to happen.

Christopher was eager to accept. From his point of view, shooting the film would be ten times as much fun as writing it. But the job would keep him in England for another two and a half to three months. He couldn't be separated from Heinz for that much longer; Heinz would have to be brought back. How he would behave during such a long stay as Kathleen's guest—how his demands on Christopher's time would be tolerated by Viertel, the all-demanding—were questions which Christopher chose not to think about until they stared him in the face.

So he began making arrangements for Heinz's coming. He mailed Heinz money for the journey and money to show the British immigration officials as a proof that he would be able to support himself while he was in England. Christopher also sent an invitation, dictated by himself, handwritten by Kathleen, asking Heinz to come and stay with her for an unspecified period, but making no mention of Christopher.

On January 5, 1934, Christopher went to Harwich to meet Heinz's boat. Wystan came with him, at his request. Luckily, Heinz was arriving at a time when the school at which Wystan was then teaching was still on its Christmas holidays. Christopher wouldn't have wanted any other companion on this mission. And a curious foreboding made him unwilling to face it alone.

When the boat arrived, Heinz was on it, enormously to Christopher's relief. He had been dreading some last-minute hitch. He and Heinz exchanged a brief formal greeting; Christopher dared not even hug, much less kiss, lest some police spy should be watching them. "Everything will be all right," he told Heinz, and sent him off to the passport and customs inspections.

He and Wystan waited outside the office where the aliens had to show their passports. He wasn't really anxious but he made himself worry a little, out of superstitiousness; overconfidence was unlucky. At the same time he remembered the ease with which Heinz had been admitted to England, when they had arrived together, last September. Meanwhile, Wystan, that positive thinker, was talking about his job and his pupils, as if this passport inspection were the merest formality, unworthy of comment. Indeed, it seemed to be so, as more and more of the aliens emerged—a few with expressions of glad relief, most of them taking it as a matter of course —and went on their way to the customs.

But Heinz didn't emerge. And, at last, when Christopher had begun to tremble with impatience and when his conversation with Wystan had died away because he couldn't keep his mind on it, a man appeared at the door of the office and called his name. Wystan followed him in.

Once inside, Christopher saw instantly that something was very wrong indeed. Heinz sat opposite his questioners, looking humiliated and resentful. He was the sullen peasant boy, despite his middle-class clothes.

Christopher decided to play the gentleman, very superior, with a "What's this little fuss about?" air. But it was as a gentleman that they attacked him. On their table lay Kathleen's letter of invitation, side by side with Heinz's passport containing that damning word *Hausdiener*. Why, they wanted to know, should a lady like Mrs. Isherwood, the mother of a gentleman like himself, invite a young working-class foreigner to her home? Could it be that she herself planned to employ Heinz—without a work permit and perhaps on substandard wages?

Christopher felt on safe ground here. After remarking severely that his mother wasn't in the habit of exploiting illegal alien labor—a rebuke which didn't seem to abash them in the least—he added that Heinz was in no need of employment; he had enough money of his own.

They had been waiting for him to say this. Instantly, a second letter was played like a trump card: "Was this written by you, Mr. Isherwood?" With a sick shock, Christopher recognized it as the letter of instructions he had sent to Heinz in Berlin. He had neglected to tell Heinz to destroy it, so Heinz had brought it along with him. And when the examiners, who had already become suspicious, had asked for proof that the money was really his, he had shown them the letter. This wasn't mere stupidity. It was perhaps a subconscious bitchery which develops in people who have become accustomed to do exactly what they are told. In the military profession it has sometimes caused famous acts of heroism costing ninety percent casualties. Heinz's not to reason why.

("If they ask how you got the money," the letter said, "tell them your grandmother gave it to you. That'll sound better. They can't prove she didn't. And it's yours, anyhow.")

"I presume you're aware, Mr. Isherwood, that this could be construed as an attempt to deceive His Majesty's Immigration Service?"

This was from the man who had asked most of the questions. He was small, bright-eyed, smiling.

"I don't see it makes any difference who gave him the money. I did, as it happens."

"Rather a generous gift, wasn't it? It couldn't by any chance have been just a loan?"

"I've told you once already—"

"And then this letter of yours. A bit curious, isn't it, the way it's written?"

"I don't see why."

But Christopher did see, only too clearly. He had written that he was counting the days until Heinz's arrival, that he'd been so lonely without him. Nothing stronger than that. But far too much, under the circumstances.

"You don't?" The voice was teasing, playful. "I'd say

it was the sort of letter that, well, a man might write to his sweetheart."

Christopher glared at him in helpless amazement. *How dare he?* And he looked Christopher straight in the eyes, smiling.

The examiners consulted together for a moment. In a daze, he heard them telling him that Heinz wouldn't be granted permission to enter the United Kingdom. He would have to leave by the next boat. Christopher was incredulous. How could this be happening, when they hadn't proved their case? Then he realized that they didn't have to prove anything. An alien has no rights whatsoever; he can't force anybody to receive him. "I shall appeal," Christopher said, and was told that that was certainly his privilege; he could write to the Home Secretary, if he wished. "But I think you'll find, sir, that he'll endorse our decision. He gives us pretty wide powers."

When all the miserable arrangements had been made and a sad leave had been taken of Heinz and they were back in the train on their way to London, Wystan said: "As soon as I saw that bright-eyed little rat, I knew we were done for. He understood the whole situation at a glance—because he's *one of us.*"

Christopher hated having to tell people what had happened at Harwich, even in a strictly censored version. Richard was an exception, of course—Christopher could tell him anything. But Richard lacked experience; he couldn't always feel what Christopher had felt. Kathleen's obstinate, one-sided love grasped nothing but the fact that Christopher was unhappy. For this she blamed both the immigration officials and Heinz; Heinz more than them, since he had caused all the trouble by being, so tiresomely, a foreigner and working-class.

And now Christopher had to return to work on *Little Friend*. A former theatrical colleague of Viertel's—Christopher's diary refers to her only as Frau G.—was visiting him and helping him revise the screenplay. She was a brisk cheerful Viennese Jewess, full of energy and ideas. Christopher didn't in the least resent the intrusion of this new broom, even when it swept away some of his favorite scenes. Although he had written them, literally speaking, he always thought of Viertel as their author.

But, at this particular moment, Frau G. was more than unwelcome. For Christopher had to explain to Viertel in her presence what had become of the German friend whose arrival he had unwisely announced beforehand. This embarrassed him so acutely that he broke off in the middle and ran into the next room, where he threw himself down on a couch and shed tears of rage, shame, and self-pity. Frau G. followed him without the least hesitation, in her thick-skinned motherly way, and tried to comfort him. To her, he had become a child, with a childish, touching, but funny sorrow. Christopher hated her a little for this; hated Viertel as well. These Jews were certainly more aware of suffering than the insensitive Gentile masses around them; but it had to be suffering of their own brand, for their own exclusive cause. Civilized liberals that they were, they no doubt deplored the cruelty of their Book of Leviticus, which set the world an example in 500 B.C.: punishing homosexual lust by death. Homosexual lust they could laugh at, now, and tolerate in a sophisticated manner. Homosexual love they put to death by denial; like Kathleen, they refused to admit that it existed. For the next few days, Christopher could barely endure being with them. It was like a lack of oxygen; his nature gasped for the atmosphere of his fellow tribesmen. As never before, he realized that they were all his brothers—yes, even those who denied their brotherhood and betrayed it—even that man at Harwich.

(In 1935, during a visit to England, Christopher met Viertel again for the first time since the filming of *Little Friend*. Christopher then became aware that Viertel's attitude had greatly changed, perhaps because of the influence of Beatrix Lehmann. There was no need for a confession. Viertel showed that he knew all about Christopher's sex life and that he was prepared to treat it with respect.

Thus they began to become really friends; the tension between them on this subject eased. It had almost ceased to exist by the time Christopher settled in California, in 1939. Walking together on the beach at Santa Monica, they would sometimes play a game: Viertel would point out the boys he guessed Christopher might find attractive. He enjoyed doing this, though he was seldom right.)

On January 20, after the screenplay had been revised and delivered to the studio, Christopher left for Berlin. He was determined to get Heinz out of Germany again as soon as possible. As usual, his concern was mixed with aggression against Kathleen. She had to be shown that Heinz was the one whose safety he put before every other consideration. Her England—the England of Nearly Everybody—had rejected Heinz. Before long, he would be rejecting her England.

He brought Heinz from Berlin to lodgings in Amsterdam, where Heinz was to live until *Little Friend* was finished. Christopher stayed there with him for ten days. Then it was time to return to London.

Despite his separation from Heinz, Christopher wholeheartedly enjoyed himself throughout the next two months, while *Little Friend* was being filmed. He missed Heinz but he no longer had the worry of knowing that he was in Germany, and there were many distractions which kept him from thinking of Heinz for more than a few moments at a time. He was unwilling to admit to Kathleen how much fun he was having, but she must have been well aware of it, for they were on good terms again and he used to amuse her with stories of the latest studio intrigues and crises every morning at breakfast before he left for work.

The beginning of the filming brought an end to Christopher's life as Viertel's victim, imprisoned in his flat. But their move to Gaumont-British didn't separate them. They were now thrown even more closely together, as allies against the Others. Their relationship, while they were on the set, was in the nature of a performance. When they walked into a corner to confer in German, the actors and crew watched them with curiosity, wondering what decisions they might be making. They were public figures, director and dialogue director, emperor and courtier. The Emperor regarded himself as being in the midst of enemies. Some of these were real, most were imaginary. Christopher had to take his side against both kinds and did so enthusiastically. He felt a loyalty to the Emperor which he had never felt to the Clown.

One of the Gaumont-British executives took a strong dislike to Viertel, because of some clash of temperaments between them. Thus Christopher got a lesson in the subtleties of racism. The executive exclaimed angrily to Christopher that Viertel wasn't a Jew at all but one of these mongrel Ashkenazim, mixed-up scum from Poland or God knows where. The only real Jews were the Sephardim, to whom the executive's family belonged. They were all aristocrats. In Spain, his family had had a fine mansion with a balcony. And when they emigrated to England, the Jewish community had been exclusively Sephardic. The Ashkenazim had pushed themselves in later, disgracing the Jews by their un-Jewish ways.

The executives ate their lunch at the Kensington Palace Hotel. This was a grand dull expensive place. Viertel, as Emperor, insisted on going there often because, as he said, "the animals must see their tamer." When he and Christopher entered the dining room, he would glance sharply around him, as if on the lookout for plotters against his regime. The two of them sat at a table apart. If anyone ventured to greet Viertel, he bowed grimly.

Christopher much preferred lunching at a pub near the studio called the Goldhawk. It was cheaper and its customers were friendlier and more interesting. Robert Flaherty, white-haired, ruddy-faced, and patriarchal, often came there; he was getting his latest picture, *Man of Aran,* ready for screening. Viertel admired him greatly, sometimes calling him Neptune (because he had ruled over this film which featured 300-foot-high Atlantic waves) and sometimes "The Last Romantic" (because, according to Viertel, he began by falling in love with a primitive culture in a remote place, then visited it and was disappointed, then made a picture about it as he had expected it to be). Flaherty told Christopher: "The film is the longest distance between two points"—a statement which I still sometimes ponder over and interpret in various ways.

Christopher loved the world of filmmaking and felt at home in it at once. Psychologically, its technicians were old-fashioned craftsmen, not modern employees. These cameramen, electricians, and carpenters reveled in the precision with which they had to work on camera angles, lighting, and the details of construction. It was their dedication to precision which made their work a game, not a job. Being thus dedicated, they belonged to a higher caste than their employers, the businessmen who ran the commerce of the studio; and they knew it. They feuded with each other, they grumbled about being overworked and underpaid, but their lives were spent in the happy absorption of children at play. Their jokes were about their game.

A different kind of joke was unintentionally contributed by Christopher. Felicity, the *Little Friend* girl, has been given a present, a big mysterious box—which is later found to contain a puppy. Trying to guess what is inside this box, Felicity exclaims: "It doesn't rattle and it doesn't smell—oh, Mummy, what is it?" Yes, he, Christopher, had actually written that line! It was only when he heard it spoken that he realized how ridiculously obscene it sounded and joined in the roar of laughter which went up from the crew. They continued to quote it for several weeks.

Viertel had no real enemies on the set, despite his frequent eruptions of fury. "Stubborn monkeys!" he yelled. "No—not monkeys! Donkeys!" Forgetting his liberalism, which anyhow ill befitted an emperor, he would say with relish: "In Russia they would all be shot." But the crew didn't resent any of this. They accepted him as a player in their game; his behavior only made the game more exciting. I think many of them were fond of him.

Viertel talked as if the entire studio were an antiquated death trap. According to him, every take was made at the risk of disaster: lamps falling from the catwalk, sets collapsing and bursting into flames, cables electrocuting the unwary. "This morning, they are going to attempt a technical maneuver of extreme peril: Connie Veidt will walk right across the set with the camera following him. No doubt there will be several dead."

Conrad Veidt was then playing in the film of Feuchtwanger's *Jew Suss*. Whenever Christopher had the opportunity, he would watch. Two memories remain. My first is of a scene in which Veidt had to read a letter of bad news and, at a certain point, burst into tears. There were three successive takes and in each one—despite the intermediate fussings of the technicians and the makeup man —Veidt wept right on cue, the great drops rolling down his cheeks as if released from a tap . . . My second memory is of the beginning of the scene of Suss's execution. Veidt sat in a cart, his hands manacled, on his way to death—a wealthy and powerful man ruined, alone. However, just as the filming was about to begin, something went wrong with the lights. There was to be a delay of five minutes. Veidt stayed in the cart. And now a stenographer came up to him and offered him a piece of candy.

The gesture was perhaps deliberately saucy. Some stars would have been annoyed by it because they were trying to concentrate on their role and remain "in character." They would have ignored the stenographer. Others would have chatted and joked with her, welcoming this moment of relaxation. Veidt did neither. He remained Suss, and through the eyes of Suss he looked down from the cart upon this sweet Christian girl, the only human being in this cruel city who had the heart and the courage to show kindness to a condemned Jew. His eyes filled with tears. With his manacled hands he took the candy from her and tried to eat it—for her sake, to show his gratitude to her. But he couldn't. He was beyond hunger, too near death. And his emotion was too great. He began to sob. He turned his face away.

Christopher now acquired a new status among his friends. He was "in the movies" and therefore enviable but a trifle declassed. This wasn't the kind of situation which most of them could even imagine themselves being involved in. Christopher was amused and flattered by their reaction and he didn't contradict them when they took it for granted that he was earning a huge sum of money. (I forget how much his salary was; certainly nothing remarkable.) He, who had been apt to beg from his friends and be stingy during the Berlin days, now enjoyed paying for taxis and picking up the bills in restaurants, saying, "I'm *immensely* rich."

He tried to get Beatrix Lehmann the part of the mother in the film. First he took Viertel to see her play the young Elizabeth on stage in *The Tudor Wench*. Viertel was enormously impressed. Then he arranged for them to meet. Beatrix arrived dressed—or so my memory assures me—in an incredible femme-fatale outfit consisting largely of green feathers. She can't seriously have thought that this was the costume of a mother, even an erring one. More likely, it was one of her curious satirical impersonations—film vamp meeting Hollywood director. Anyhow, her instinct was correct. Viertel was charmed. Almost at once, they were intimate. As they laughed together, they looked strangely alike; perhaps it was the tribal resemblance of two tragicomedians. (Viertel did give her a part, not in *Little Friend,* but in his next film, *The Passing of the Third Floor Back.* She played an embittered spinster and made herself hideous as only she knew how.)

When the filming started, Christopher was able to invite his friends to the studio and treat them to the fascinating spectacle of Viertel directing a scene. This is described in *Prater Violet:*

> It isn't necessary to look at the set; the whole scene is reflected in his face . . . He seems to control every gesture, every intonation, by a sheer effort of hypnotic power. His lips move, his face relaxes and contracts, his body is thrust forward or drawn back in its seat, his hands rise and fall to mark the phases of the action. Now he is coaxing her from the window, now warning against too much haste, now encouraging her father, now calling for more expression, now afraid the pause will be missed, now delighted with the tempo, now anxious again, now really alarmed, now reassured, now touched, now pleased, now very pleased, now cautious, now disturbed, now amused . . . When it is all over, he sighs, as if awakening from sleep. Softly, lovingly, he breathes the word "Cut."

Among the visitors to the set was Forster. Viertel made some remark about Forster's eyes. Christopher later passed it on to Forster, who replied in a letter:

> The fact that he praised my eyes is very reassuring, because one's eyes are always with one, they do not vary from day to day like the complexion or the intelligence. Let him gaze his fill . . .

Then, referring to the studio:

> It *is* a milieu—so energetic, friendly, and horrible. I
> can't believe everything isn't going to crash when such
> a waggon gets so many stars hitched behind. Every film
> I ever see will now appear incredibly good . . .

When *Little Friend* was released, in the summer of 1934,
it did quite well at the English box office. It also got a
much better reception in the United States than most
British films of that period. *The New York Times* said that
it was "very close to being a masterpiece of its kind" and
Film Daily believed that it "should find a warm welcome
from American women of all ages and degrees."

Some of Christopher's friends were indulgent. They
declared that the film was really quite good—far better
than one could have expected. Others, less impressed,
took it for granted that he couldn't be held responsible
for the film in its final form, since, obviously, the Gaumont-British vulgarians must have altered every word of
his screenplay. The least charitable assumed that he *had*
written the film they saw and heard on the screen. But
they excused him because they regarded him as an amusingly cynical whore. (On a later occasion, speaking of
Christopher's movie writing in the States, Auden told
him: "You, at least, sell *dear* what is most dear.")

Christopher laughed and half agreed with them. Yes,
he *was* partly responsible for the film's sentimentality.
(This had only become subtler, not less distasteful,
through having been expertly glossed over by Viertel
and his cameraman.) Then why didn't Christopher feel
ashamed and repentant? Because he now realized that,
quite aside from his desire to earn money, he had needed
psychologically to do a job like this; would need to again,
from time to time. He, the arrogant dainty-minded private artist, needed to plunge his hands into a vulgar
public bucket of dye, to get them dripping with it, to

subdue his nature temporarily to it and do the best he was capable of under the circumstances. His friends apparently didn't need this experience. He couldn't quite explain to them why it was so important for himself. All he did know was that the making of *Little Friend* had been a new and absolutely necessary phase of his education as a writer.

TEN

On March 26, 1934, Christopher left London to rejoin
Heinz in Amsterdam. Thus he symbolically rejected
Kathleen's England. But this short journey was to be
only the first phase of his rejection. To remain in Amsterdam would be like lingering undramatically backstage
after making your final exit. No, Heinz and he must go
much farther away—far enough to impress that audience,
partly real, partly imaginary, of which he was always
conscious.

Tierra del Fuego? The Seychelles? Tristan da Cunha?
Lhasa? These were attractive chiefly because of their remoteness. If he could spend only one day in each, his
place snobbery would be satisfied. He would be able to
say, I have been there.

Much more compelling were the two names which had
haunted him since boyhood—Quito and Tahiti. The
magic of Quito had almost nothing to do with Quito the
place; Christopher had then no idea what it looked like.
What excited him was the concept of a city poised at ten
thousand feet above the equator, with days and nights of
eternally equal duration and the round of seasons repeated every twenty-four hours: spring in the morning,
summer at noon, autumn in the afternoon, winter at

night. An earthly model of paradise—or of limbo, according to the way you thought of it.

Tahiti was no mere concept to Christopher. He had seen many photographs of it and of its opposite island, Mooréa, whose wildly, magnificently scrawled skyline has the authority of a famous signature, guaranteeing this to be the world's most dreamed-of landfall. Tahiti also offered you a dreamed-of manner of life; you could be a beachcomber there, like Gauguin.

Quito would be rather difficult to reach. Tahiti was easy. A French boat could take you all the way there from Marseilles, via the Panama Canal. The ticket wasn't too expensive. But, when Christopher inquired further, he was told—incorrectly, I now suspect—that there was a limit on the length of your stay, unless you were a French citizen. Also, that beachcombers were being deported.

And where would Heinz and he go, after Tahiti? There was Western Samoa, with Stevenson's home and grave; there was the bay in New Zealand where Katherine Mansfield spent her childhood summers; there was Thirroul in Australia, where Lawrence wrote *Kangaroo*. All these were sacred shrines for pilgrimage and also places where one might settle down and work. But Australia and New Zealand belonged to the Commonwealth, and Western Samoa was administered by New Zealand. Mightn't they exchange lists of undesirable aliens with the British? Christopher's fears were probably groundless, but he was now overanxious about such dangers.

Then somebody suggested the Canary Islands; a compromise but an attractive one. They weren't very far away but they did (in those days) seem adequately remote. At least Christopher would be able to think of himself as having escaped from Europe; politically the islands belong to Spain but geographically they are part of Africa.

Early in April, Christopher and Heinz sailed on a

Dutch boat from Rotterdam, by way of Vigo, Lisbon, and Funchal, to Las Palmas, the chief city of the Canaries, on the island of Gran Canaria. They stayed at the Towers Strand, a hotel built in Germanic-modern style beside the beach. Their room was a kind of hut on top of the building. It was ordinarily used by servants. They had been given it with apologies because the hotel was so full; but for them it was desirably private. They had the big flat roof to themselves to sunbathe on, with a view out over Las Palmas to a background of volcanic hills that formed the center of the island. Hot sunshine on the playa and the sea, rainclouds massed around the hills, cocks crowing and goats cropping on housetops, smoke blowing from ships' funnels and laundry flapping in the sea wind, drunks huddled asleep against walls daubed with slogans presaging a civil war, which was then only two years ahead.

Late in May, Christopher wrote to Forster, telling him that Heinz and he had made friends with some of the young islanders:

> They sit out under the palm trees until two o'clock in the morning, talking about painting, or meet in each other's rooms to listen to the Kreutzer Sonata, like undergraduates.

They had also made friends with a Swiss lady, Frl. Leonora Pohly, whom they had first met "wandering about the mountains at sunrise, with her arms full of flowers." She reminded Christopher of a cocker spaniel, with her curly red hair hanging around her ears and her warm eager doggy nature. She came to visit them every day and was always anxious to advise and help them. On being told as much as she could be told of Heinz's difficulties at Harwich, she had insisted on going with him to the German consul and explaining that "domestic servant" was a misleading description of his profession. Christopher wasn't present at the interview and I can't now remember what was said, but Heinz came away with his passport altered from *Hausdiener* to *Sprachstudent* (student of languages).

This was the Consul's own extraordinary choice. He might as well have written "Archdeacon." However, now that Heinz is a language student, he has decided to learn languages, any languages, the more the better. He stops the guests in the corridor and says, beaming all over his face, in Spanish: "My friend is very ill." This is so far his only Spanish sentence. It gives rise to misunderstandings, as you may imagine.

On May 23, Christopher told his diary: "I am stuck. I can't write *The Lost*."

The Lost had become Christopher's title for the novel about Berlin on which he kept trying to work. He had originally thought of this title in German, loving the solemn rolling sound of *Die Verlorenen*. He applied it to his subject matter with at least three separate meanings. It meant "those who have lost their own way"—that mass of Germans who were now being herded blindly into the future by their Nazi shepherds. It meant "the doomed" —those who, like Bernhard Landauer, were already marked down as Hitler's victims. And, in a lighter, ironic sense, it meant "those whom respectable Society regards as moral outcasts"—Sally Bowles the "lost" girl, Otto Nowak the "lost" boy, and Mr. Norris, who has committed the unpardonable crime of having been found out.

Confronted by all his characters and their stories, Christopher was like an official who is called upon to deal with a crowd of immigrants and their belongings. They wait, absolutely passive, to be told where they are to live and what their jobs will be. The official regards them with growing dismay. He had imagined that he could cope with them all, somehow or other. Now he is beginning to realize that he can't.

Christopher had already made one plan for accommodating his immigrants—it was as follows:

Peter Wilkinson, newly arrived in Germany, has been invited to a party at the Wannsee villa of the Landauers, whom he has never met. He arrives early and has to kill time by wandering along the beach of the lake. Here he is picked up by Otto Nowak, who takes him into the woods and seduces him. He then goes to the party and meets the Landauers, Sally Bowles, her boy friend Klaus, and Baron von Pregnitz, a homosexual official in the German government. Sally finds Peter sympathetic and decides to rent one of the rooms in his landlady's flat. Bernhard Landauer falls in love with Sally and/or Klaus —which means that he will soon be needing Peter as a go-between. The Baron is snobbishly drawn to Peter because he is a young Englishman of good family. (The favorable impression Peter makes upon everybody at the party is chiefly due to his extraordinary state of elation, caused by his adventure with Otto. Usually he is taciturn and inhibited; now he seems witty, charming, even sexually attractive.)

Peter has made an appointment to meet Otto later that evening, at the brothel run by Olga. While waiting for Otto, Peter gets acquainted with Mr. Norris, who has come there to receive one of his erotic whippings. Norris takes no particular interest in Peter until Peter happens to mention that he knows Baron von Pregnitz. Norris has been trying for some time to get an introduction to the Baron, whom he hopes to interest in selling German military secrets to the French. So now his attitude to Peter becomes suddenly cordial . . . Thus, Christopher had contrived to pack all his characters into one structure. But there were far too many of them and the packing was too tight. They couldn't move without getting in each other's way.

Christopher never worked out in detail what the action

of this novel would be. All I have is his description of its projected ending:

> Peter has returned to England after a row with Otto. He is miserable. One evening, he is asked out to dinner at the house of some aunts. Their chatter drives him to such a point of desperation that he feels he must get in touch with Otto at once. There is only one place where he can ring up—at Olga's. He slips off into another room, carefully closes the door, and gives the number.
> Meanwhile, at Olga's, a drunken party is going on. Otto has already gone out. (He is, in fact, going to his death—for he is murdered that night by his enemies in another street gang.) A drunken boy picks up the receiver and, half as a joke, half through stupidity, holds a conversation with Peter, saying that he *is* Otto. Finally, when Peter realizes that he isn't, the boy hangs up the receiver. The book ends with Otto lying dead in the snow under the girders of the overhead railway.

There is one other note about *The Lost* in Christopher's diary:

> The link which binds all the chief characters together is that in some way or other each one of them is conscious of the mental, economic, and ideological bankruptcy of the world in which they live. And all this must echo and reecho the refrain: It can't go on like this. I'm the Lost, we're the Lost.

This sounds like a "method" stage director instructing his leading lady, Sally Bowles, to be aware of the world's mental, economic, and ideological bankruptcy as she lights her cigarette. Christopher often wrote such memos to himself—half serious, half satirical—when he was trying to arrive at a literary decision; they helped him make

177

up his mind. Here he is poking fun at his own love of concepts. In the novel as he has been planning it, the chief characters are really prototypes created to demonstrate his concept of the Lost. However, you can't demonstrate all the aspects of a concept if you haven't enough prototypes; and Christopher was now being forced to admit that he couldn't get all of his prototypes into one novel. He was therefore forced to ask himself: "How can I call my novel *The Lost* if I don't fully explain what I mean by 'lost'?" To which the shockingly simple answer was: "You can't."

But Christopher wouldn't at first accept this answer. He was still under the spell of his sonorous conceptual title. He went on thinking of his novel as *The Lost* even after he had decided to make it exclusively the story of Mr. Norris, casting out Sally Bowles, the Landauers, the Nowaks, and many minor characters.

It has been my experience that the embryos of novels tend to start their growth as interlocked Siamese twins or triplets, which can only be separated by the most delicate surgery. I remember a long morning during which Christopher paced the hotel roof, back and forth, back and forth, performing this surgery inside his head and freeing Norris from the stranglehold of his brothers and sisters. Having done so, he quickly sketched out a first chapter.

Then, at the beginning of June, he and Heinz took a bus into the hills and spent three days exploring them on foot. From the bottom of an extinct crater, now fertile farmland, they scrambled slowly up to its rim and made their way along dizzy ridges to the pedestal of a sheer and sinister-looking rock called El Nublo, The Cloudy One. Seemingly unclimbable, it had lately been climbed by a party of Nazi tourists, who had planted their swastika flag on its top. The flag had been blown away already, but the flagpole remained.

On such occasions, Heinz was at his most lovable and his most German—not the German Boy but the German Child; a child out of Grimm's fairy tales, setting forth innocently into the unknown. He was astounded by everything he saw. He laughed delightedly. He sang. His favorite wander song can be translated as follows:

> *My journey I'm makin'*
> *With five pennyworth of fat bacon*
> *Which I love to chew on*
> *And no one ain't takin'.*

> *And who does that*
> *I'll bash him on his hat*
> *Bash him on his smeller*
> *Till it's flat.*

Another of Heinz's songs was about a fight between Communist workers and the police, in the early 1920's. Two comrades take part in this fight and one of them is killed. So the other writes a letter, "with trembling hands," to his dead friend's mother. The fight actually took place at a town called Leuna. But Heinz found it amusing, when singing this song, to change Leuna to *Leihhaus,* thus making the letter announce:

> *The cops shot your son. Now he's lying*
> *In the pawnshop and will not return.*

Although suffering from spasms of vertigo and blisters on his feet, Christopher was serenely happy in the company of the German Child and in his newly found confidence that he would now be able to write his novel.

Next day, they plodded downhill through seemingly endless ravines which brought them at last to the southernmost point of the island, Maspalomas. A tall slender lighthouse stood in what looked like a tiny patch of the Sahara desert, transplanted from across the water. That night they slept in a room with a hole instead of a window. The bed contained one—but only one—crab louse. It was beautiful, golden with a spot of black on it; quite different from the drab vermin which Christopher had sometimes hosted in Berlin. When they started off to catch their bus back to Las Palmas next morning, he left something in the bed which was even more exotic than the louse, a British hundred-pound note. He had been carrying it with him throughout this journey—"for emergencies," he vaguely, evasively told himself. On this point, I lose psychological contact with the Christopher of those days. This refusal to rely exclusively on his traveler's checks, this clinging to "real" money, must have been a reflection of Kathleen's insular attitude when she and her parents toured Europe at the end of the nineteenth century . . . He remembered the note after he had walked only a few yards and rushed back to retrieve it from under the pillow.

On June 6, they left Gran Canaria for the island of Tenerife. Christopher felt that he would be able to work better there, with fewer distractions. Also, he wanted to "have" his novel—as a woman might wish to give birth to her child—under the auspices of a celebrated romantic place name. (He even considered putting "Tenerife, 1934" at the bottom of the last page. But, by the time the novel was finished, something had decided him not to. Maybe it was the fact that Forster had put anti-romantic "Weybridge" at the end of two of his novels. Wasn't "Tenerife" a trifle vulgar?)

They settled into a pension called the Pavillon Troika, near the village of Orotava. It was thrilling to know that you were living on the slopes of a volcano, twelve thousand feet high. They had seen it from the rock pedestal of El Nublo, towering above a cloud pedestal far out on the ocean. But, here, it was too close to be visible. Here, you were merely an atom of Gran Canaria's magnificent view. From the Pavillon Troika, all you could see, most of the time, were glimpses through warm rolling sea fog of farms on the lower mountainside and of the waves beneath them.

The pension was run by a middle-aged Englishman who dyed his hair a very dead black. He warmly approved of the relationship between Christopher and Heinz, but not of Christopher's occupation: "After all, old boy, I mean to say, will it matter a hundred years from now if you wrote that yarn or not?" He kept urging Christopher to make better use of his youth, while he still had it, by spending more time down at the beach, swimming. But the beach was dirty and too distant, and the Englishman's advice wasn't disinterested. He had a gramophone with a powerful loudspeaker which he would have liked to play from morning till midnight. Christopher had protested that he couldn't possibly work while this noise was going on, and had threatened to move out. So it was agreed that the music shouldn't start until four in the afternoon. The Englishman hoped that it would then lure customers in to enjoy the cocktail hour. It seldom did, for there were few potential customers.

Christopher wrote always in the garden. Beneath the spotted leaves of a rubber tree, with banana plants and hibiscus around him, he banged away at his little Corona. (A baby typewriter it would seem today—the skeleton of a baby, for you could look right through it, between the thin ribs of its keyboard. But it was astonishingly sturdy. He would be using it for another fourteen years.)

This was a period of contented absorption, measured in chapters, not weeks. The solving of a literary problem became a major event, but the excitement it caused him was introverted, since there was no one he could run to and read aloud a just-completed passage. Christopher wasn't about to expose his art to the philistine judgment of the Englishman; and Heinz would hardly have made a perceptive critic, even if Christopher had been writing in German.

181

At odd moments, he gave Heinz lessons in English, geography, and modern history. While Christopher worked, Heinz kept himself occupied, writing long letters to his friends and playing with the Englishman's puppy and the many cats. With his genius for communication, he somehow made the gardener's boy and the old woman who cooked the meals understand a mixture of German, English, and Greek, laced with occasional words of Spanish. His head was now toothbrush-bristly all over. Christopher had cropped Heinz's hair at his own request. The Englishman had told him that this would promote hair growth and Christopher had encouraged Heinz to believe it because he found bristles sexy.

After supper, they often got mildly drunk and capered on the small marble dance floor in the patio. The Englishman told them wild tales of his life in the United States. He had jumped ship while working as a steward and had spent several years wandering around the country, lovemaking. He strongly advised Christopher and Heinz to go and do likewise.

On July 9, Christopher began a two-day holiday from his novel. He and Heinz set out to climb the volcano, the Pico de Teide. They had hired a guide, and two mules to carry food and blankets. Someone must have talked them into making the expedition so elaborate; it was still quite cheap but it wasn't their style. At the last moment, they impulsively invited a young German, a schoolmaster on holiday, to come with them. He seemed pleasant enough. The back of his neck had an ugly Prussian look, it was red and stiff; and his face was prematurely lined, wooden, rather silly. But he had nice blue eyes.

They spent the night in a rest hut on the lava plateau which surrounds the cone of the Pico. After sunset, the temperature dropped sharply. The hut had a fireplace but no chimney; it filled with smoke when they started a fire. Their only light was from a pair of bicycle lamps.

Christopher was acutely aware of the altitude; it made him feel tense, apprehensive, slightly crazy. It seemed to affect the schoolmaster too, but differently. He became dogmatic and talked in slogans from Nazi propaganda: "A people must have a national ambition. It is natural for one people to wish to impose its culture upon all others." When Christopher challenged him to define what he meant by German culture, he was unable to and shrugged the question off as irrelevant. None of this was really surprising. But Christopher, in his present state of mind, saw the schoolmaster as supernaturally sinister, transformed before his very eyes into a demon who threatened Heinz's existence. No—it was even worse than that. For Heinz evidently couldn't see the demonic aspect of the schoolmaster, regarding him as an ordinary human Nazi whose political opinions should be ignored, rather than spoil the enjoyment of this trip. Which meant that Heinz, being German, had within him a peculiarly German tolerance of Nazi ideas—a tolerance which could betray him into the demon's power. Not only Heinz's existence was threatened but his soul.

Next morning, panting in the thin air, they followed a fairly easy path up to the top of the cone. Hot sulphur fumed through greenish holes in its sides. When the guide held a lighted match to one of them, all the other holes began to fume more violently. And there was a place where you could hear a noise like the roaring of subterranean fire. As the sun rose, they stood silent in the enormous emptiness, looking out over fleecy cloud fields to where the guide had told them the coast of Africa lay. Then Heinz let out a great joyful yell and, using his walking stick for a brake, glissaded down the cone in a swirl of pumice dust. Without a smile or a word, his soul's enemy took off in pursuit of him. Christopher descended more sedately, sulking. Since waking up that morning, he had avoided speaking to the schoolmaster and had urged Heinz not to speak to him either. Heinz had gone on doing so, greatly to Christopher's annoyance. The schoolmaster seemed anyhow quite unaware of Christopher's hostility.

Then followed the long downhill trail, on which Christopher felt glad that they had hired the mules, because he could ride one of them and thus isolate himself from Heinz and the schoolmaster. However, the decreasing altitude restored him gradually to sanity. By the time they reached the Troika, he had had to admit to himself that the demon was a human being after all, hateful but relatively powerless.

While Christopher was struggling to write his huge novel about the prototypes of the Lost, he had decided that it must be narrated in the third person, objectively, camerawise. The camera would record only outward appearances, actions, and spoken words—no thoughts, no feelings, nothing subjective. In this kind of storytelling, the author is playing a game with the reader. The author gives him all the necessary objective data, challenging him to interpret it and guess what will happen next. The more often the reader misinterprets and guesses wrongly, the greater is the author's success. This is the technique of the classic detective story.

But now Christopher was attempting an altogether different kind of novel, in which Mr. Norris wasn't a prototype, wasn't designed to demonstrate a concept. Here, he was a character in the simplest sense. Meeting him must be its own reward.

Christopher wanted to make the reader experience Arthur Norris just as he himself had experienced Gerald Hamilton. He could only do this by writing subjectively, in the first person, describing his own reactions to and feelings about Hamilton; otherwise, his portrait of Mr. Norris wouldn't be lifelike. He could, however, permit himself to invent as much dialogue, as many situations and additional characters as he needed. One does that even when one is telling a story to one's friends which is allegedly true.

But the narration problem wasn't to be so easily solved. *Was* Christopher claiming that the Narrator of this novel was, in every respect, himself? No. Most importantly, he wasn't prepared to admit that the Narrator was homosexual. Because he was afraid to? Yes, that was one reason. Although his own life as a homosexual was lived fairly openly, he feared to create a scandal. He even hesitated to embarrass Kathleen. And there was Uncle Henry—if he were sufficiently shocked, he might cut off Christopher's allowance.

There was a second reason, a literary one. Christopher doesn't mention it in his diaries or letters of that period. But I think that, subconsciously at least, it must have influenced his decisions.

Christopher wanted to keep the reader's attention concentrated on Norris; therefore, the Narrator had to be as unobtrusive as possible. The reader had to be encouraged to put himself in the Narrator's shoes—to see with the Narrator's eyes, to experience his experiences, to identify with him in all his reactions. For example, the Narrator is at a Beethoven concert, he sees and smells a juicy steak in a restaurant, he wakes in the night to feel his cheek being licked by the tongue of a non-venomous snake. The ordinary reader, being convinced of the Narrator's ordinariness, will take it for granted that he is feeling pleasure in the first instance, appetite in the second, and terror and disgust in the third. The reader will share these feelings.

But suppose that the Narrator shows no pleasure in the music? Suppose that he shows disgust on seeing and smelling the meat? Suppose that he shows no fear of the snake and even starts to pet it? Suppose, in other words, that he proves himself to be a tone-deaf, vegetarian herpetologist? The ordinary reader may be repelled by, or sympathetic to, such a Narrator's reactions, but he will never identify with him. He will always remain aware that the Narrator is an individual who is very different from himself.

This is what would have happened if Christopher had made his Narrator an avowed homosexual, with a homosexual's fantasies, preferences, and prejudices. The Narrator would have become so odd, perhaps so interesting, that his presence would have thrown the novel out of perspective. It could no longer have been exclusively a portrait of Mr. Norris. The Narrator would have kept upstaging Norris's performance as the star.

Christopher dared not make the Narrator homosexual. But he scorned to make him heterosexual. That, to Christopher, would have been as shameful as pretending to be heterosexual himself. Therefore, the Narrator could have no explicit sex experiences in the story. ("This sexless nitwit," one reviewer was to call him.) The unlucky creature is, indeed, no more than a demi-character. It is as if Christopher has told him: "Don't call any unnecessary attention to yourself; don't get more involved with anybody than you absolutely have to." There are moments in the novel at which some of the other characters seem actually aware of the Narrator's demi-nature. When, for example, Helen Pratt calls him "a nice little chap," it is with a strange contemptuous tolerance. She knows what she knows. But Christopher won't allow her to say more.

Thus Christopher both acknowledged and disowned his kinship with the Narrator. In *Mr. Norris,* he expressed the ambivalence of his attitude by giving the Narrator his two superfluous middle names, William Bradshaw. They had always embarrassed him and, lately, he had grown to hate them because, joined to Christopher and Isherwood, they formed a tedious procession of ten syllables which wouldn't fit into the allotted space on any of the official documents he was required to sign during his travels. In *Goodbye to Berlin,* and two later novels, he changed the Narrator's name to Christopher

Isherwood, saying to himself that William Bradshaw was a foolish evasion. But the evasiveness is in the Narrator's nature, not in his name.

Christopher set out to write what he called a "dynamic portrait." He used this term to describe a novel whose interest depends on the gradual revealing of a character, rather than on action, crisis, and confrontation. What the action of such a novel does is to remove layer after layer of the "skin" of outer appearance—thus taking the reader inward from his first superficial impressions and too hastily formed judgments until he is face to face, at last, with the "real" individual. (This only means, of course, that aspect of the individual which the author has arbitrarily decided is the essential one.)

In those days, Christopher was fond of saying that what most interested him in writing fiction was to present the bizarre as though it were humdrum and to show events which are generally regarded as extraordinary forming the daily routine of somebody's life. He had chosen Norris for his first subject because, of all his Berlin characters, Norris was the most bizarre.

However, in the process of writing the novel, Christopher was seduced away from his original intention. Toward the end of it, he abandons Norris and his portrait for a whole chapter, while he takes the Narrator and some minor characters to Switzerland and involves them in an espionage intrigue. Here the bizarre is merely bizarre.

(I now realize that what seduced Christopher was his recent experience with the screenplay of *Little Friend*. This had shown him that he could invent situations in areas of life which were quite unknown to him; invent them without shame, although part of himself regarded this newly discovered faculty as being a kind of betrayal. Henceforth, from time to time, he would be unable to resist using it. It was so much fun.)

In his two novels about Berlin, Christopher tried to make not only the bizarre seem humdrum but the humdrum seem bizarre—that is, exciting. He wanted his readers to find excitement in Berlin's drab streets and shabby crowds, in the poverty and dullness of the overgrown Prussian provincial town which had become Germany's pseudo-capital. Forty years later, I can claim that that excitement has been created—largely by all those others who have reinterpreted Christopher's material: actresses and actors, directors and writers. Christopher was saying, in effect: "Read about us and marvel! You did not live in our time—be sorry!" And now there are young people who agree with him. "How I wish I could have been with you there!" they write. This is flattering but also ironic; for most of them could no more have shared Christopher's life in Berlin than they could have lived with a hermit in the desert. Not because of any austerities Christopher endured. Because of the boredom.

Christopher finished the novel on August 12. I remember that he had to hurry to get his last page typed before the Englishman started the music. Christopher wrote in his diary:

> The gramophone keeps reiterating a statement about Life with which I do not agree.

When he mailed the manuscript to the Hogarth Press, it was still called *The Lost*. But, not long before its publication in 1935, he decided to alter its title to *Mr. Norris Changes Trains*. This, too, was a title which he had originally thought of in German: *Herr Norris Steigt Um*. It was intended by Christopher to mean not only that Mr. Norris keeps changing trains—that is to say, keeps having to change countries in a hurry, to escape his creditors and the police—but also that he keeps changing allies and political affiliations, jumping from one bandwagon onto another.

When Stephen Spender heard of the new title, he protested in a letter:

> *The Lost* is an excellent title. The other is arty. Anything would surely be better and less Hogarth Pressy. It gives one a sense of earrings.

I still can't agree with Stephen. And I enormously regret that Christopher let himself be persuaded to make a change in the title of the American edition of the novel. Somebody in the office of William Morrow, his U.S. publisher, assured him that Americans always said "transfer" and therefore wouldn't understand what "changes trains" meant. Christopher knew nothing at that time about American idioms, so he took this extremely dubious statement for fact and offered an alternative, *The Last of Mr. Norris*. He thereby created the false impression that these are two different novels, one the sequel to the other. Which has led to much wearisome correspondence with readers, setting the record straight.

On August 15, Christopher and Heinz began a week's tour of the three westernmost Canary Islands: La Palma, Gomera, and Hierro. This was sheer travel snobbery; the islands had little to offer but their remoteness and La Palma's claim to possess the largest extinct crater in the world. The length of the tour was made necessary by the intervals between visits of the coastal steamer. Still, they killed time happily, clambering up cinder cones, playing billiards in fondas, or lying in bed. Heinz was a good person to be bored with; he never blamed Christopher for his boredom. And they did meet two fascinating characters—tourist beggars of contrasting types—about whom Christopher later wrote a story called "The Turn round the World."

Then, on September 6, they left the islands for the Spanish mainland. Landing at Cádiz, they took a bus to Algeciras, visited Gibraltar, and later crossed by steamer to Ceuta, in what was then Spanish Morocco. As Christopher came ashore down the gangplank, the hundred-pound note was picked from his pocket. There was nothing effective to be done about this, so he relieved his feelings by making a token fuss at the British consulate. The vice consul naturally thought it insane to carry such a sum of money around. Not being also a psychologist, he didn't find Christopher's insanity even the least bit interesting.

After this, there is a gap in Christopher's diary and a blank in my mind. Memory refuses to attach itself to the snapshots they took in Tetuán and in Xauen—then still thought to be dangerous because of the recent fighting between the Moors and the Spanish. I gaze at these glimpses of winding alleys and muffled figures and can remember only a visit to Tangier twenty years later, which was made unforgettably melodramatic by an initiation into hashish taking.

Having left Africa, they traveled north through Spain by way of Granada and Madrid. I forget what the reasons were which decided them to settle in Copenhagen, early in October. I suppose that, for the moment, there seemed nowhere else for them to go.

Thus ended Christopher's grand journey of home rejection and defiance of Nearly Everybody. What followed this was no longer defiant; just a succession of moves on a chessboard, compelled by a stronger opponent. In fact, a retreat.

ELEVEN

Writing to Stephen Spender from Copenhagen on October 9, 1934, Christopher reports that he and Heinz have met Stephen's elder brother, Michael, and his wife, Erica, by chance on the street and that Erica has been most kind to them. She has found them a flat in the same block as the Spenders', at Classensgade 65, and has helped them buy a few pieces of furniture and move into it.

> One has to wait three or four months, as a foreigner, before applying for permission to remain in Denmark at all; and the authorities refuse to say in advance whether permission is likely to be granted. This rather disinclines me to buy anything for the flat which isn't absolutely necessary. Heinz is making meatballs in the kitchen and I am typing this in a very "dictator" room; quite bare except for a ventilator, a table, and a map of Europe.

Compared with his brothers, Michael appeared rugged and masculine and altogether less sensitive, but he had his share of the Spender good looks. Christopher had met him briefly before this and had then been inclined to accept Stephen's view of him. Stephen, the hyper-subjective, had made fun of Michael for having claimed that he had never in his life held a subjective opinion. Michael certainly was a pragmatic type of scientist who made a cult of efficiency and despised the lack of it in others. However, he was also aware of his own limitations and more modest than Stephen would admit. Christopher found Michael's conversation fascinating precisely because it was free of the subjective exaggerations in which he himself was so apt to indulge. It was a welcome change to listen to Michael's strictly objective stories of Greenland, which he had recently visited on some scientific mission.

One story I still remember because it is such an apt parable, applicable to any failure in understanding between two cultures:

An Eskimo, on being shown a photograph of Copenhagen harbor full of ships, was unimpressed and puzzled. He asked: "But how can people live in your town? They must all be starving. I see no fishing canoes."

On the whole, Michael approved of Christopher, finding him less subjectively minded than most of Stephen's friends. This was because he had read *The Memorial* and had been impressed by its display of objective details—such as the names of musical pieces performed at Mary Scriven's concerts, the technical gossip of Maurice's friends about cars and motorbikes, the obscure places visited by Edward Blake in Asia Minor, the description by Eric of a bankrupt mining town in South Wales. Michael, with endearing innocence, took it for granted that Christopher knew what he was talking about; that he had produced these facts out of a vast store of knowledge. Christopher, like many other writers, was shockingly ignorant of the objective world, except where it touched his own experience. When he had to hide his ignorance beneath a veneer, he simply consulted someone who could supply him with the information he needed. Nevertheless, he accepted Michael's compliments gracefully.

Erica Spender was a German girl with a somewhat boyish attractiveness. She was full of temperament, fun, and aggression and made tactlessly frank remarks. She regarded the Christopher–Heinz relationship with an amused horror. Once she said to Christopher: "When I see the two of you walking down the street together, buttoned up in your overcoats, I think: My God, they must bore each other to death, how can they *bear* it?" He didn't take offense, for her interest in them was at least genuine. The three of them became friends.

When Christopher was a child, he had thought of Copenhagen as the capital of Hans Andersen Land. As an adult, he was still under Andersen's spell. (In conversation, he even maintained, more than half seriously, that "The Little Mermaid" is a more profound and true-to-life tragedy than *Madame Bovary* or *Anna Karenina.*) But, now that he was actually in Copenhagen, he saw it merely as the capital of Denmark. Its connection with Andersen seemed to be only through relics and historical landmarks. Maybe if Christopher had been alone and had had a love affair with a young Dane, he would have rediscovered the Andersen magic, sparkling somewhere deep down in the modern boy's collective unconscious.

From a practical point of view, Copenhagen was a good place for them to live. German was a second language there; all educated people spoke it to some extent, so Heinz was less of a foreigner. The foodstuffs—butter, milk, eggs, fish, and meat—were extraordinarily appetizing, and now Christopher and Heinz could cook for themselves. The city was clean, and bright with blond Scandinavian heads. That particular winter happened to be mild; there were many days of sunshine. It was only when icy rain or snow gusts drove down the Classensgade that Christopher felt the awful melancholia of the North.

At the beginning of November, Auden sent Christopher the manuscript of a play called *The Chase.* He had developed it from an earlier play written by the two of them, *The Enemies of a Bishop.* Auden asked for suggestions and Christopher was eager to make them, especially since *The Chase* was almost certainly going to be produced by Rupert Doone's Group Theatre. The Group Theatre had already produced Auden's *The Dance of Death* in February of that year, with Doone himself in the leading role.

During the weeks that followed, Christopher's correspondence with Wystan about the play became a collaboration. Christopher outlined some new scenes and some revisions of existing scenes. A few he wrote himself, others he asked Wystan to write. Wystan always enjoyed being set such tasks; they were a challenge to his immense creative powers. I can't remember that he ever refused or ever failed to produce what had been asked for.

Christopher's diary, November 24:

Every day I go out to buy the milk, sneaking round the corner to look at the posters. *Krigs Fare* (War Danger) and so forth. The Danish papers take a sadistic delight in exaggerating every new alarming report.

Why am I in such an awful funk? Partly of course because I don't want to die. Much more because I dread the Army itself—like going back to school again —and I dread leaving Heinz. But it is the waiting which is so awful. The little money I have would stop if war were declared. We should never be allowed to stay here. In the end, I know, I should have to return to England.

Heinz said to me this morning, "You seem to have no interest for anything any more. You're making me as miserable as you are yourself. If war comes, it'll come."

There was, in fact, no major political crisis in Europe just then. But Christopher and all his fellow worriers in that war-doomed period were like patients with a terminal disease—apt to become acutely aware of their condition from time to time, even if there were no symptoms of it to remind them.

His diary entry continues:

I have failed to do my duty. My place is in England with the Communists. I am a deserter and a potential traitor.

A letter from Edward Upward, earlier that year, reveals that Christopher has written to Olive Mangeot in the same tone:

Olive showed me your letter in which you said something about being silently judged. Of course that's all trash, because—though Marx may not have said it—each of us helps the revolution best by using his own weapons. And your best weapon is obviously writing. It's my misfortune that I have to fight as a fifth-rate teacher.

A religious devotee sometimes cultivates moral scruples and tells them to his father confessor, who dismisses them as a form of self-regard which is essentially hypocritical. Christopher seems to have been cultivating political scruples in the same manner. Edward, like a wise confessor, calls them "trash." I think that Christopher was merely homesick for his friends in England, both Communist and non-Communist. Much more candid and revealing is his statement that he is a potential traitor—in other words, that he suspects himself of not belonging to the Communist side as wholeheartedly as he pretends to.

On November 30, Christopher went over to Malmö, where he had been invited to give a lecture on "My Experiences in an English Film Studio." When the ferry from Denmark docked, Christopher was greeted by a party of hospitable Swedes who at once began sympathizing with him. How miserable it must be for him, they said, to live in Copenhagen. Doubtless he hadn't had a square meal or a real drink since his arrival there; the Danes understood nothing about pleasure. They rushed him into a restaurant and stuffed him with Swedish delicacies, washed down by full-strength Swedish punch. Finding himself at length standing dazed and unsteady on a platform, he was at first scared; never before had he tried to lecture when drunk. Then he realized that most of the audience was drunk, too. He laughed at them. They laughed back at him, and applauded. The lecture was a success. Afterwards, they paid him their highest compliment, telling him that he wasn't like the ordinary Englishman.

The year 1935 came in dark with new worries. Christopher had found that he would have to pay Danish income tax. Also, the Danish police suspected Christopher of being a "political" writer—refusing, however, to say exactly what they meant by "political." It seemed clear that he and Heinz wouldn't be allowed to stay in the country indefinitely, even if they should want to do so.

But then, on January 10, Auden arrived—by airplane. He had got Faber and Faber, his publishers, to advance the money for his ticket on the ground that this was to be a business discussion. Wonderful, unpredictable Wystan! Christopher was hugely impressed. Flying still seemed an act of daring to him. He didn't venture to try it himself for another two years.

Together, they worked through the play, making minor alterations. They had now agreed to call it *Where Is Francis?* Its final title, *The Dog beneath the Skin,* was suggested later, by Rupert Doone.

Wystan was the best possible cure for Christopher's depression. His presence demanded entertainment and intellectual response. By entertaining him, Christopher automatically became a better version of himself; he cheered himself up. This must have made poor Heinz's life more cheerful too.

On February 7, Christopher sent Kathleen a postcard, asking her to get in touch with his press-cuttings agency and warn them to be on the lookout for reviews of *Mr. Norris Changes Trains,* which the Hogarth Press would be publishing soon.

Christopher had asked Kathleen to do him other such favors from time to time. But this was something much more; it was the inauguration of a new relationship between them. Henceforward, Kathleen, with Richard as her assistant, would be Christopher's London representative. During the next few years, she would be continually writing letters and making phone calls to editors and publishers. She would also badger those who had failed to keep promises or follow up leads—including, quite often, Christopher's official literary agent. Christopher rewarded her occasionally by telling her that she was worth ten agents put together. His excuse to himself for loading her with all this work was that she enjoyed it. Probably she did, for she was thus able to have a share in his life.

Christopher to Kathleen, February 11:

Here we skate but are sad. Very soon, compulsory military service will be reintroduced in Germany. What is Heinz to do? If he goes back, he becomes part of the machine and won't be allowed out again for the next five years, perhaps longer. If he doesn't, he is an exile for the rest of Hitler's stay and that may mean a lifetime. He is horrified at the thought of going. In Germany he has only his old grandmother, who will soon die, two married aunts, and his father, who didn't bring him up and whom he never sees.

If he stays with me he must make some kind of life for himself. He wants to live in the country and keep animals. But where?

In 1938, his passport will expire. He will have to get another nationality somehow, I suppose, but this is fearfully difficult and takes a great deal of time.

Christopher to Kathleen, February 26:

Lately, I have been seriously thinking of emigrating to South Africa! South Africa is undoubtedly the best dominion for Germans. And Heinz might gradually turn into a Boer and from a Boer into a Briton. Also, if we had a couple of acres of land there and a cottage, it could be in his name and give him a kind of status.

Even his father now frankly advises him not to return, so his conscience is becoming easier on the subject.

Stephen Spender to Christopher, March 7:

You will know by now that your novel is highly praised in the Telegraph and the Statesman and the Spectator. I also saw the Woolfs last night and Leonard told me that he had just arranged for a second printing.

I am terribly sorry for you and Heinz about this German conscription. Leonard says now that a war is inevitable, as the world has got into the vicious rearmament circle of 1912. Morgan Forster also has given up hope of there being peace.

Why don't you go to America? I think I would

emigrate now, if I thought I could write about anything if I were away from Europe. I somehow feel that you would be able to write there, perhaps even better than in England.

I think all a writer can do, the only completely revolutionary attitude for him today, is to try and create standards which are really civilized.

Christopher to Kathleen, March 12:

Mr. Norris is certainly getting more appreciation than The Memorial, though I can't say that I find any of the critics particularly intelligent in their remarks. I am much shocked at the callousness with which they all completely ignore the tragedy at the end. They seem to find German politics just one long laugh.

How curious of Uncle Henry not to like the book. I'd felt certain that it was just the Dickens aspect of Mr. Norris which would have appealed to him. Indeed, I feel that Mr. Norris, far from being modern in conception, is almost too faithful to the English Comic Tradition that one gets so sick of hearing about. This is obviously what pleased Compton Mackenzie.

(What Henry had chiefly objected to was Christopher's use of the name Bradshaw for his Narrator. According to Henry's social mystique, Isherwood was a mere tradesman's name while Bradshaw epitomized the family's claim to aristocratic status and historical importance. Therefore, Christopher had committed sacrilege by dragging William Bradshaw down into the company of criminals and proletarians. No doubt, Henry also deplored the coarseness of the novel's humor—not because it shocked him personally, but because it might shock the titled ladies whose friendship he so greatly valued.)

Another psychological surprise is the attitude of Mr. Norris himself. Now that the book is out, he has forgotten all feelings of injury. He eagerly searches the press for reviews and notes successes with proprietary pride: "We got a very good notice in the Telegraph," etc!

Yesterday I got the following telegram: "Very glad indeed to meet fascinating Mr. Norris. Sincere congratulations. Viertel."

Christopher's next letter to Kathleen—his last from Copenhagen—refers to Hitler's official declaration of March 16 denouncing the clauses of the Versailles Treaty which agreed to German disarmament and proclaiming the immediate introduction of conscription:

As soon as Heinz has been formally called up and has formally refused to return to that madhouse, he becomes, of course, from the Nazi point of view, a criminal. So he must get another nationality, either by adoption or by settling in some foreign country. Adoption would probably be the easier, if one could find the right sort of people to undertake it. Failing that, some nationality which can be bought outright.

This is Christopher's first mention to Kathleen of the possibility that Heinz might change his nationality by purchase. Gerald Hamilton must have suggested it.

Gerald was then in Brussels, and it was to Brussels that Christopher and Heinz went first, after leaving Denmark on April 13.

Christopher to Stephen, from 44 Avenue Longchamps, April 19:

Brussels seems very lively after Copenhagen. It is raffish and shabby, with dark monkeyish errand boys and great slow Flamands with faces like bits of raw meat. And there are kiosks and queer dives and the Host is carried to the dying through the streets with people kneeling as it goes by. Also there is the Manneken-Pis, the stone pissing fountain of which you'll have seen photos. You can buy brass reproductions of it in all shops, with a rubber tube and bulb attached, to squirt water at your friends. All this rather goes to one's head after the endless twilight winter in our attractive but terrible flat. I feel delivered from all kinds of vague suffocating apprehensions.

Also, of course, there is Gerald, in the pink of health and parted forever from his wig. He hasn't changed in the least.

About Heinz and conscription. I have thought the whole thing over, all ways, for weeks. But, look here, surely the fact that one is taking on responsibility isn't in itself an argument one way or the other? There would be just as much responsibility (or more) in sending him back to Germany. Suppose the war came before he'd finished serving and suppose he was killed; who'd be responsible *then?* And, looking at it from the moral standpoint, isn't it much less defensible to go and lick their boots now, when you've every intention of deserting them later? My plans are to leave Europe as soon as possible for a country where Heinz can settle down and work. And, in the meanwhile, if he is called up, to do everything possible to avoid giving a direct No, employing dummy medical reports and similar devices. This all sounds rather desperate, perhaps. But I don't feel that way about it; at least, not just now. I believe, in my place, you'd do much the same.

(This sounds as if Stephen must have written to Christopher, pointing out that, by encouraging Heinz not to return to Germany, he was making himself responsible for Heinz's whole future. This letter of Stephen's has been lost, if indeed it ever existed. Anyhow, the above can also be read as part of a continuing dialogue which Christopher was having with his own conscience.)

At the end of April, Christopher visited London, leaving Heinz in Brussels. He returned on May 12. Next day, they crossed the frontier to Rotterdam, because Heinz's permit to stay in Belgium had to be renewed by a Belgian consulate abroad. The Belgians refused to grant the permit. Germans were not popular with them, especially when they had no very convincing reason for wanting to live in Belgium. Christopher and Heinz weren't unduly dismayed, however. They agreed that they would just as soon live in Holland.

On May 20, Christopher wrote to Kathleen from Amsterdam, telling her that they had taken a room at Emmastraat 24. This was where Heinz had stayed while Christopher was finishing work on *Little Friend*. They got on well with their landlady, a German who had married a Dutchman.

Christopher felt very much at home in Amsterdam. It was a place of comfort for a worrier, because it created a snug, smug atmosphere of security—never mind how false. A bitterly humorous refugee later told him that the Dutch were convinced they would never be invaded because, as they said, "We can flood the whole country" and "A queen is on the throne."

What does "Amsterdam" evoke for me now? The staircase of a seventeenth-century house, so steep that you can touch the steps above you with your chin, while climbing; the smell of canal water in the summer sun, gamy but pleasing; the crowds of wind-reddened cyclists, Christopher and Heinz amongst them, pedaling across the flat land, below the level of the sea they are going to swim in and the dunes of Zandvoort where they will make love. What I can't recall is the taste of milk chocolate eaten between gulps of beer. Christopher was fond of the combination in those days, especially when drunk. Now I can't even bring myself to try it.

Joe Ackerley, whom Christopher must have met by this time, had just begun editing the art and book pages of *The Listener*. He invited Christopher to become one of his reviewers. Christopher gladly accepted, not only because he needed the extra money but because this was another challenge, like film writing. Between 1935 and 1937, he reviewed about thirty-five books. He asked Joe to send him, whenever possible, contemporary autobiographies by people who weren't celebrities—a horse trainer, for example, or a prison doctor, or an ordinary seaman. These required no special knowledge and no research; you judged them purely on the basis of their contents. Such a book is probably the only book which its author or authoress will ever write. It is thus, in a sense, a masterpiece, the definitive statement about an individual life. It will, nearly always, have something in it which can be sincerely praised—a moment of artless frankness, a warmth of innocent joy, an anecdote so incredible that it could never have been invented.

When, however, Christopher was obliged to write about the work of his literary colleagues, he found himself becoming either overpolite or demurely bitchy. His tone always rang a little false.

Forster to Christopher, May 11:

> Have now read Mr. Norris twice and have much admiration and enjoyment. I liked it less the first time because it is not altogether my sort of book—dwells on the contradictions rather than the complexities of character, and seems to reveal people facet by facet whereas The Memorial if my memory serves tackled strata. However, I got over that and managed to read what you've written, I think.
>
> The construction is fine and Margot was a complete surprise to me. It's marvellous too the way you've maintained standards of right and wrong and yet left

Norris an endearing person. And you've made him both silly and witty, like a character in Congreve. He's awfully good.

The necessity of combining knowingness and honesty in William renders him more of a problem, for in art these are uneasy bedfellows. However, you bring him through pretty well. I was a little worried in Switzerland to what extent he was paying his employer's way with the Baron. Did he go the whole hog or turn a pig-skin cheek? I don't the least mind, but feel that in the first case he would violate the fastidiousness and in the second the integrity of his character.

Actually, the novel makes it clear that, by the time they start for Switzerland, the Baron no longer finds William sexually attractive. So there is no question of their going to bed together, even if William would have agreed to it. Forster must surely have realized this. It now seems to me that the concern he expresses about William's integrity is really a concern about Christopher's own character. Seeing certain weaknesses in it, Forster administers an oblique, affectionately gentle, but nevertheless earnest warning.

At the end of May, Christopher went alone to Brussels for the weekend, as the guest of Gerald Hamilton. Gerald wanted Christopher to help him revise the manuscript of an autobiography which he had written. It was to be called *As Young as Sophocles*—a title taken from a passage in William Johnson Cory's poem, "Academus":

> *I'll borrow life, and not grow old,*
> *And nightingales and trees*
> *Shall keep me, though the veins be cold,*
> *As young as Sophocles.*

And when I may no longer live
They'll say, who know the truth,
He gave whate'er he had to give
To freedom and to youth.

It was characteristic of Gerald's peculiar kind of vanity
that he was able, in all seriousness, to apply the last four
of these lines to himself.

During that weekend, he took Christopher to lunch
with a millionaire, one of his prospective client-victims.
Being in the presence of great wealth went to his head
like alcohol. He sparkled with epigrams. Although the
millionaire spoke quite fluent English, Gerald insisted
on talking French, his favorite language. Referring to
the capitalist system, he said gaily, *"Je proteste mais j'en
profite."*

Because of Heinz, Christopher was now more deeply
involved with Gerald than ever before. Gerald was the
only person he knew who could get the permits Heinz
needed and perhaps help him change his nationality.
Gerald was then "working on" (as he put it) Heinz's
permit to live in Belgium, but he admitted that it might
take several more months of negotiation with the police.
This was Christopher's incentive to help Gerald with his
autobiography.

Christopher wasn't irked or humiliated by their involvement, for he really liked Gerald. With him, you
never had to pretend. Gerald inhabited a world into
which Christopher had barely peeped; one might call it
"real," for it was without hypocrisy, its ends and means
were frankly criminal. It was a world in which appalling
things could happen to you as a matter of course; ruin,
prison, even murder, were its occupational accidents.
Gerald had suffered some of these but he was still determined to remain in it and survive. Christopher was sometimes shocked and repelled by the glimpses he got of this
world. Nevertheless, Gerald's example encouraged him
to live his own life more boldly.

It must have been in May that Erika, Thomas Mann's eldest daughter, arrived in Amsterdam with her cabaret company, Die Pfeffermuehle (The Peppermill). Its sketches were mostly satirical and anti-Nazi. It had already performed with success in other countries bordering on Germany where German was understood. Through Klaus Mann, who was also in Amsterdam at that time, Christopher met Erika, a slim dark-eyed handsome woman of about his own age. On the stage, she had the air of a political leader rather than of a performer, confronting the Fascist foe with scornful humor and beautiful poise and courage. Also in the company was the unforgettable actress Therese Giehse. My most vivid memory of her is in a scene in which she nursed the globe of the world on her lap like a sick child and crooned weirdly over it.

One day, Erika said to Christopher with an embarrassed laugh: "I have something rather personal to ask you—will you marry me?" She had been told that the Nazis were about to take away her German citizenship, since she was now a public enemy of the Third Reich. By marrying an Englishman, she could become a British subject instantaneously.

Christopher felt honored, excited, amused—and reluctantly said no. The reason, as he vaguely phrased it to Erika, was that "it would cause difficulties with my family." This was true, in a sense. Kathleen, who still obstinately hoped for grandchildren produced in wedlock, would have been horrified by such a marriage of convenience. If Christopher had been feeling aggressive toward her just then, it might have pleased him to cross her. But he wasn't, and anyhow he had stronger motives for refusing Erika. One of these was that he was afraid of compromising Heinz, who might well have been exposed to the ensuing publicity and branded by the Nazis as the minion of the husband of their enemy. I don't think Christopher was mistaken, here.

His other motive was far less reasonable but as strong —his rooted horror of marriage. To him, it was the sacrament of the Others; the supreme affirmation of their dictatorship. Even when his heterosexual friends got married, Christopher found their action slightly distasteful. When his basically homosexual friends got married —declaring that they were really bisexual, or that they wanted children, or that their wife was "someone who understands"—Christopher expressed sympathy but felt disgust. Later, many of these would start having sex with men on the side, while still maintaining that marriage alone is meaningful and that homosexuality is immature —i.e., disreputable, dangerous, and illegal . . . However, I must admit that Christopher himself was behaving immaturely when he shrank from marrying Erika lest somebody, somewhere, might suspect him of trying to pass as a heterosexual.

Christopher suggested that he should write to Auden, explain the situation, and ask if he was willing. Erika agreed. Auden wired back: "Delighted." When the telegram arrived, Christopher felt a little envious. Sir Wystan had won the glory of a knight-errant who rescues the lady from the monster. Nevertheless, he never seriously regretted his own decision.

No time was wasted. Erika went over to England and was married to Wystan at Ledbury, Herefordshire, because it was near the Downs School, where he was then teaching. On June 15, the very day of the wedding, Goebbels—unaware that the joke was on him—solemnly announced that Erika was no longer a German.

(In 1939, not long after their arrival in the United States, Wystan and Christopher visited Thomas and Katia Mann, who were then living at Princeton with Erika, Klaus, and some of their other children. A photographer from *Time* happened to be present. Thomas asked Wystan and Christopher to pose with them for a group portrait. "I know Mr. Auden's your son-in-law," said the photographer, "but Mr. Isherwood—what's his relation to your family?" Thomas's prompt reply made everybody laugh but the photographer, who didn't understand German: "Family pimp.")

In a letter to Kathleen, June 21, Christopher tells her that he has started a novel, the day before:

> I hope it's going to be really good. Not so superficial as Norris and yet, in its own way, funnier. Its hero is a sort of van der Lubbe, an embodiment of the madness and hysteria of our time. He is the type of ideal liar who no longer has the least notion that he isn't telling the truth. I think I can make him rather heroic.

Christopher had been planning this novel for some time. He had decided to call it *Paul Is Alone.* Here is an outline of its action, put together from various notes in his diary:

> Part One: Ambrose [Francis] is living on the island of St. Nicholas. One night, Paul makes a dramatic appearance there by swimming across from the mainland. He is in a state of near-collapse from hunger. Ambrose has him fed and given a place to sleep.
>   Paul proves to be an efficient cook. He takes charge of the kitchen, bosses the Greek boys around, and serves excellent meals. He tries to impress Ambrose by playing the mystery man. He admits that he has no money but won't say how he got to Greece. He calls himself Paul von Hartmann and claims to be a German baron. He mentions several Englishmen of titled families as being his friends. From his descriptions of them, Ambrose realizes that he must indeed know them. But Ambrose is more puzzled than impressed, because

Paul speaks English like a native and with a slight Cockney accent. Ambrose later finds that Paul's German is also that of a native, but educated, upper-class.

Within a few days, a charming, good-natured, unaffected young German turns up. His name is Fritz. He tells Ambrose that he has been wandering around Greece, after escaping from Germany, where he was arrested by the Nazis as a Communist. At first, Paul tries to become Fritz's special friend. But soon Fritz is so popular with Ambrose and the Greeks that Paul gets jealous of him. Paul steals a ring belonging to Ambrose and makes it appear that Fritz stole it. So Ambrose sends Fritz away.

Then an English friend of Ambrose arrives to stay. He at once recognizes Paul as a waiter from a club to which he belongs in London. Paul was dismissed from the club for theft. The Englishmen he has claimed as his friends were, in fact, members of the club; Paul only knew them by waiting on them. He has come to Greece as a steward on a tourist-liner and jumped ship. Paul is utterly humiliated when the Englishman tells this to Ambrose. He leaves the island at once.

Part Two: Paul is back in London, down and out. An Austrian film-director named Bergmann [Viertel] meets Paul while he is strolling the streets at night, is amused by his talk and concerned about his half-starved condition and therefore brings him home. Bergmann's wife Magda immediately takes a strong interest in Paul which, at first, is motherly.

Paul plays up to both of them by becoming what he senses they want him to be—a thief and a liar who is nevertheless romantically innocent. He tells them that he is British, of Anglo-German parentage; that he has posed as a German baron (his German mother was merely upper-class and unhappily married to a working-class Englishman); that he has been a waiter; that he has stolen from his employers and from Ambrose.

He implies that he is unable to stop stealing or lying; he needs the Bergmanns' help.

Bergmann and Magda, who are the real innocents in this situation, are eager to help him. Since Paul speaks German and is also efficient and quick to learn, Bergmann hires him as a secretary-assistant. Sometimes Paul goes with him to the studio where Bergmann is directing his film; sometimes Paul works for Magda at their apartment.

Magda fancies herself as a psychologist. She believes that she can cure Paul of his kleptomania by showing him love and trust. She begins giving him jobs which involve him in handling their money. At first, he proves worthy of her trust; he also responds to her love, as long as it is motherly. But, when she tries to seduce him, he is repelled and embarrassed—all the more so because he is homosexual. He runs away, taking a large sum of money with him.

Part Three: Paul is staying at a hotel in the Canary Islands. Thanks to the Bergmanns' money, he is well-dressed and temporarily well-off. He poses as a film-actor who will shortly appear in his first starring role —under a new name which he isn't at liberty to tell until the studio is ready to start its publicity-campaign for him. He makes this sound convincing by his descriptions of life in the studio as he has seen it while working with Bergmann.

Meanwhile, stressing the German side of his ancestry, he makes friends with several Germans who are living in the islands. One of these, a young schoolmaster, is the leader of a Nazi group. Paul falls in love with him and becomes his disciple—although he has expressed violent anti-Nazi views while living with the Jewish Bergmanns.

The schoolmaster and Paul climb the Pico on Tenerife. That night, at the rest hut, the schoolmaster preaches Hitlerism to him with Nordic ruthlessness. This scene ends in a sex-act. Paul is now so infatuated that he agrees to spy on one of the German residents who is a professed Nazi but whom the schoolmaster suspects of being a traitor.

Paul cultivates the friendship of this man until he is trusted by him. When news comes that Hitler has killed Roehm, the man says delightedly that this will mean the downfall of the Nazi regime. Paul reports his words to the schoolmaster and the rest of the Nazi group. They go to the man's house and beat him up so badly that he isn't expected to live. Paul, terrified, leaves by the next ship. It happens to be going to Denmark.

Part Four: In Copenhagen, Paul marries a German-Jewish girl whose passport is about to expire, in order to give her British nationality. She is a Communist and this earns him the respect and trust of the other Communists in the city. He goes to live with the girl and her lover, who is also a German Communist.

Paul pretends to have worked with the Communists in Germany at the time of Hitler's coming to power. He tells, as his own adventures, the stories Fritz told him on St. Nicholas. Since Fritz was from Munich and the girl and her lover are from Berlin, Paul runs very little risk of being found out.

Then the lover goes back to Germany on a mission to the Communist underground. Time passes. He doesn't return. It is nearly certain that he has been caught.

And now Paul becomes the victim of his own fantasies and lies. He can't resist making the grand gesture —volunteering to go into Germany himself and find out what has happened to the lover. The other Communists agree to this, believing that Paul is an experienced activist and that he has as good a chance of surviving as any of them, if not a better. Whereas, of course, he has almost no chance; he has never even been in Germany before.

Paul crosses the frontier and that is the last they ever hear of him. In due course, they begin to honor him as one of their martyred dead. But the reader, knowing Paul much better than they do, may have certain doubts.

(Paul wasn't a portrait of any particular individual. The general idea of the character was based on an Englishman whom Christopher had known briefly during his early days in Berlin. This young man was a kleptomaniac—or perhaps he posed as one to make himself seem more interesting. Christopher preached Homer Lane to him and proposed a cure in the classic Lane tradition—the young man was to go on stealing but he was also to keep a ledger in which he entered the estimated value of everything he stole, as though he were running a business. This was to make theft unromantic. The cure didn't work. But Christopher later pretended, to Stephen and others, that it did.)

Like *The Lost, Paul Is Alone* was an attempt by Christopher to pack a section of his past life into a plot structure —in this instance, his experiences since leaving Berlin, up to and including the Auden–Mann marriage. When he described the novel in outline—much more sensationally than I have done here—to Upward, Auden, Spender, and Lehmann, they were all enthusiastic. Only he himself was full of misgivings. Again and again, by talking about it to his friends, he talked himself into continuing; again and again, he lost faith in it. He tinkered with it, on and off, for at least a year, but produced no more than a couple of chapters.

Finally he realized that he simply wanted to describe his life as he had lived it. What inspired him was the commentary he would make on it, not the melodrama he could make out of it. Certainly, he would fictionalize many episodes in order to simplify them and thus reveal their essence; a change-over from fact to fiction often begins with the weeding out of superfluous details. But he could tell his own lies; he didn't need a Paul to tell them for him. That would merely put his fiction at a double remove from fact.

On July 7, John Lehmann came to Amsterdam to talk to Christopher about *New Writing,* the magazine he was planning to edit and publish next spring. Christopher would soon owe a great debt to John. His continuing demand for material forced Christopher to do what he was stupidly unwilling to do—publish the rest of his Berlin writings as disconnected fragments, suitable in length for the magazine, instead of trying to fit them into a stodgy, plot-ridden story. Thus John became responsible for the informal form of *Goodbye to Berlin.*

Many of their discussions during that visit were held while walking through the Amsterdam streets. A favorite walk took them along the edge of an athletic field full of teenage boys. Among these were a few types of exotic beauty, products of Holland's colonial presence in the East Indies—Nordic blond hair and peach skin, with Indonesian cheekbones and liquid black equatorial eyes. At one corner of the field was a boxing ring. The boys didn't fight, they only sparred, with a sportsmanlike restraint which verged absurdly on politeness. But it was just the caressing softness with which their big leather gloves patted each other's naked bodies that Christopher found distractingly erotic. His attention would stray far from literature, and his voice, though continuing to talk about it, must have sounded like a programmed robot's: "Oh yes, indeed—I *do* agree—I think he's quite definitely the best writer in that genre, absolutely—"

In a letter to Kathleen, July 30, Christopher reports that Gerald Hamilton keeps sending postcards, each under a different name, to one of the Dutch publishers, urging him to publish a translation of *Mr. Norris* in Dutch; he has sent forty of these cards already. (The publisher, nevertheless, refused the book, giving the odd-sounding reason that it was "too topical." Perhaps by "topical" he meant anti-Nazi, and was thus hinting that he feared its publication might expose him to reprisals by Nazi sympathizers in Holland.)

Early in August, Kathleen paid them a short visit. She went sightseeing with her usual energy, although Dutch culture was a little too Germanic to suit her taste. One evening, while they were out for a stroll, Christopher unintentionally led her onto the Zeedijk, where ladies in negligee sat at the windows of invitingly lit parlors. Kathleen behaved as though this were a street on which picturesque native craftsmen were selling their artifacts. She asked, in would-be appreciative tourist tones: "Oh, is this what they call the red-light district?"

On August 24, Forster and his friend, Bob Buckingham, arrived; also Brian Howard and his friend, Toni. (Since I have just used the word "friend" twice in one sentence, this is a good place to comment on it. Admittedly, it is ambiguous. In Christopher's case, for example, it had to cover his relationships with Upward, Forster, Auden, and Heinz—each one of which differed greatly from the others in character. Nevertheless, when a male friendship includes sexual love, I dislike referring to either of the friends as a "lover" or a "boyfriend." Except in the plural, "lover" suggests to me a one-sided attachment; "boyfriend" always sounds condescending and often ridiculously unsuitable. So I shall go on using "friend" and try to show what the word means when applied to any given pair of people.)

On August 27, Forster and Bob, Brian and Toni, Stephen Spender (who had appeared unexpectedly the day before), Klaus Mann, and Gerald Hamilton all went with Christopher and Heinz to The Hague, where Gerald had arranged a birthday lunch in a restaurant for Christopher. (Christopher's birthday was the twenty-sixth but he had become accustomed in childhood to celebrating one day later, because the twenty-seventh was the birthday of his Grandfather John.) Soon after their arrival, a rainstorm forced them to take shelter in the nearest public building. It happened to be the Gevangenpoort prison, now a museum. This was an emergency which demanded all Gerald's art as a host. He had to entertain his guests without benefit of alcohol or even chairs, amidst a depressing display of antique torture instruments.

This all-male party was oddly assorted. Gerald himself sparkled with jokes to which he wasn't quite attending; he had an air of nervously expecting the police to appear. Stephen simmered with sly giggles, aware of the Joke behind the jokes yet also basically inattentive, perhaps because he was composing a poem. Klaus Mann, charming and civilized, with his quick eager speech, talked pessimistically but cheerfully about the times they were living in. (He had described his latest book, *Flucht in den Norden,* to Christopher with a grin as "oh, another pre-war novel.") Brian Howard's dark, heavy-lidded, keenly searching and testing eyes missed no nuance of the situation but were made restless by his need for a drink and his anxiety lest Toni should say something gauche. Handsome Bavarian blond Toni, ill at ease in his expensive clothes, was only anxious not to offend, also in need of a drink, and enjoying himself least of anyone present. Forster, beaming through his spectacles, was probably enjoying himself most, since Bob Buckingham was with him. They kept exchanging glances full of fun and affection. Bob's thick-featured broad face was made beautiful by its strength and good nature. Heinz had felt drawn to him immediately and it seemed to Christopher that they had a kind of resemblance, due to their working-class kinship. He himself was feeling unusually happy.

After his return to England, Forster wrote:

> As for Amsterdam, my only objection to it is that I had no time there whatever alone with you. There was nothing I wanted to imbibe or impart, still it would have been an additional enjoyment. After all, we are both of us writers, and good ones.
>
> I think you did realize how much we both liked Heinz.

This was the first of Forster's letters which began "Dear Christopher" and which was signed "Morgan."

Gerald, the ever punctual, ever polite, used to say that Brian Howard had "the manners of a very great genius" —by which he meant that Brian was unreliable, unpunctual, noisy, and quarrelsome in public, apt to get drunk or doped—and that he didn't have the talent which would have excused such behavior. Here, Gerald—who hadn't much literary taste—was wrong. Brian did have talent as a poet. What was inexcusable was that he used it so seldom. His self-indulgence was babyish; he was one of the most fascinating and dangerous babies of his generation. If you flattered yourself that you could wean him away from babyhood, he was delighted to let you try, for as long as your patience held out. But you couldn't complain later that he hadn't warned you you'd fail—and maybe end by acquiring his vices, into the bargain. Indeed, he warned Christopher, that would-be healer: "What you *must* realize, my dear, is that *you* can never understand someone like me—someone who's devoted his *entire life* to pleasure." Brian contrived to pronounce the word "pleasure" in a tone which brought a chill to Christopher's spine and suggested the grimmest austerities of the medieval monks.

Christopher had enough sense not to get too involved with Brian personally, but for a while it seemed that circumstances might throw him and Heinz together with Brian and Toni as a foursome. Toni had been refused permission to live in England—on the ground that he had associated with a drug addict during a previous visit —so now he and Brian, like Christopher and Heinz, were looking for a country where they could settle.

September 1. Dinner with Brian and Toni. They have now heard from Ireland and it seems doubtful whether it's worth going there, as there is an exchange of alien lists with England. Brian wants to go to Portugal, buy a ruined palace, and keep hens and goats and grow oranges. Toni keeps making objections and warns Brian in advance that he won't clean the shit off the goats. Brian got angry with him and alarmed that his lack of enthusiasm would put us off. Actually, I don't want to go unless we can get Gerald or Stephen to come with us.

September 6. Last night we went out with Brian and Toni and sat in the cafe by the Concert Hall. The boys played billiards. Brian discussed the various fittings of the cafe, piece by piece—the lamps, the vases, the ornaments—and described the artistic pedigree of each: sham Louis XIV, bastard Oriental mixed with Second Empire, pre-war arty German (balls on strings) etc, etc. He knows a good deal about the history of bad taste and was very amusing.

Christopher's diary also describes a teatime scene in the lounge of a hotel where Christopher and Brian are sitting together. Brian produces from his pocket a twist of paper containing some white powder. "Do you know what *this* is, my dear?" he says aggressively and very loudly, to embarrass both Christopher and the other guests. "Take a *good* look at it—no, it isn't salt, my dear,

and it isn't sugar, my dear, it's *cocaine,* my dear, CO-
CAINE!" He sniffs ostentatiously at the powder as he
explains that this isn't good cocaine, however. "Good
cocaine is sparkling white, so dazzling that you can't look
at it." Continuing to sniff, he tells Christopher that cocaine "gathers in a knot in the chest and is like ozone,"
that hashish "is like toffee, it makes you feel like the
gateway to Hell," and that heroin "spreads like a stone
flower from the stomach to the legs and the arms." Christopher asks him to describe his sensations at this moment.
He answers: "Imagine yourself partly a wonderful calm
Venetian palace in the sunshine and partly Joan of Arc."

And then there was another evening on which they
had all been out together. Having said good night to
Brian and Toni, Christopher and Heinz walked at a lei-
surely pace down the street toward their lodgings. Meanwhile, Brian ran down a parallel street, waited for them
at the next corner, and jumped out at them, with his black
furry greatcoat over his head. They screamed, first with
surprise, then with laughter, as he chased them . . . In
retrospect, this seemed to Christopher to have been a
beautifully imaginative act of affection. "How many
other people we know," he asked himself, "would have
cared for us enough to do that?"

(Brian and Toni did go to Portugal, in October of that
year. But they didn't stay long. Christopher and Heinz
saw little of them when they, too, came to Portugal
later.)

On September 12, Christopher and Heinz went to the
Belgian consulate in Rotterdam and made another attempt to get Heinz a permit to stay in Belgium. Again
they were refused; Gerald Hamilton had, in fact, accomplished nothing for them. Returning disgusted and depressed to Amsterdam, they found a letter from a friend
suggesting that they should try for the permit at the

Belgian consulate in Luxembourg. One could get into Luxembourg without any formalities.

On September 14, they entered Luxembourg, went to the Belgian consulate there, and were given a thirty-day permit for Heinz within five minutes. Next day, they took a bus trip through what is called the Luxembourg Switzerland, a hilly region of forests, which Christopher imagined as looking like the country of Ruritania in *The Prisoner of Zenda*. At Echternach, the bus made a detour across the frontier into Germany and back. Their driver assured them that the German officials wouldn't ask for passports. Some passengers were nervous and preferred to remain behind and be picked up on the return journey, but Christopher and Heinz couldn't resist the adventure. At a café just inside Germany, they were allowed to get out of the bus and spend a quarter of an hour drinking beer and writing postcards. A young man in S.S. uniform was sitting there, but he seemed as unreal and theatrical as the Jew-Hate placard nailed to the wall. They mailed a postcard to Gerald but the shock which they had intended it to give him was neutralized, because they arrived in Brussels before the card did.

September 19. We moved in here yesterday evening, a second-floor flat overlooking the Boulevard Adolphe Max (number 22). The living-room has fish-net curtains, huge sideboards covered with silver cake-dishes and fancy ashtrays, a pair of sofa dolls, two table lamps whose silk shades are the skirts of ballerinas—the kind used in brothels—six large and small photos of Clark Gable and six of Ramon Novarro, a miniature aeroplane propellor supporting a whole bunch of snaps, good-looking young airmen mostly (one of them signed: "pour Claire, l'audacieuse"), and a grandfather clock (whose chime I have had stopped) with weights like small artillery shells. The bedroom has a handsome white bath, a dangerous gas-heater for the water, and a big painting of Leda with her swan.

Our landlady ("Claire l'audacieuse") is gay, talkative, haggardly chic with waved greyish hair and darkened eyelids, in a sleeveless white satin blouse. She is amazingly generous, gets breakfast and cleans our rooms for nothing and is now washing all our clothes, for which she asks only the price of the soap.

Claire was a tragic figure. I think she must have been on the verge of starvation. For a while at least, she had nowhere to live and Christopher and Heinz discovered that she was sleeping in the kitchen of the flat without telling them. This was an intolerable situation; they had absolutely no privacy. At last, though feeling terribly guilty, they somehow got her to leave.

By the middle of October, the Ethiopian crisis was at its height. Italy had invaded the country and the League Assembly had voted to impose sanctions. Meanwhile, Heinz had been refused a six-month permit to stay in Belgium and his thirty-day permit had expired. Gerald arranged for his expulsion to be delayed from week to week, but it was obvious that a move must be made soon. Stephen was in Brussels with the young man who is called Jimmy Younger in *World within World,* and the two of them had agreed to come with Christopher and Heinz to Portugal. But they couldn't leave for at least another month—I forget why.

October 19. Heinz has got spectacles, now. The oculist said to me: "His world is not our world, Monsieur. All his life, vertical lines have been practically invisible to him, while horizontals have appeared abnormally distinct. When he looks at a circle, he sees it as an oval but, since he has learned by experience that it is circular, he retransforms it into a circle within his brain."

The other day, for the first time in his life, he went to bed with a whore. She had no breasts and wanted a hundred francs. It was not a success.

During November, Christopher finished writing *The Nowaks* and sent it to John Lehmann, who was going to publish it in his first issue of *New Writing,* the following spring. It would thus become the first fragment of *Goodbye to Berlin* to appear in print.

On December 10, Stephen, Jimmy, Christopher, and Heinz sailed from Antwerp on a Brazilian boat which would take them to Lisbon on its way to Rio.

TWELVE

At the time of sailing, Christopher felt lightheaded with relief. This voyage, at least, was going to be a holiday from worry about Heinz's permits. And the company of Stephen and of Jimmy Younger offered relief of another kind; they would help him decide what was to be done, when they had landed in Portugal and faced new problems. During Christopher's wanderings with Heinz, he had made all the decisions alone—grumbling to himself that this was a heavy burden he had to bear. He would have done better to realize that Heinz was no longer a boy and needed responsibility.

Jimmy Younger was ready to run their whole expedition, if they would let him. He had served in the Army and believed in getting things organized. His appearance was attractive: curly red-brown hair, sparkling yellow-brown eyes, big smiling teeth. He would call Stephen "yer silly thing!" and tell him, "Don't be so daft!" with a Welsh (Cardiff) accent. He was full of fun and the love of argument—left-wing political or just argument for its own sake. He used the jargon of a left-wing intellectual, but his own kind of intelligence was intuitive and emotional. He had a Welsh ear for the music of poetry and could genuinely appreciate the work of Spender, Auden, and their fellow poets. Telling Christopher about his first meeting with Stephen, he said: "That was when the curtain went up, for me."

I remember the voyage in terms of opera, with the four of them relating to each other either as quartets, trios, or duets. As a quartet, their performance was directed toward the other passengers. Taking it for granted that nobody on board could possibly guess what they were really like, they amused themselves by behaving with deliberate oddness—exchanging private-joke signals, grimaces, and asides in full view and hearing of their audience.

The trio was between Stephen, Christopher, and Jimmy. It now seems to me that it was performed for Jimmy's benefit, to make him feel that Stephen and Christopher regarded him as one of themselves. They didn't, altogether, and Jimmy must have been aware that they didn't. But, perhaps, for the time being, it satisfied Jimmy's pride that they even made the effort to pretend.

Christopher's duet with Heinz was more intimate than it had been for some time; being with Stephen and Jimmy made them very conscious of themselves as a couple. This didn't mean, however, that they had yet begun to criticize the other two. Heinz, who could now speak a hesitant basic English, also had a duet with Jimmy—of necessity, since they often found themselves alone together. The duet between Stephen and Christopher was long-established and had a continuity which bridged their separations; they discussed books and politics and abstract ideas and other authors, but very seldom the people they happened to be living with. There was no duet between Stephen and Heinz or between Christopher and Jimmy, perhaps because both Stephen and Christopher were afraid of being drawn into relationships which might have made them disloyal to each other. Christopher did eventually have a duet with Jimmy, but that was much later and under altered circumstances.

223

The quartet's conscious effort to enjoy itself produced a travel diary. Its entries were written in a tone of shipboard humor and were meant to be read aloud at once, before they could go stale. Here are a few excerpts:

Thursday, December 12. 1935. [Written by Stephen]: On Tuesday, when we left Brussels for Antwerp, Gerald came to say goodbye to us, wearing a huge fur-lined coat with a skunk collar in which his chinless, thick-lipped, flat-nosed face nestled. He was wearing no jewelry, but there was such a smell of scent in the room after he had come in that I said, "What lady has been here with scent?" "I'm still here," he answered, bridling a little. We all kissed him goodbye.

This boat is very old and goes very slowly. There are two lounges, one a drawing-room, very decorative, with a yellow-keyed grand piano, the other an Olde Tudor lounge, clawed over by five enormous electric fans, hanging from the ceiling like vampires. Here we read or write. In the other room, Jimmy strums on the piano and Heinz sings.

There is a fat woman, from Northern Ireland but half Belgian, who speaks several languages and is very taken by Jimmy.

21.00 hours. Same day. [Written by Christopher]: We are standing off Le Havre. The day has been dominated by the Irish-Belgian lady. "Oh, but you'd like Rio—you should see ut. If you've got an artistic 'eart—that is, heart—well, art and heart, I mean both—nature must speak to you there." But she was shocked when Jimmy said he didn't like the Royal Family; she ordered him off to the gymnasium: "Away with you and shake up your liver!"

Later, Jimmy played the piano: "And the cares that

hang around me through the week—seem to vanish like a gambler's lucky streak."

Isherwood then asked Spender what he was thinking.

Spender: "I was thinking about the lucky streak. If I'd written that, I thought, I should have made it somehow terrible and terrific. And how boring, I thought to myself, that I can only write about things terrifically."

At some time during the crossing of the Bay of Biscay (December 14–15)—calm at first, then rough; but not rough enough to make any of them actually seasick—the Irish-Belgian lady read their palms and told them their characters. Christopher reports this:

> Stephen is self-willed, violently pursues his ideas and changes them frequently, listens to advice and has a nature of gold. Heinz is conceited, ambitious, and will succeed. Jimmy is Welsh—and therefore conceited—strong-willed and mad on girls. And I—ah, I am the kind of boy Madame has adored all her life: wherever I travel, whatever I do, I'll always remain real hundred per cent English—just a shy, modest, charming boy. The doctor then offered his palm, disclosing a toothpick which he had been gripping all through the meal like a dagger. She refused to say what she saw in it—it would shock us.

(The quartet made a joke out of pretending to wonder whether this doctor was really a doctor at all—because *Portuguese Doctor,* not simply *Doctor,* was printed above his cabin door. Might not this phrase have some quite other significance, as "Dutch wife," "French letter," and "Spanish fly" do?)

Heinz wanted to borrow a German book from the library and this led to the discovery that there is only one to be had—and that much mutilated. We then applied to the Germans, who told us that this boat was originally a German boat and that the Brazilian government seized it during the war. The guilty consciences of the Brazilians caused them, according to the white-haired German, to throw overboard all the German books in the library. The white-haired German is discreetly bitter—the thin-haired younger German less bitter and less discreet and his wife an idiotically sincere chatterbox who protests, very loudly in the lounge, that Germany Wants Peace—by which she means, as Stephen says, that Germany wants to grab everything without having to fight for it.

Since his college days, Christopher had associated port with solemn toasts proposed and tedious anecdotes told by the elderly Others in curtained dining rooms. But at Oporto, where they landed for a few hours on the sixteenth, porto was simply a local wine which they drank out of doors in the midday sun; sickly-sweet, too warm, and too strong. Christopher boozily scribbled on a postcard to Kathleen: "The ship has a hole in her side." Stephen found some vast metaphysical humor in this (true) statement and laughed till the tears ran down his cheeks. Heinz laughed at Stephen's laughter, with equal violence. Jimmy nursemaided them back on board.
· That evening, a party of silly Brazilian girls declared brightly, in Heinz's presence, that they hated all Germans. Christopher got up and walked out of the lounge. He enjoyed making such gestures of righteous indignation but didn't pause to consider how much Heinz must be embarrassed by them.

On the morning of December 17, their ship entered the estuary of the Tagus. By that evening, they had settled into the Hotel Nunes at Sintra, fifteen miles outside Lisbon. Here are Christopher's first impressions, gathered during the next few days:

Sintra is a large village composed chiefly of palaces, ruinous and to let. The overhanging cliffs are sprouting with fern-shaped trees and subtropical plants, like an enormous rock-garden. In the woods, one comes upon locked gateways, extravagantly sculptured, leading nowhere, and rococo summer-houses where an eighteenth century poet might find inspiration for the dullest of all tragedies in heroic couplets, with a prologue, epilogue, and fourteen acts.

The castle of Pena is easily the most beautiful building any of us have ever seen. In fact, it has the immediate staggering appeal of something which is sham, faked, and architecturally wrong. It could hardly be more effective if it had been erected overnight by a film company for a super-production about the Middle Ages. Clamped on to the highest spike of rock on our local range of hills, its Moorish-Gothic-Renaissance towers and ramparts command a view of all this part of Portugal . . . Inside the castle are the touchingly shabby royal apartments, with their railway-carriage upholstery and uncomfortable beds. Copies of *Country Life* and other English Society magazines lie about on the tables, faded yellow and dated 1910. (The year the last king of Portugal was deposed.) In the billiard-room is a horse-racing game of the kind still found on seaside piers.

Up here there is mist and thin rain. The sky has been gloomy ever since our arrival; still we have been busy and haven't felt unduly depressed. Already we have found a house—not *the* house which we still hope one day to discover, but quite a nice cottage with a sitting-room, a dining-room, and five small bedrooms, furnished brightly but with a certain note of despair, as if for spinsters. The house is called Alecrim do Norte (which is the name of a kind of evergreen bush) and it is in San Pedro, a suburb of Sintra, higher up the hillside. It has a wonderful view, right down the valley to the sea.

They moved into the cottage on December 21. Their landlady was a gray-haired, vigorous, tweedy English-woman who lived nearby. She had spent most of her life in Portugal and could tell them everything they needed to know about local merchants and food prices. As a matter of principle, she was determined that they shouldn't be cheated. They undoubtedly *were* cheated, quite often; but Portuguese prices were so much lower than English that it hardly mattered. Indeed, it seemed to them that it was they who were doing the cheating. The landlady found them a cook and a maid—for tiny wages, which, she assured them, were well above standard. They had bad consciences about this—Jimmy especially—but nevertheless resigned themselves to being exploiters.

By the beginning of 1936, they had all of them settled down to daily occupations. Stephen was working on a book *(Forward from Liberalism)* and a play *(The Trial of a Judge)*. Jimmy was acting as his secretary, keeping the household accounts and supervising the servants. (Their cook cooked fairly well but fatalistically; when Jimmy found cause for complaint, she frustrated him by agreeing that the meal had turned out badly.) Heinz now had an assortment of creatures to look after—a black and white mongrel puppy, named Teddy, which made messes; six hens and a rooster; and some rabbits. He also kept the garden tidy. Christopher was trying to write *Paul Is Alone.* He was the least contented member of the household because his work wasn't going well. So he wasted time indulging in anxiety, his chronic vice. As always, he had an excuse: Heinz's situation in Portugal was far from secure. The German consulate in Lisbon knew the whereabouts of all Germans. Sooner or later, it would send Heinz an order to come and register for conscription. When he failed to do this, it would report him to the Portuguese police as a German whose citizenship might perhaps be taken away from him. Since Heinz didn't even have the status of a Jewish or political refugee, the police might well decide to regard him as an ordinary criminal and expel him from the country . . . Christopher's anxiety, however well-founded, didn't help Heinz; it infected him and weakened his courage.

Meanwhile, their group diary kept up a lively patter, recording domestic events and encounters with the local inhabitants. Teddy had been cured of a tapeworm and got fat but continued to wet the carpet. Heinz, on being offered oysters at a Lisbon restaurant, insisted, with a curious Prussian pedantry, that there was a correct way of eating them which he must be shown before he could start. They all tried to show him, including the waiter, but Heinz was unimpressed. There *was* a correct way, he repeated, though obviously none of them knew it. So his oysters remained uneaten.

As newcomers, they were objects of curiosity and got invited to parties by their neighbors. In Holland and in Belgium, Christopher and Heinz had lived surrounded by the tribe of the Emigration and had felt themselves part of it. ("We've elected you an honorary Jew," a refugee had once told Christopher, as a joking compliment.) When refugees gathered together, there was much wit but no joy. Hitler always seemed invisibly present, just out of earshot; it was more like a conspiracy than a party. Here in Portugal, their hosts were mostly English, Scots, or Irish—refugees from nothing except the North European climate and the higher cost of living elsewhere. They were a gossipy, inquisitive, hospitable bunch of individualists, always on the lookout for new ears into which to whisper their elderly scandals.

Several of them were preoccupied with what Christopher dismissively called "magic." One lady painted spirit portraits and gave readings from the tarot cards. Another had prepared a large-scale map of Fairyland. Another had written down her adventures in a previous life, as a Syrian lad, during the Roman Empire.

Stephen describes a meeting with members of this psychic fringe:

I heard some rather odd fragments of conversation from the sofa on which Miss H. and Mrs. J. were sitting. Miss H. said in her matter-of-fact voice: "I really think it was very inconsiderate of him, especially when you prepared him a special high mass." "Oh well," said Mrs. J., "we can't expect him to behave otherwise. The other day, when he was here, I had the most terrible two hours of my life. I had to think ahead of his thoughts all the time. It was very stiff going, particularly at the corners."

Meanwhile, Jimmy was having a conversation with Miss W. He said he thought there was going to be a war. "No," she said, "not unless the ether is reactionary." Jimmy took her to be referring to the British Broadcasting Corporation, so he assured her that our friend Mr. Ackerley of *The Listener* is quite advanced politically, though not as materialistic as one could wish.

Some weeks later, Miss W. did a spirit portrait of Stephen. (Christopher thought it looked much more like his own brother Richard, whom Stephen anyhow slightly resembled.) She also gave Stephen a reading of the tarot cards. This was so discouraging that she became increasingly apologetic. The King of Cups was crossed by the Falling Tower, and then the Devil himself appeared, and then a heart pierced by three swords . . . When she had finished, Stephen, wanting to reassure her that he was a good sport and not discouraged, asked in a tone of mock-innocence: "Could we have a second game?" Miss W. winced slightly at the word but didn't seem offended. Later she assured him that he was destined to be one of the leaders of the new age, one of the truly great, and that she was proud to be the first person to tell him this. She was obviously less impressed by Christopher. But he got good marks for knowing Gerald Heard. To his surprise, she spoke of Heard with awe, as a master of the occult.

On January 18, Christopher wrote to Kathleen, thanking her for sending him the program of *The Dog beneath the Skin*. She had seen the first performance of it by the Group Theatre Company at the Westminster Theatre on January 12. (The regular run of the play began on January 30.) Auden had worked with its director, Rupert Doone, to cut and revise the script, during rehearsals. They had altered the ending—rightly, I now think—and taken out the Destructive Desmond episode—wrongly, I still think. At that time, Christopher grumbled over all the alterations, merely because he hadn't been consulted in advance. But he must have understood, even then, that this would have been impossible. There was no time for an exchange of letters and the Group Theatre couldn't have afforded long-distance telephone calls to Portugal.

In the same letter, Christopher told Kathleen he had just heard from Bob Buckingham that Forster had had a bladder operation and that he would soon have to have another, much more serious. Before leaving for Portugal, Christopher had visited England from November 30 to December 5 and had spent a day with Forster. He now realized that Forster must have already known then that this ordeal was ahead of him and that the risk, in his own case, was (as the surgeon put it) above normal. Yet he had said nothing about this to Christopher, hadn't even hinted at it, and had indeed appeared to be his usual lighthearted, amusing self. Later, after Christopher had written to him, he replied:

Yes, I never told you I wasn't well when we parted. There seemed so much to say and I was so happy seeing you.

Christopher was tremendously moved. This, to him, was the authentic tone of the anti-heroic hero.

During January, they had two visitors, Humphrey Spender and Gerald Hamilton. Humphrey was with them, on and off, for several weeks, making a trip to Spain and then returning. He was worried about losing his hair and finally consented to undergo Heinz's treatment; Heinz shaved him completely bald. Thereafter, Humphrey wore a beret when strangers were present, even indoors.

Gerald stayed for a few days only, at a hotel in Sintra. (No doubt he had sinister business with some Portuguese government official.) Gerald's code of cleanliness demanded the use of a bidet whenever he had been on the toilet. There was no bidet in his hotel room, so he unwisely hoisted himself onto the washbasin. It was unequal to his weight. The entire fixture was torn out of the wall and the bowl shattered, wounding him embarrassingly in the buttocks. Gerald left for Tangier to nurse them and also his hurt dignity—for nobody could help laughing at this unkind accident.

On February 4, Stephen, Humphrey, Jimmy, Heinz, and Christopher paid a long-projected visit to the casino at Estoril, which Christopher calls "that almost legendary haunt of vice," in the group diary:

> Of course it all seemed very harmless: two large modern rooms crowded with pink English tourists in dinner jackets and women in evening dress. Soon we were playing according to our respective natures: Stephen, with bulging blue eyes and angry lobster cheeks, played at the highest table madly but carefully, and won nearly four hundred escudos. Humphrey sneaked about, with his sly diffident smile, betting at all the tables and working up his unobtrusive gentlemanly little pile, two and a half escudos at a time. Jimmy,

slightly more reckless but very domestic, was seated with his counters arranged before him primly, like knitting. Heinz, studious and bespectacled, played away in a corner, crossly, all by himself, betting only on numbers and in complete ignorance of the rules— he refused utterly to tell anybody whether he was winning or losing—keeping his counters clenched fiercely in his very hot hand. As for me, I prowled around the tables, imagining myself like Dostoevsky, Tolstoy, Lord Byron, or any of the characters in the novels of Balzac or Disraeli, paused to count my money, tried to think of systems, got rattled, apologized, and hoped that nobody else was winning, either. By the end of the evening, we had all lost except Humphrey, who admitted coyly to seventy escudos. We left soon after midnight.

Next day, they woke up burning with gambling fever and certain that they would win. Too impatient to wait for the evening, they arrived at the casino when it opened at 3:30. The afternoon casino, with its blinds drawn to shut out the sunlight, was an altogether different world from the harmless-seeming tourist resort of the previous night.

Only one table was being used and this was already full up. Not a single English tourist—their place was taken by a sinister clique of professional gamblers—a fat hairy unshaved man wearing greasy clothes powdered round the collar with scurf, a pig-jowled brute with a gold bracelet, a horrible old woman with long lank gray hair, who kept dipping for counters in a shabby midwife's bag. The room was quite silent, except for the croupier's voice; the play was rapid and underhanded. Several times, our winnings were simply grabbed. And when Stephen protested—his face like a scarlet indignant poppy, accusing history for all wars and wrongs—he was snarled at or brutally snubbed. In this atmosphere, we rapidly lost our money. At half past six, three very woebegone would-be bank-breakers crept into their taxi; the boys, more obstinate, stayed on to risk some last shillings and returned an hour later, giggling nervously, having lost all.

Christopher to Kathleen, March 1:

I think the life we are leading at present is far more satisfactory than anything we have tried before. The great thing is to be involved in one's surroundings and we are involved already, even if only as bogus English colonists. The word has gone round that we are such nice boys; and nice boys are a rarity in this colony of ladies.

However, Christopher, writing one day later in his own private diary, reveals that Stephen and Jimmy have already decided to leave Sintra in the middle of the month, for Spain, Greece, and Austria:

It's all very friendly and we are perfectly pleasant about it, but of course we all know that our attempt at living here together has been a complete flop. The schemes of taking another and larger house have been tacitly dropped.

There had been some domestic friction—chiefly on account of Teddy, the puppy. Teddy was exclusively Heinz's dog, but the others also had to live with the messes he made. And Heinz had his own peculiar way of handling a pet; if Teddy bit him, he would bite Teddy back, quite hard, so that he uttered nerve-jarring squeals. Christopher chose to regard Heinz's behavior as admirably natural; he was simply treating Teddy as his equal. When Stephen and Jimmy called Heinz cruel, Christopher called them sentimental hypocrites. However, he later had to admit that

Stephen and Jimmy have honestly done their best to get along with Heinz, who certainly can be maddening when he sulks. Although sharing the expenses for the animals, they now hardly dare look at them, for fear of precipitating another row.

It now seems astonishing to me that Christopher should ever have supposed Stephen would stay at Sintra for long, Heinz or no Heinz. He was temperamentally restless and needed frequent changes of scene—they were probably helpful to his work. Christopher, in Stephen's place, might have wandered about, too. Tied down by Heinz's permit problems, he was inclined to envy Stephen and therefore accuse him of desertion.

March 4. Yesterday, Stephen and Jimmy sneaked off to Estoril. They lost, between them, nearly five pounds.

Today Gerald Hamilton has written, very pessimistic about the chances for Heinz's future. I feel awfully depressed, but it's no use moping—I must find someone in this country who can help us. Dogskin was advertised last Sunday as being in its last weeks. And the plague amongst the hens, which we thought was over, has broken out again. Another died today. Heinz is going off gloomily to gamble at Estoril. Still this cold miserable rainy and windy weather. Snow in the mountains. Floods everywhere.

After supper, for no particular reason, my spirits rose. Read aloud to Stephen and Jimmy out of Laurence Binyon's *The Young King,* imitating various styles of hack Shakespearian acting. Stephen did the footsteps off, clank of armour, etc. We all laughed a lot. It was an evening of the kind I haven't spent more than half a dozen times since Cambridge, when Edward Upward and I did this sort of thing nearly every night. The others went to bed but I sat up, quite cheerful, reading *Abinger Harvest* and feeling, without the least cause, that quite probably everything will turn out all right somehow, in the end.

Then Heinz came in. He had won a thousand escudos. He was very uncertain whether to tell the others or not. If he does, he says, he must invite them to a celebration lunch, and he doesn't want to because he has never really forgiven them for the Teddy row. I said he must do as he likes.

March 5. Heinz did tell them, at breakfast. With his endless longing to be approved of and liked, he had planned his announcement and invitation as an important peace-gesture. But what actually happened was that Stephen asked "How much did you win last night?" "A thousand." *"Did* you?" Stephen's tone was cold and disapproving. He was instantly afraid that this success would make Jimmy anxious to visit Estoril again. "Perhaps," said Heinz, "one day soon, I'll invite you." Stephen not unnaturally took this to mean that Heinz would invite him and Jimmy to go gambling at the Casino. "Well, we're not going to," he answered at once, rather crossly—before Jimmy should have a chance to say anything.

Heinz, somewhat dashed, explained what he really meant; but the mischief was done. Stephen couldn't warm up again so quickly. "Oh—" was all he said. "That'll be very nice." Perhaps he didn't take the invitation very seriously—at any rate, his tone implied that he didn't. He and Jimmy began talking of something else. And Heinz retired, chilled and hurt, to feed the hens.

March 8. Yesterday, Hitler denounced the Treaty of Locarno and sent troops into the Rhine Zone.

We went to the Casino and gambled for a couple of hours. Heinz stayed on there, "waiting for a number to come up."

In the evening, our landlady invited us in to hear the

news. This is what the last three years have been, I thought—going into strange houses to hear the wireless announce a disaster. Hitler's shrill mad voice was relayed from a gramophone record. One had the feeling that he was dancing up and down on the tips of his toes.

Heinz came in at half past three, having lost everything.

Today it is pouring with rain. I haven't been out. A letter from Bob Buckingham to say that Morgan has had the operation and is very weak. Worked on the *Abinger Harvest* review.

On March 10, Christopher wrote to Kathleen enclosing a politely menacing note from Leonard Woolf:

I hear a rumour that Methuens are publishing a book by you. I presume that this must be a mere rumour in view of the fact that you have agreed to give us the first offer of your next novel, and that you told me that you would probably be sending it to us to consider in the autumn?

Christopher added:

Clearly, it's no use going on hedging with him; would you please ring up Curtis Brown and tell them I definitely wish them now to explain the whole situation to him? I am also writing to Woolf myself.

"The whole situation" was that Christopher was suffering from pique. Although *Mr. Norris* had been well reviewed and had sold well, Virginia Woolf hadn't invited him to meet her. Therefore, when other publishers approached him with offers, he had entered into an informal agreement with Methuen, the highest bidder. It was understood that they were to become his publishers as soon as he could get free from the Hogarth Press.

No doubt, Virginia Woolf's peculiar mental condition made her shrink from confronting Christopher, whom she may well have pictured to herself as a member of an aggressive, uncouth, hostile younger generation. Without question, Christopher behaved unprofessionally, childishly. Nevertheless, I sympathize with his hurt feelings.

As things turned out, the Hogarth Press published three more of Christopher's books. Meanwhile, he met Virginia several times and was even more fascinated by her than he had expected to be. It wasn't until 1945, four years after her death, that he published his first book with Methuen, *Prater Violet.*

March 15. Litvinov has said that war is inevitable. Gerald writes alarmingly from Brussels: Germans are being sent out of the country every day. Heinz is innocently busy with the rabbits. Where will he be in a month from now?

Stephen and Jimmy left yesterday morning for Spain, where churches are being burnt and right-wing newspaper offices sacked. In the afternoon, I went down to the railway station to try to get an evening paper. As I passed the prison, a great deal of shouting and laughter was going on inside—it sounded more like a school during the lunch-interval. A dark jolly-looking unshaven man looked out of one of the small barred windows and asked me, in very good French, for a cigarette. I told him I hadn't got one—I was sorry. "Just going for a walk?" he asked. "That's right," I said. "Well, enjoy yourself." "Thank you." We waved to each other politely. No guards were to be seen.

On March 16, Auden arrived to begin working with Christopher on their next play, *The Ascent of F6.* Since the near-success or, at any rate, non-failure of "Dogskin," Rupert Doone and his friend, the artist Robert Medley (who had designed the masks for *The Dog*), had been urging them to produce something else which could be staged by the Group Theatre. But Wystan and Christopher would have continued playwriting together in any case; it had now become a function of their friendship.

Considering that *F6* was written, revised, and typed out within one month, I assume that the two of them must have pre-planned it to some extent during a previous meeting which I can't recall. But Wystan was anyhow an extraordinarily fast worker. Christopher, who was merely writing prose dialogue, had difficulty in keeping up with the pace of his verse production. Wystan's first drafts were usually close to the final version. Christopher's were crude beyond belief. (I remember how astonished Wystan was when he found one of them lying around and, to Christopher's dismay, read it.) For Christopher was afflicted—as I now am to a far greater degree—by a species of laziness which made him have to force himself to write down something, anything, in order to "break the ground." The resulting nonsense would then shame him into asking himself seriously what it was that he wanted to say.

Some memories of the visit: Wystan writing indoors with the curtains drawn; Christopher writing out in the garden, with his shirt off in the sunshine . . . Wystan insisting on scrambling up a steep part of the Sintra hills, saying that they must get themselves into the mood of the mountaineers in their play; this was accompanied by laughter, lost footings, slitherings, and screams . . . Christopher and Heinz taking Wystan to see the horrible old afternoon gamblers at Estoril, thus inspiring him to write "Casino" ("Only their hands are living—") . . . Wystan and Christopher sitting side by side on a sofa, posing for Heinz's camera, as Wystan murmured a quotation from Yeats: "Both beautiful, one a gazelle."

It was then that Ernst Toller, the dramatist, poet, and revolutionary, came with his wife to stay at Sintra for a few days.

Toller I liked extremely; he reminds me very much of Viertel. When we talked about Hitler, he simply couldn't bring himself to utter the words *Mein Kampf.* First he said, "Mein Krampf," and then, "His book."

Thus Toller met Wystan, who, only three years later, would write his epitaph.

April 17. Wystan left by train today, taking with him the manuscript of our new play. I have really enjoyed his visit very much, and this month, because he has been here and we have worked more or less continuously, has seemed much brighter than the last.

Wystan hasn't changed in the least. His clothes are still out at the elbows, his stubby nail-bitten fingers still dirty and sticky with nicotine; he still drinks a dozen cups of tea a day, has to have a hot bath every night, piles his bed with blankets, overcoats, carpets, and rugs; he still eats ravenously—though not as much as he once did—and nearly sheds tears if the food isn't to his taste; he still smokes like a factory chimney and pockets all the matches in the house. But although I found myself glancing nervously whenever he picked up a book, fiddled with the electric light cord, or shovelled food into his mouth while reading at meals; although I was often very much annoyed by his fussing and by the mess he made—still I never for one moment was more than annoyed. I never felt opposed to him in my deepest being—as I sometimes feel opposed to almost everyone I know. We are, after all, of the same sort.

This explains why the collaboration was such a success. I can't imagine being able to work so easily with any of my other friends. Fundamentally, Wystan and I are exceedingly polite to each other.

Our respective work on this play was fairly sharply defined. Wystan did act one, scene one; the dialogue between Ransom and his mother in act one, scene three; the dialogue between Ransom and the Abbot in act two, scene one; Ransom's monologue in act two, scene two; the whole of act two, scene four; all songs and choruses, the speeches by the A.'s, and all other speeches between the scenes. We interfered very little with each other's work. The only scene on which we really collaborated was the last. It was understood, throughout, that Wystan's specialty was to be the "woozy" and mine the "straight" bits.

"Woozy," in their private jargon, meant grandiloquent, lacking in substance, obscure for obscurity's sake. It described the style of the kind of verse plays they despised. When Christopher uses the word here, however, he isn't suggesting any criticism of Wystan. Certainly, Wystan loved grandiloquence, but he used it to say something substantial. An ardent solver of puzzles, he found it amusing to be obscure; but he insisted that he always provided clues to his meaning which the reader could find if he looked carefully enough.

Actually, no part of *The Dog* or *F6* can properly be described as "straight," i.e., realistic. The prose scenes which Christopher wrote are full of surreal parody, satire, and pastiche; the characters are like figures in cartoons. Even the subtitling of *F6* as "a tragedy" implies that its authors are mocking the established theatrical values.

Much of what Christopher called Wystan's wooziness was essentially religious in content. Wystan's mother was a deeply devout Christian—unlike Christopher's Kathleen, whose Christianity was chiefly inspired by her urge to conform socially—and Wystan was still under his mother's influence. He now outwardly supported Marxism, or at any rate didn't protest when it was preached, but this was halfhearted and largely to humor Christopher and a few other friends. Christopher was of course aware of Wystan's Christian leanings. He made fun of them, in order not to have to take them seriously, which might have led to a quarrel. "When we collaborate," he wrote, "I have to keep a sharp eye on him—or down flop the characters on their knees; another constant danger is that of choral interruptions by angel-voices."

Christopher to Forster, May 12 and May 23:

I love Portugal. The people are charming. They lean over the wall when we are having meals in the garden and wish us a good appetite. But how they do sing! The two maids sing in harmony, very old folk-songs with hundreds of verses, until I have to ask them to stop as I can't hear myself write. And the farmer, ploughing with oxen just beyond the garden wall, sings a song to the oxen which lasts all day.

The Ascent of F6 is about an expedition up a mountain and attempts to explain why people climb them . . . Which brings me to T. E. Lawrence. I am awfully glad you are editing his letters and hope you'll write a long introduction. Please don't expect our *F6* to cast a dazzling light on the subject. I only say the play's about him for shorthand-descriptive purposes. The whole conflict is entirely different and much clumsier, as it seems to have to be on the stage. It's only about Lawrence in so far as the problem of personal ambition versus the contemplative life is concerned.

Heinz is very well. Having finished the big house for the ducks and chickens, he is now building a skyscraper for rabbits. It is very high indeed and we fear it may fall over in a gale. Meanwhile, I study the Portuguese irregular verbs and occasionally go over and

take a peep into the wardrobe, groan, and hastily shut
the door again. The reason I groan is because there are
thirteen books in there waiting to be reviewed for *The
Listener.* (You needn't tell Joe this.)

We have a new friend, a very nice Lisbon advocate
named Dr. Olavo. We visit him on Sundays. Scrambling into his chair, he rests his chins on his chest, his
chest on his stomach, and his stomach on his thighs;
then he dangles his little legs high above the ground,
orders whiskey and soda, and regards me with anticipation, waiting for me to compose a sentence in French
about Liberty, of which we both approve. The sentence is never forthcoming, but it doesn't matter
much. The whiskey is followed by tea, which is followed by Madeira cognac and light port. A French
poet arrives and talks about Verlaine. The ladies come
in. Then suddenly Heinz, whom everybody has forgotten, says very carefully and slowly: Voulez-vous une
cigarette, Monsieur? And we all laugh and applaud for
several minutes.

Christopher urged Forster to come out to Sintra and
convalesce there, but Forster didn't feel strong enough
to make the journey. Then Uncle Henry wrote suggesting that Christopher should take him on a tour of Portugal in August. Christopher begged Kathleen to dissuade
Henry from this plan, and she evidently did. It had now
been arranged that Kathleen herself would visit them at
the end of June.

May 29. Today, on the way downstairs to lunch, comes
the dazzling, irrevocable decision—not to write *Paul Is
Alone* at all. It is quite clear; all I'd planned was a
daydream. I knew nothing about any of the characters.

Now I'm going to get on with my book of autobiographical fragments—entitled perhaps *Scenes from an
Education.*

Contents, provisionally, as follows: Three Years at

the Bay. In the Day Nursery. Medical. Berlin Diary, autumn 1930. Sally Bowles. Pension Seeadler. The Nowaks. Berlin Diary, winter 1932–33. On the Island. O.K. for Sound.

Christopher was thus proposing to take nearly all of his Berlin material ("Pension Seeadler" became *On Ruegen Island*) and add to it "O.K. for Sound" *(Prater Violet),* "On the Island" *(Ambrose),* and three fragments which would ultimately appear in *Lions and Shadows.* He probably didn't realize how huge this book would have been.

The final draft of *Sally Bowles* was finished on June 21. Christopher at first referred to it slightingly in his letters to friends, saying that he doubted if a story as "trivial" as Sally's belonged among his other Berlin pieces, which were all fundamentally serious. Sally might well have retorted that at worst she was no more trivial than Otto Nowak. (*The Nowaks* had now appeared in *New Writing* and had been praised by some serious left-wing critics.) But Christopher would have replied that Otto was a victim of the politico-economic conditions under which he was living and that victims can never be regarded as trivial, especially when they are proletarian; whereas Sally wasn't a victim, wasn't proletarian, was a mere self-indulgent upper-middle-class foreign tourist who could escape from Berlin whenever she chose. Christopher's scruples now seem absurd to me; a touch of triviality was exactly what the book needed. But in those days his attitude to his own writings was complicated by the left-wing standards he imposed on them.

Sally Bowles faced another obstacle to its publication. When Christopher asked Jean's permission, she hesitated; she was afraid that the abortion episode—which wasn't fictitious—would shock her family, with whom she was now on good terms. Christopher had to consider if it could be cut out of the story. It couldn't, he decided, for the abortion is the moment of truth which tests Sally and proves that no misfortune, however drastic, can shock her out of her fantasy world . . . However, Jean ended by giving her permission, unconditionally. Since *Sally Bowles* was too long for *New Writing,* John Lehmann got the Hogarth Press to publish it, as a small separate volume, in 1937. Its instant popularity made Christopher realize that it would also have to be part of *Goodbye to Berlin.*

June 26. Yesterday, at last, it happened.

Coming back from a lunch party in Estoril, we found the envelope from the German Consulate on the hall table. Heinz is to report some time in the near future to get his orders for military service.

At present, my only reaction is a fierce warm sick feeling. My thoughts scamper round inside my head like scared hens.

What on earth shall we do? To go to the Consulate means, most likely, getting the passport confiscated. To bolt seems equally futile. Can Gerald help us? I doubt it.

June 29. We went to see Dr. B.S., the famous Lisbon lawyer. A large round-faced man, with round glasses and round, cold, not unkindly eyes. No, he said, he was sorry—it was all quite hopeless: Heinz couldn't possibly be naturalized without doing his military service first. "The best advice I can give him is to return to Germany."

I came out into the street feeling stunned. It was absurd, of course, to be so upset. What else had I expected? But, of course, secretly, I'd been hoping. Back to lunch at the T.'s. Mrs. T. was extremely kind; Mr. T. a bit uncomfortable—why *shouldn't* Heinz go back? Everything seemed to be slipping away down into a bottomless black drain. It is an awful moment when the absolute confidence of childhood—"Nanny'd never let that happen to *me*"—is shaken. I was probably in a high fever. So absolutely doomed did I feel, wandering up and down the hot sunlit streets, that it even seemed strange that we were still allowed at liberty. Going into the post-office, I tried to send a telegram to Gerald, but no words would come. We ordered ginger beer but couldn't drink it. Later we did telegraph.

That evening, we interviewed Olavo, who was very elastic and bright. He waved the difficulty aside. He would make all enquiries, be responsible for everything. We were not to worry. Heinz couldn't be extradited. He, Olavo, would prevent it. We returned home soothed.

The next day, Kathleen's ship docked at Lisbon. This is from her diary:

Christopher came on board and all was well as he managed all the getting through the customs and the tipping and had a taxi waiting. It was all winding roads with trees through great wide stretches of country and the castle at the top of Sintra dominating the view . . . And then the Villa Alecrim do Norte. It seemed all rather Italian. And the two Portuguese maids did too . . . Steps from the front door descend to the cheerful little colour-washed sitting-room. Away and away miles and miles of wild open undulating country, away to blue hills, changing lights, a train winding across the country . . . otherwise, the bees buzzing over the flowers and perfect stillness (but for the maids, who chatter and do not work much).

Poor Christopher. One of the usual upheavals has just arisen again, re Heinz and the possibility of conscription . . . C, after supper, to telephone to Hamilton in Brussels, who it is supposed could assist over changing Heinz's nationality . . . My room all white and green, and that marvellous open view, like one used to get at Wyberslegh. It is all most attractive.

246

The diary continues with descriptions of sightseeing tours taken with Christopher and of meetings between Kathleen and members of the British colony in Lisbon. Kathleen was welcomed warmly by them, as an elderly lady of distinction. Her presence at Alecrim do Norte made the Christopher–Heinz relationship suddenly respectable, as Christopher had foreseen that it would. There are, however, very few references to Heinz in Kathleen's diary. Here is the only extensive one:

July 4. A lovely day again, enjoyed sitting in the pretty little sitting-room, opening on to the gay little garden and the wide ever-changing view. Heinz in and out with the chickens. Anna in attendance with food, and Christopher too. It is really the most domestic life they have had and now it is all threatened . . . Fairly encouraging but necessarily expensive news from Gerald Hamilton . . . Heinz joined us for tea. He does not speak unless spoken to. In some way difficult to explain *how* or *why*, he tones in with Christopher's life wonderfully well. They divide everything and every evening Heinz makes up "our accounts" and asks C just what he has spent during the day; and their personal and household expenditure is all entered. If *only* there wasn't this constant worry, on Heinz's account, over their plans.

Meanwhile, in his diary, Christopher was writing about Kathleen:

It is amazing—the barrier, even now, between us. Mostly of shyness. But, in getting older, she seems to have got heavier and harder. I'd imagined myself falling on her neck, appealing to her to forget and forgive the past, to regard Heinz as her son—but all that, in her presence, seems merely ridiculous. She is infinitely more broadminded, more reasonable, than she was in the old days—I like talking to her, in fact I talk to her better and more amusingly than to anyone else; but the ice is never really broken. To Heinz she is pleasant, gracious, chatty. She treats him—in a perfectly nice way—like one of the servants.

Kathleen left Portugal on July 10, for England. That same day, Heinz went to stay briefly with an English couple who were relatives of the landlady. This move had been arranged by Christopher in a mood of panic. By now, he had almost persuaded himself that the Nazis at the consulate would take the trouble to kidnap Heinz and put him on board a German ship. He had written in his diary: "Every time the doorbell rings, we jump out of our skins." Meanwhile, as the neglected chickens ran about the garden in confusion, telegrams and telephone calls darted back and forth between Christopher and Gerald, producing nothing but promises that Heinz would somehow get his problems solved before too long.

However, a few days later, sanity reappeared in the person of William Robson-Scott. He was touring Portugal and paid a visit to Christopher, whom he had known since the Berlin days. There was something toughly resilient in William's makeup. He could bend before storms without breaking. His hair was short and vigorous, like grass clinging to the edge of a cliff. He laughed with nervous violence, turning red in the face and pressing his hands between his knees. Temperamentally mild and polite, he stated his opinions almost apologetically, but with fearless frankness. When the occasion demanded, he would become imperious in an old-fashioned British way, brushing difficulties aside like insects. (Christopher borrowed some of William's mannerisms for the character called Peter Wilkinson, Otto Nowak's lover, in *Goodbye to Berlin*. In real life, William and Otto never even met.)

When the Nazis came into power, William was teaching at the University of Berlin. The daily confrontation between him and his students must have been ironically comic. Here was a roomful of young Germans being lectured to by a seemingly typical representative of the ruling class of England—Germany's natural ally, according to *Mein Kampf.* It was to be presumed that he regarded himself as belonging to a master race born to rule the "lesser breeds without the Law." Hitler admired this attitude and taught his followers to imitate it. However, William's students soon became aware that their professor, far from being an ally, regarded Nazi Germans as the very lowest of the lesser breeds. William made this clear to them, in his nonchalant style, over and over again. Some of the students were outraged and walked out of the classroom. Complaints were made to the university authorities. These reached the ears of an older Englishman, a colleague of William's in the English department. This Englishman was a joker. When told that William ought to be dismissed, he said: "I wouldn't do that, if I were you. Might create international tension. You see, the fact is, the fellow's a cousin of the King of England." Incredibly enough, the Germans believed this. William suddenly found himself being treated with mysterious respect. Later, he discovered the joke. So did the Germans. They were not amused. William had to resign.

William could offer Christopher no practical advice, but his mere presence was immensely reassuring. Christopher simply couldn't picture kidnappers arriving to carry off Heinz, now that William was on the premises. And, if they did come, William would refuse to acknowledge their existence. "Nonsense!" he would snort, and they would disappear like a disease which has been unthought by a Christian Science practitioner.

Through William, Christopher met his friends James Stern the writer and his wife, Tania. The Sterns wanted to rent a house and spend several months in the neighborhood. Christopher was immediately drawn to both of them and it was agreed that they should share Alecrim do Norte with him and Heinz.

Christopher found Jimmy Stern sympathetic because he was a hypochondriac like himself (though with far more reason); because he grumbled and was humorous and skinny and Irish; because his brainy worried face was strangely appealing; because he had been a steeplechase rider in Ireland, a bartender in Germany, and a cattle farmer on the South African veldt; because he was terrified of snakes and had been bitten by one (he implied that it had followed him around patiently until his attention was distracted by watching a rare bird); because he had written a book of extraordinary short stories, called *The Heartless Land.*

As for Tania, she was one of the most unaffected, straightforward, sensible, and warmhearted women Christopher had ever encountered. She was also one of the most beautiful: small, dark-haired, dark-eyed, and with a body as beautiful as her face. She was a physical-culture expert and taught a system of exercises invented by herself. When she looked at you, she seemed aware of all the faults of posture which betrayed your inner tensions; but you never felt that she found them repulsive or even absurd. She was ready to help you correct them, if you wanted her to.

Tania was a German who had lived for some time in Paris before she married Jimmy. She had two brothers who were Communists and who had barely managed to escape from Nazi Germany. She herself had no fear of the Nazis when they were no longer on their home ground. She suggested going with Heinz to their consulate and demanding to know exactly what would happen to him if he refused to obey their conscription order. She was sure that there was nothing they could do, except threaten. "But what if they take his passport away?" Christopher asked. "We won't bring it with us," said Tania, laughing. Her plan seemed outrageously daring and yet practical. Christopher was three quarters convinced by her assurance. Besides, his anxiety ached for the relief of a showdown—to know something, anything, definite after all these months. Heinz, who adored Tania, would have gone with her fearlessly. However, Jimmy, quite rightly I think, refused to allow her to get herself involved.

Christopher asked himself: Why shouldn't *I* go with Heinz to the consulate? He had to answer: I am afraid. Not of those officials, but of how he would behave. He was afraid of being questioned about his relations with Heinz, of losing his nerve, of being reduced to impotent rage, of being unable to play the scene through to a finish. That was why he had let Frl. Pohly go with Heinz to the consulate at Las Palmas for him. He couldn't forget that confrontation at Harwich.

Sometimes, Jimmy would shut himself up in his room for a whole day or more, seeing nobody but Tania. But his sensitive nerves and spells of melancholy created no tension in the household. Christopher wrote in his diary: "Jimmy's jumpiness is quite without venom towards the outside world. He is much too busy hating his father to have any malice left over for us." And Tania took everything in her stride. She devoted herself to Jimmy yet found sufficient time to be with Christopher and Heinz and also very efficiently managed the housekeeping. This seemed—in the short run at least—a perfectly workable arrangement and I believe that—had the run been long —they might all have lived together in harmony for months or even years.

On July 18, Franco started the revolt in Morocco which spread at once to Spain itself and became the Civil War.

July 28. Here I am, on the granite verandah of Dr. Olavo's house in the Beira Alta, looking out over the vines and olive woods of the Mondego Valley. Behind those mountains, across the Spanish frontier, they are fighting.

We have sat up each night until past two o'clock

listening to the wireless—and although the news was better yesterday, it doesn't seem at all certain yet that the Fascists will be beaten.

Not that Dr. Olavo doubts this for an instant. He stabs an accusing finger, swallows his Madeira, springs to his feet: "Never shall they win! Never! I understand the mentality of these generals. Ah, these butchers, these monsters, these analphabetics—they would dare to assault the noble great-hearted generous Spirit of Democracy—very well, I defy them!"

Certainly he defies them. He is astonishingly incautious. From this house you can see the property of his brother, the former minister of war, who was murdered during the putsch which put the present regime into power. And yet Olavo is not merely free, his opinions are tolerated; he even has an important post in the civil administration. As I told him, he's lucky not to be living in Italy or Germany.

Forster to Christopher, July 30:

I am rattled by the news from Spain this evening and feel I am saying farewell to you and Heinz. You know those feelings and can discount them: the last parting is never when or as one supposes. I had been planning to come to Portugal in the autumn. Now all seems impossible.

This nightmare that everything almost went right! I know that you have it over the Communist failure in Germany. As a matter of fact, one's activities (and inactivities) must have been doomed for many years. I'd throw in my hand if all these metaphors weren't nonsense: there's nowhere to throw one's hand to.

Dear me, Amsterdam was good. We often talk of it. I can't believe it was only last year—two big wars since, two operations on myself, and so on, place it on another planet.

252

Christopher to Stephen, August 11:

About Spain, you can imagine how I feel; if they win this time, it's the end. The end, even, of the British Empire, you'd think; and yet the majority of the British colony here are screaming against the Spanish government and praying for the rebels.

The other evening, we had a picnic with Mr. and Mrs. T. and Mrs. Y. and a really violent and embarrassing argument started, Mrs. T. pro-govt and Mrs. Y. pro-reb. Mrs. Y. kept exclaiming, "But I tell you, they're just a lot of dirty Communists and they murder women and burn churches; and the others are our *sort,* I mean, I can't argue, but one feels they're *clean* and they've kind of been to a sort of decent school, if you know what I mean."

I like both of them very much as women and they've both been decent to Heinz since all this wretched business with the Consulate, but all the same I find I avoid going to see Mrs. Y. now. The papers here are hundred percent pro-reb, so we get no reliable news. I feel awfully depressed.

THIRTEEN

Kathleen's diary reference to "necessarily expensive news" from Gerald Hamilton suggests that Christopher had prepared her, while she was still in Portugal, for a financial shock. Christopher later joked to his friends that he had done this by gradual stages, in the manner of a Victorian announcing someone's death to a relative: "There's been an accident. Yes, he's hurt. Rather badly, I'm afraid. No, he's in no pain. Not now . . . You must try to be brave." What Kathleen had to try to be brave about was that Heinz's change of nationality was going to cost, approximately, one thousand pounds.

It is possible that Christopher had been too tactful in breaking this news and that Kathleen had returned to England supposing that he had exaggerated or that the crisis wasn't immediate. But now came the outbreak of war in Spain. The mails from Portugal were held up. Instead of vaguely worded letters from Christopher, Kathleen got a peremptory cable in which he told her to write directly to Hamilton's lawyer in Brussels and arrange to send him the money. The lawyer answered Kathleen in a tone which she describes as "pretty cool," by which she means insolently casual. He would accept Heinz as a client on receipt of the money. But he refused to guarantee that any naturalization papers could be obtained with it or that such papers, if obtained, would prove to be valid.

Kathleen turned for help to her cousin and adviser, Sir William Graham Greene. "Cousin Graham" held an important post at the Admiralty. He was a friend of Winston Churchill and an uncle of Graham Greene the novelist.

Through the clear eyeglasses of this honorable worldly-wise man, Kathleen began to see the situation in an even more sinister light:

I feel more and more that there is something very shady behind it all. The lawyer might even in the end double-cross us.

This gangsterish expression sounds comic, coming from Kathleen. She must have felt that she already had one foot in the underworld.

August 13. A cable came from Christopher who, following my suggestion, is coming back. It is impossible to get anything settled at this distance, specially with the posts taking so long.

August 18. Letter from Christopher. They have left Portugal and are now in Belgium, at Ostende. I'm sorry, as Christopher will now see Gerald Hamilton before coming home. I also have suspicions about the lawyer.

August 21. Christopher arrived in time for lunch, having spent last night at Dover with William Plomer; he had also seen E. M. Forster, who is down there with his mother. In the afternoon, Cousin Graham came to talk over the Belgium, Ecuador, Brazil possibilities with Christopher.

I have forgotten the technicalities involved in becoming a citizen of these countries, but I am fairly sure that, in Heinz's case, certain documents could only be obtained by bribery. For example, you might have to have a certificate declaring that you had been a resident of the country for a large number of years, or that you had served in its armed forces—when, in fact, you hadn't. Such certificates could of course be proved false if a hostile official chose to investigate your past, at any time in the future.

Belgium was too near Nazi Germany. In the event of a German invasion, Heinz might find himself in worse danger with a Belgian passport than without one. Under the new Nazi laws, the penalty for attempting to change your nationality was a long term of imprisonment; it could even be death. So Christopher was now making up his mind to emigrate with Heinz to some country in Latin America. From there, he said to himself, they would perhaps later be able to make a second emigration—to the United States.

During these conferences with Kathleen and Cousin Graham, Christopher had mixed feelings. He was suspicious of Gerald, on this as on so many occasions, and of the lawyer also because he was Gerald's ally. Yet, after all, it was the lawyer who was taking the risks. How could he be expected to send written guarantees which might one day be used as evidence against him? Christopher didn't want Kathleen to be swindled; but he felt out of place siding with her against Gerald and the lawyer. If they were lawbreakers, well, so was he. He liked and respected Cousin Graham. But, whenever Heinz's name was mentioned, Christopher was all too aware of Graham's self-restraint. He was making an effort not to show his disapproval of this imprudent and costly relationship in which Christopher had got himself involved. As for Kathleen, her exaggerated concern about the money *as* money irritated Christopher. Whatever happened, he fully intended to pay it back to her. So, if he was prepared to risk losing it for nothing, what right had she to make such a fuss? Deep down, his attitude toward her was sadistic. Let her suffer a bit of anxiety and embarrassment, as a punishment for her condescending attitude to Heinz.

Christopher finally prevailed upon Kathleen to send the money to a bank in Brussels, through which it could be paid to the lawyer. Having done this, he left to rejoin Heinz at Ostende. Early in September, he wrote to tell Kathleen that the lawyer had now established connections with some officials at the Mexican legation in Brussels. Getting Mexican nationality for Heinz through them would be "absolutely legal, foolproof, and aboveboard" and it could be done in about two and a half months. (Christopher was merely repeating the lawyer's assurances. He knew nothing at first hand.)

In the middle of September, Christopher and Heinz moved from Ostende back to Brussels. At the end of the month, Christopher went over to England for six days. Richard supplies a glimpse of him at the station as he was leaving again for Belgium, giving a performance as a left-wing prig—probably to entertain Richard:

You asked the young man at the bookstall if he had a copy of the Daily Worker. He said decidedly, No, he didn't stock it. You said, You should, you're a worker. To which he replied virtuously, It's people who don't like work who read that paper.

Christopher had now returned to work on an earlier project of his: the story of his life from the end of his schooldays to his departure for Berlin. At that time he planned to call it *The Northwest Passage*—a title which is explained in its fifth chapter:

The truly strong man, calm, balanced, aware of his strength, sits drinking quietly in the bar; it is not necessary for him to try and prove to himself that he is not

257

afraid, by joining the Foreign Legion . . . leaving his comfortable home in a snowstorm to climb the impossible glacier . . . [He] travels straight across the broad America of normal life. But "America" is just what the truly weak man, the neurotic hero, dreads. And so . . . he prefers to attempt the huge northern circuit, the laborious terrible northwest passage . . .

From Christopher's and Wystan's point of view, the Truly Weak Man was represented by Lawrence of Arabia, and hence by their character Michael Ransom in *F6*.

In 1937, the American author Kenneth Roberts published a best-selling adventure novel, *Northwest Passage*. So Christopher had to call his book by a different name, and decided on *Lions and Shadows*.

At the end of October, Christopher reports to Kathleen that an official of the Mexican legation in Brussels has left for Mexico City, taking with him the necessary documents on Heinz's case and seven hundred pounds, for which the lawyer has a receipt. Heinz will receive his naturalization papers before the end of November, at the Mexican consulate in Antwerp. "In the meantime," Christopher adds, "we are taking steps to get an actual letter from the Legation, acknowledging the whole transaction officially and promising specific time-limits." (This letter was never forthcoming.)

On November 8, Christopher writes that the lawyer has told him that the official has arrived in Mexico City and is attending to their business; a telegram can be expected in five or six days, confirming this. Then the naturalization papers will be sent by airmail. The lawyer now promises that the total cost, including his expenses, will be *under* one thousand. Meanwhile, a gentleman has been introduced by the lawyer to Christopher as a representative of the Mexican legation—the only one he has met (or would ever meet). This gentleman has a distinguished appearance and speaks fluent American English with a slight Spanish accent. He assures Christopher that their business is going well and will soon be terminated satisfactorily. Christopher finds him charming. (Their meeting didn't take place at the legation.)

Heinz must have spent a depressing autumn. In Brussels he had no daily occupation. He missed his dog Teddy and his chickens and rabbits. Moreover, he had had so much trouble with his nose and throat that the doctor had recommended two operations: removal of his tonsils and repair of his squashed nose. Having had the first of these, he dreaded the second. It was postponed again and again and not performed until December 7. Christopher was shocked by the sight of him after it: "Just a mouth wide open groaning, surrounded with bandages." When the scars had healed, everybody agreed that Heinz looked much handsomer. His perfect profile even reminded Christopher of the beautiful Pharaoh Akhnaton's. But Christopher still privately regretted the old one.

Late in November, Stephen wrote to tell Christopher that he was going to marry a girl named Inez Pearn, whom he had only recently met, at an Aid to Spain meeting. Stephen attempted to win Christopher's sympathy for what he had done. He pointed out that he and Jimmy Younger were already living apart and independent of each other at the time of his engagement but admitted that Jimmy was nevertheless very much upset. Referring to his feelings for Inez, Stephen continued:

I am sure you will understand this necessity for a permanent and established relationship, because I know that you have always felt it so strongly yourself.

This was clever pleading but it didn't placate the implacable Christopher. However, he gave Stephen no hint of his reactions—until much later—and only showed them by an increased warmth toward Jimmy. Stephen and Jimmy had planned to come to Brussels for Christmas. Now Stephen wouldn't be coming. Christopher wrote to Jimmy, urging him to come anyway. This pleased Stephen, who was worried that Jimmy might begin losing contact with their mutual friends.

On December 10, while Hitler and Mussolini were threatening Europe's peace by intervening openly in the Spanish war, Edward VIII performed the relatively minor drama of his abdication. Christopher listened to the abdication speech with John Lehmann, who was briefly visiting Brussels. John and he were in a bar and they insisted on having the radio on and the record player off until Edward had finished, despite the protests of non-English-speaking customers. I remember the strangeness of hearing Edward's voice for the first time, with its unkingly twang.

Later, Christopher wrote to Kathleen:

It is generally believed on the Continent that Edward was really kicked out because of Nazi influence in his entourage; in that case, why can't the slimy old hypocrite have the courage to say so, instead of trying to make it a moral issue?

Aside from feeling mildly sentimental about Edward as a faded but once great beauty, Christopher took little interest in him. Nevertheless, he had negatively supported Edward's cause during the crisis by detesting his enemies and quarreling with Kathleen about him when they had last met. By "the slimy old hypocrite" Christopher meant Cosmo Gordon Lang, the Archbishop of Canterbury, who had opposed Edward's intended marriage to Mrs. Simpson on the grounds that she was a divorced woman. Christopher was utterly unable to believe in moral attitudes other than his own; he refused to admit that the Others sincerely hated adultery, homosexuality, or any of the sins they denounced. Kathleen he regarded as a mere snob. If Mrs. Simpson had been royal like Marina, he said, instead of being an American commoner, her previous life would never have been held against her. Kathleen, who enjoyed baiting Christopher, though she was quite unaware that she did, had written to him that one of her friends had been much moved by the Archbishop's statement. Hence Christopher's outburst.

At about this time, Christopher heard a rumor that Auden was planning to go to Spain. Then came a letter from Olive Mangeot which might be interpreted as hinting at the same news. Rightly or wrongly, Olive now believed that she was a target of police informers, telephone tappers, steamers-open of letters, and other agents of Fascism; she therefore tended to use phrases so cryptic that even her friends couldn't understand them. The rumor was soon confirmed, however, by Wystan himself:

I'm going to Spain in early January, either ambulance-driving or fighting. I hope the former. Is there any chance of seeing you in Paris on my way through? In case of accidents, remember that you and Edward are executors.

Meanwhile, Stephen wrote that Jimmy had enlisted in the International Brigade. He was still coming to Brussels for Christmas but he would be on his way to Spain, and another enlistee, Giles Romilly, would be with him. Giles had left Oxford in the middle of term to join the Brigade, in which his brother Esmond was already fighting. They were nephews of Winston Churchill.

Christopher and Heinz did their best to give Jimmy and Giles an appropriate, ungloomy send-off. They ate some memorable meals, under Gerald Hamilton's guidance. The best was in a famous restaurant's private dining room where a Belgian royal personage had once entertained his mistresses. Gerald said that, after supper, the waiter used to bring in the key of the room on a salver and present it to the personage. The room still had a couch in it. The four of them also frequented a large noisy working-class dance hall where nobody minded if men danced together.

To Christopher, during this visit, both Jimmy and Giles appeared tragically vulnerable—Giles because he looked physically fragile, boyishly pretty; Jimmy because of the softness of his nature. The fact that Jimmy was an ex-soldier seemed irrelevant; the peacetime British Army couldn't have prepared him for the Brigade in combat. It was noticeable that Jimmy had stopped repeating his revolutionary slogans; his present predicament was too personal for dialectics. Like Giles, he made a brave show of high spirits.

1937 opened with an announcement from Stephen that he, too, was going to Spain, with the writer Cuthbert Worsley. They were to find out what had happened to the crew of a Russian ship, the *Komsomol*, which the Italians had sunk in the Mediterranean. It was suspected—correctly, as was later proved—that the crew was interned by the rebels. This was an assignment which any properly accredited neutral correspondent might have undertaken without much risk. But Stephen wasn't neutral. He was a recently joined member of the Communist Party and a long-time publicly declared enemy of Fascism wherever it appeared. He was being sent on this investigation by the *Daily Worker.* Therefore, if he and Cuthbert did penetrate behind the rebel lines, they would risk getting arrested as spies and imprisoned or even shot.

Luckily, when they tried to go from Gibraltar to Cádiz, they were turned back at the frontier by Franco's guards. Stephen then left Spain but very soon returned. This time, he saw Jimmy Younger. Jimmy had been appalled by his war experiences and was desperate to get out of the Brigade and leave the country.

On January 11, a telegram arrived from Wystan in London. His departure for Spain had been delayed but now he was about to start. Next day, Christopher met him in Paris, at the Hôtel Quai Voltaire.

The British press had turned Wystan into big news. Even those editors who obviously regarded him with cynicism or ill will helped to publicize his journey—to his own embarrassment, for he was afraid of being prevented by the authorities from entering Spain. To thousands of young people he was now a hero—a Byron or at least a Rupert Brooke, going forth to war. Byron had written that "the land of honorable death" awaited him. Brooke had consoled himself with the thought that the foreign place where he fell would become "for ever England." Wystan's dedication to his chosen cause was certainly as sincere as theirs had been, but his reactions were absurdly different. The poem he had just finished, later to be called "Danse Macabre," was a dazzling explosion of ironic fireworks and a send-up of the Warrior-Hero which seemed to poke fun at Wystan himself.

Christopher could never have done alone what Wystan was doing. He was too timid to have taken such a step independently. Would he have gone to Spain with Wystan, if it hadn't been for Heinz? I think he would, despite his timidity, because he could have found no other good enough excuse for staying behind. As things were, he didn't feel guilty about this, only regretful for what he was missing.

Christopher wasn't seriously afraid that Wystan would be killed in battle. The government would probably insist on his making propaganda for them, rather than fighting. Still, Byron and Brooke had died by disease, not weapons, and a war zone is always full of potential accidents. This was a solemn parting, despite all their jokes. It made them aware how absolutely each relied on the other's continuing to exist.

Their friendship was rooted in schoolboy memories and the mood of its sexuality was adolescent. They had been going to bed together, unromantically but with much pleasure, for the past ten years, whenever an opportunity offered itself, as it did now. They couldn't think of themselves as lovers, yet sex had given friendship an extra dimension. They were conscious of this and it embarrassed them slightly—that is to say, the sophisticated adult friends were embarrassed by the schoolboy sex partners. This may be the reason why they made fun, in private and in print, of each other's physical appearance: Wystan's "stumpy immature fingers" and "small pale yellow eyes screwed painfully together"; Christopher's "squat" body and "enormous" nose and head. The adults were trying to dismiss the schoolboys' sexmaking as unimportant. It was of profound importance. It made the relationship unique for both of them.

On January 13, Christopher saw Wystan off on the train. Wystan had a bad cold but was otherwise cheerful. His only anxiety was about his luggage, which had been sent ahead, by mistake, to the Franco–Spanish frontier. He was afraid that it was lost forever. Luckily, he was wrong.

During January, Christopher worked on translating the lyrics which are printed between the chapters of the *Dreigroschenroman*, the novel which Brecht based on his *Dreigroschenoper*. This translation of the novel, by Desmond Vesey, was called *A Penny for the Poor*.

I think Christopher's translations are generally adequate. But he made one mistake which is worth describing because it was deliberate and because it illustrates a fundamental difference in outlook between the translator and his author. "Polly Peachum's Song" tells how Polly behaved to her suitors before she met the right one, Macheath. In each verse, a boat is mentioned. Polly and one of the suitors get into it. In the first two verses, the boat is cast loose from the shore, and Polly adds, "But that was as far as things could go." In the third and last verse, however, the boat is "tied to the shore," when she has got into it with Macheath.

Christopher found this incomprehensible, because he took it for granted that the proper poetic metaphor for sexual surrender would be the casting loose of the boat. So, quite arbitrarily, disregarding the meaning of the German text, he transposed the lines and had the boat tied up in the first two verses, only to be cast loose in the last verse when Polly is possessed by Macheath.

No one protested. The book appeared with Christopher's version of the poem. It was only when Christopher met Brecht for the first time, in California about six years later, that he had his misunderstanding corrected. Brecht told him mildly, with the unemphatic bluntness which was so characteristic of him: "A boat has to be tied up before you can fuck in it."

No news came from Mexico City. Christopher took this calmly because the lawyer himself had now announced that he was going to Mexico, on other business, at the end of the month, and would be able to find out what was happening.

There was also another, stronger reason for optimism. During a recent visit to London, the lawyer had talked to some officials at the Home Office and inquired about Heinz's case. According to the lawyer, it was indeed on "moral" grounds that Heinz had been refused permission to land in England; but the officials admitted that the refusal was only based on suspicion and might be reconsidered. The lawyer had therefore reapplied for Heinz's admission, insisting that Heinz was a respectable person with highly respectable friends, such as Mr. E. M. Forster. Forster's name was said to have made a most favorable impression on the officials. And Forster himself followed this up by writing them a letter.

So, for a few days, it seemed that the Mexican passport might become unnecessary. Then, however, the lawyer was informed by the Home Office that Heinz's application had been refused. Unofficially, he was advised to try again, later in the year. As a routine precaution, the authorities would refuse to admit any alien whose background was even slightly questionable, until after the coronation of George VI in May.

On February 3, Christopher went to London. *The Ascent of F6* was soon to be produced at the Mercury Theatre in Notting Hill Gate. Wystan and he had agreed that he should watch the rehearsals, since Wystan didn't expect to return from Spain for some time.

As before, Rupert Doone was the director. Christopher got along with him much better than Wystan had. Being both small men and both prima donnas, Rupert and Christopher were natural allies as long as they didn't compete; and there was no question of their competing. Their roles were clearly defined. Christopher sincerely admired Rupert's talent and was charmed and amused by his behavior—the regal way he carried his head, the absoluteness of his gestures of command, his uninhibited treatment of actors, especially when they were giving him trouble. "He hit high C," Rupert would say, "but I hit D." Rupert behaved as Christopher imagined himself behaving, in his fantasies, but never could, in real life. In public, Christopher showed Rupert the greatest respect, never speaking to the actors about their parts except when Rupert had invited him to do so.

The Mercury Theatre was a tiny building. Below the auditorium was a basement in which the Ballet Rambert rehearsed; there was constant running up and down stairs and mingling of the ballet with the *F6* company. Christopher fancied one of the Rambert dancers and summoned up the courage to ask him to come out to a nearby teashop. The young man was also acting as assistant stage manager and found it entirely natural to be asked by anybody to do or fetch anything. Registering only the word "tea," he darted off, returned with a cup of it, and vanished again before Christopher could even thank him. Momentarily frustrated, Christopher consulted Rupert, who took the affair in hand without hesitation. Stopping the young man in the passage, he said imperiously, "Will you please show Mr. Isherwood round the theatre?" The young man was bewildered for a moment. There was almost nothing to show. Besides, he was aware that Christopher had been coming to the Mercury for several days already and must know the premises inside out. Then, grasping the situation, he grinned and said: "Well, that's the stage—" And thus the ice was broken.

One of the bonds between Christopher and Rupert was a shared admiration for Mickey Rooney, then a world-famous teenager with a lewd Irish grin. On the day of the dress rehearsal, they were unable to resist the temptation to go and see him in his latest film, *The Devil Takes the Count* (called *The Devil Is a Sissy* in the United States). Having once sat down in the cinema, they couldn't tear themselves away from this outrageous but potent tearjerker until it ended. By the time they reached the Mercury, the cast had been kept waiting for nearly an hour. Rupert, showing not the faintest trace of guilt and offering no explanations, started work immediately.

For Christopher, the production of *F6* was an even more enjoyable experience than the shooting of *Little Friend,* because it was such an intimate affair. Rupert, Robert Medley, Benjamin Britten, and he became united like a family in making their decisions; there were no studio executives to interfere with them. I remember Robert as large, smiling, unflustered, always ready with suggestions for scenic effects and solutions to technical problems; Ben as pale, boyish, indefatigable, scribbling music on his lap, then hurrying to the piano to play it. I can't remember Christopher doing anything in particular, except laughing a great deal.

On the opening night, February 26, the audience was as big as the theater would hold. Kathleen and Richard were there and also Wystan's mother. Beside this solemn intense woman with her austere nose, Kathleen seemed frivolously feminine. Kathleen always had the impression that Mrs. Auden disapproved of her.

If *F6* didn't quite succeed as a whole, it at least pleased many people by the variousness of its parts. The duologue between Mr. A. and Mrs. A. formed an independent playlet, which nearly everybody enjoyed. Ransom's rantings and his woozy conversation with the Abbot of the monastery provided necessary tragic relief from the BBC comedians. Hedli Anderson's singing of Britten's music was a performance which needed no support— especially in the overwhelming funeral dirge, "Stop all the clocks." Doone saw to it that the changes of scene and mood were made very quickly.

The effect of Edward Lamp's off-scene destruction by the avalanche was unexpectedly convincing. It was created by setting up a microphone in the backstage lavatory and flushing the toilet. The amplified noise was awesome.

(When *F6* was performed in New York by the Drove Players, in 1939, its director, Forrest Thayr, Jr., created an even more powerful effect in a totally different way. The play was staged in a studio with a staircase at one end of it. This staircase represented the mountain. The actors leaned over the rail of the staircase, looking down toward the ledge on which Lamp was supposed to be standing. They began yelling to him that the avalanche was coming —but no sounds were made backstage to represent it. There was a pause of dead silence. Then, somewhere in the back of the building, with terrific violence, a door was slammed.)

Wystan returned from Spain on March 4, sooner than expected. He was unwilling to talk about his experiences, but they had obviously been unsatisfactory; he felt that he hadn't been allowed to be really useful. Also, he had received certain negative and disturbing impressions which I shall mention later.

On the night of his return, he went with Christopher to see the play. Not long after the curtain had gone up, the changes in the text made by Christopher and Rupert began to be evident. They were none of them drastic. But Wystan turned to Christopher and said, in a loud reproachful whisper: *"My dear,* what have you *done* to it?"* Most of the audience heard him and were amused.

At a much later performance, the audience was similarly amused by Margot, Countess of Oxford and Asquith. This formidable patrician was greatly taken with Hedli Anderson. When Hedli left the stage, Margot dozed off and woke to find herself in the midst of a scene which she neither understood nor enjoyed. She demanded indignantly: "What have they done with that *charming* little Danish girl?"

F6 got some excellent notices and was a considerable success. In April, it was transferred to a bigger theater— the Little. Two years later, it was revived at the Old Vic.

On March 17, Christopher returned to Brussels. Nothing had yet been heard from Mexico City, but Christopher had new plans for the immediate future. While in Paris, seeing Wystan off to Spain, he had visited the Sterns, who were now living in a flat on the Quai de l'Horloge. Christopher had told Tania Stern how frustrated Heinz was feeling in Brussels, with nothing to do. Tania had been sympathetic and, as usual, practical. She suggested that Heinz should learn a trade. Here she knew a silversmith who would give him lessons. So it was arranged that he and Christopher should move to Paris for a while. They hadn't done this sooner because the lawyer had had some difficulty in getting Heinz a French visa. But now the visa had been granted. They left Brussels a few days after Christopher's return there.

Cyril Connolly was in Paris at that time with his American wife, Jean, and a friend of theirs, also American, named Tony Bower. Jean and Tony were later to appear, affectionately caricatured as Ruthie and Ronny, in *Down There on a Visit:*

> She is a big girl altogether; big hips, big bottom, big legs. I've seldom seen anyone look so placid, so wide-open to visitors, so sleepy-slow. Her great beautiful gentle cow-eyes have sculptured lids which make me think of an Asian bas-relief—the carving of some giant goddess.
>
> I like Ronny. His impudent, attractively comic face keeps breaking into grins, and his round blue eyes sparkle with a lit-up gaiety which is in its own way courageous, because he isn't as carefree as he tries to appear.

Tony was then in the relationship of a disciple to the Connollys. He was eager to follow their advice and imitate their life style in every particular. On the day when Christopher and Heinz first met him, he was scarcely aware of his surroundings. This was because, the previous evening, he had obediently swallowed some sleeping pills which Jean Connolly had given him. They were the ones she used regularly, without any visible ill effects to herself, but they were triple strength. Tony was not only a model disciple but free with his money. He had thus gained the reputation of being enormously rich, which he wasn't. He bought the Connollys and their friends gourmet meals at the restaurants Cyril favored.

Christopher knew few Etonians because he despised them on principle, as an article of his left-wing snobbery. But for Cyril, as for Brian Howard, he had to make an exception. Cyril was certainly one of Eton's most creditable growths, as Brian was one of its most monstrous. Cyril won Christopher's admiration by the brilliant artifice of his wit and the genuineness of his passions—for landscape, architecture, classical and Romanic languages, food, wine, lemurs, and literature. His big face—flat blue eyes, tiny nose, and double chin—looked as ageless as a Buddha's; but he was more of a pope than a Buddha, for he spoke with conscious authority, implying that he knew you, as a writer, better than you knew yourself—knew you historically in relation to the entire hierarchy of letters, past and present, and could assign you a place in it. You might lose that place later, of course. If you ever did, he would tell you so, blandly but brutally. He had a terrible phrase for such outcasts: "Those whom the God has forsaken."

Connolly had praised *The Memorial, Mr. Norris,* and *The Nowaks* and he was soon to refer to Christopher in print as "a hope of English fiction." Thus fanned, Christopher's ambition burned hotly and he determined that Cyril's hopes should not be disappointed. Nevertheless, Forster's approval was still worth far more to Christopher than Connolly's. Connolly made Christopher feel competitive, Forster didn't—because the one offered fame; the other, love. Connolly and his God could forsake Christopher. Forster never would, however much Christopher's work might deteriorate.

The five of them rode bicycles around Fontainebleau and walked in the forest. I have a photograph of Jean Connolly striking an attitude; she is pretending to be Ransom urging his followers on toward the summit of F6. And I remember a coldness, only momentary however, between Cyril and Christopher. Cyril had asked Christopher, in a tone which Christopher found patronizing, how he felt about Heinz—the implication seeming to be that Cyril couldn't believe that an intelligent adult like Christopher could take such a relationship altogether seriously. To this, Christopher replied casually but nastily: "Oh, very much as you feel about Jean, I suppose." Cyril obviously found this insulting, to Jean and to himself. But he couldn't very well say so.

On April 1, Christopher went over to London on some business. He had meant his visit to be short. But, soon after he arrived, he became ill with an infected mouth. The infection flared up suddenly in a cavity from which a tooth had been only partly extracted by a clumsy dentist, a few weeks earlier, leaving an embedded fragment.

On his return from Spain, Wystan had left an overcoat at Kathleen's house. It was very dirty but Christopher had been sleeping with it on his bed; it made him feel an affectionate nearness to Wystan. Nanny now decided that the Spanish war germs in the coat had infected Christopher. "It's all that old coat," she kept muttering.

Christopher's condition got gradually worse, partly because Kathleen refused to take his illness seriously. His high fever was his fury against her skepticism. His mouth became ulcerated and his tonsils inflamed. The doctor couldn't exactly diagnose the nature of the infection and later admitted that he had been gravely worried. All he could say was that it would be unwise to extract the rest of the tooth until Christopher was better.

Meanwhile, there were plenty of visitors: Tony Bower, just over from Paris—Kathleen describes him in her diary as "a tall young man, rather like a friendly giraffe"; Stephen, sunburned from being in Spain, with his wife, Inez, "small and rather ironic"—Kathleen neglects to mention that Inez was strikingly good-looking. "Stephen's friend Jimmy has managed to fall out with the

International Brigade and been put in prison"—this is Kathleen's way of saying that he had deserted and been caught. Later, thanks to Stephen's efforts, Jimmy was pardoned and allowed to leave the country.

Kathleen was critical of Wystan, because he filled the air of Christopher's room with cigarette smoke and banged on the piano. Edward Upward, who came with his wife, Hilda, got much better marks. Kathleen felt that his recent marriage was already a success—"he looks so well and cared for." Indeed, he was so plump that Kathleen didn't at first recognize him. She found Wystan "a most restless unpeaceful person" and Edward "just the reverse."

On April 13, Wystan left for Paris. Christopher had hoped to go with him but this was now out of the question. On the seventeenth, Wystan phoned to say that Heinz was in trouble. The French police had told him that his permit to stay in France would not be renewed. It was due to expire in two days.

What had happened? Christopher later got various reports. This was, more or less, what they added up to: Heinz had had the bad luck to be sitting in a café when an Englishwoman complained to the police that her necklace had been stolen. The police questioned everybody present. Heinz, who was a bit drunk and therefore aggressive, had got into an argument with them. So, without accusing him of the theft, they had detained him temporarily and cross-examined him further. Thus they discovered that he had lost his identity card, a short while previously, in a street fight. Then they had interviewed people at the hotel where Heinz was staying and had been told *(a)* that he was a practicing male prostitute and *(b)* that he had seduced the chambermaid, who was deaf and dumb. The police had therefore decided that he was an undesirable alien.

It so happened that Tony Bower was having tea with

Christopher when Wystan's phone call came through. Tony offered to go to Paris next day and personally escort Heinz to Luxembourg. It was the only move on the chessboard which Christopher could see, since Heinz had no visa for either Holland or Belgium and couldn't get one at such short notice.

Tony was then somewhat in love with Christopher. So it was easy for Christopher, who was well aware of this, to prompt Tony to make his offer. Christopher told himself that he was doing Tony a favor, making him happy by letting him be helpful. Here he miscalculated. Tony's impulsive gesture was followed by resentment, when he began to feel he had merely been made use of. All this was soon forgotten, however, and they remained friends.

Christopher was inwardly convinced that he could somehow have prevented Heinz's expulsion from France, if he had been in Paris. No doubt he was wrong, but his conviction made him feel frustrated. Once again, England had become a prison. He vented his spleen on Kathleen, growing increasingly difficult and imperious. Kathleen writes:

> Olive Mangeot came at five and stayed till seven, and as usual Christopher was very aggrieved and irritable after being with her, though this time I dare say he was thoroughly overtired, not being fit for much talking. She brought the *Daily Worker,* which always makes him feel how unsympathetic we are with his political views. And he went to bed very offended and vexed as well as very tired. I think we are all tired and he does not realize we are trying to do our best.
>
> Nanny very tired and naturally rather aggrieved at the way Christopher takes everything for granted, and hardly answers or says thank you and we really all spend our time running up and downstairs while he poses as a sort of sultan, and very impatient, expecting a series of teas to be carried up for his friends, and finding fault with the cooking.

One day, when he felt too toxic to talk or even read, Christopher had the idea of sitting for William Coldstream, whom he had met through Wystan. Coldstream had already suggested painting Christopher's portrait and he agreed at once to come. He was attractive, amusing, and intelligent; Kathleen calls him "appreciative"— one of her highest terms of commendation. He painted Christopher on a couch, propped up against pillows, wearing a striped red and blue dressing gown given him by Uncle Henry. In this position, Christopher could doze or lie in a semi-coma of not disagreeable weakness, imagining himself to be lazily, easily dying.

The picture was duly finished and taken to Coldstream's dealer. Later, Coldstream met a friend in the street who told him: "I've just been looking at one of your paintings—I'm delighted with it—you know—that charming portrait of an old lady lying in bed—"

FOURTEEN

On April 25, Christopher was well enough to go to Luxembourg. He traveled by way of Belgium and had a dinner between trains with Gerald Hamilton, which he later described to Forster:

> After the worst crossing of my life, a very dazing nonstop-talking dinner with Mr. Norris: "Here you are, my dear boy, to the minute, I really must apologize that everything isn't quite ready, but this is the very best duck obtainable, tell me honestly, don't you think it's decidedly on the cold side, well, well, I must apologize but don't let's waste our time we must really talk about your affairs, yes, yes, what kind of journey did you have, but do start, let me see, as I was saying, my goodness, there isn't any *mustard . . ."* etc. etc. I caught the train on from Brussels by the skin of my teeth.

Heinz and Tony Bower were at the Hotel Gaisser, where Christopher and Heinz had stayed in 1935. Christopher found Tony bored, after a week of Heinz-sitting, and impatient to get away. Heinz was feeling deeply aggrieved. The police, he said, had believed all the lies told them by two prostitutes who lived at his hotel and didn't like him. He firmly denied most of the charges made against him, including an alleged statement by the silversmith that he had failed to appear for his lessons. Actually, he had only missed one, and the silversmith had told him that he was a promising pupil. In proof of this, he produced a silver ashtray which he had made for Christopher.

Christopher now believed Heinz and felt ashamed, because, as he had to admit to himself, he had taken it for granted that Heinz had done everything he was accused of having done. While in London, he had unconsciously come round to the attitude of Kathleen and others, that Heinz was still an irresponsible adolescent. Instead of having faith in Heinz, Christopher had merely forgiven him in advance, before hearing what he had to say in his own defense.

As far as the French authorities were concerned, the question of Heinz's guilt was academic. The very fact that they hadn't accused him of any particular crime made the situation hopeless. He was simply on their undesirable list—and all Germans, at that time, were becoming increasingly undesirable in France. There was no hope that they would relent in the foreseeable future. However, the lawyer assured Christopher that Heinz would have no difficulty in reentering Belgium as soon as he had his Mexican passport. It appeared that the Mexicans had suddenly announced that this would be available almost immediately.

Christopher only half believed this promise, but he wasn't much worried. To him, there was something safe about Luxembourg, just because it was so small. You even got an intimate, protected feeling when you looked at the publicly displayed photographs of its sulky-faced Grand Duchess Charlotte and her teenage son Prince Jean, with his charming grin. After Christopher's illness and Heinz's troubles in Paris, they were happy to be together again. And now their long period of waiting— waiting to begin a new life—seemed nearly over. Now at last, surely, something definite was bound to happen.

On May 4, Gerald visited them. The lawyer had told him that there would be news from the Mexicans by the end of that week. He left again next day. The end of the week came and there was no news. Christopher continued to feel optimistic. Perhaps it was the springtime which had raised his spirits.

On Wednesday, May 12—the day, incidentally, of George VI's coronation—two police officials visited the Hotel Gaisser while Christopher and Heinz were still in bed. They told Heinz that he was expelled from Luxembourg and must leave immediately.

Christopher phoned the lawyer in Brussels. The lawyer showed no surprise; he was calm and reassuring. This was nothing serious. All that had happened, obviously, was that the French police had finally got around to sending their latest list of undesirables to their colleagues in Luxembourg. Heinz's expulsion was therefore just a matter of routine. Yes, he could get Heinz an emergency short-term visa for Belgium. But Heinz would have to go back into Germany first.

It was like a very matter-of-fact nightmare. Christopher listened in a daze of dismay as the lawyer explained that Heinz must take a train to Trier, because that was the nearest German city to the frontier. He must stay at such and such a hotel. The lawyer would drive down to Trier himself, next day, and get the visa for Heinz from the Belgian consulate there. That afternoon, they would drive back together to Brussels, where Christopher would be waiting for them.

Partly emerging from his daze, Christopher began to ask questions. Why couldn't the lawyer arrange to have the visa issued by the Belgian consulate in Luxembourg? Because, said the lawyer, that couldn't be put through before tomorrow and Heinz had to leave Luxembourg today. But couldn't the lawyer come down here today and do something to delay Heinz's expulsion? No, there was nothing he could do; such things were impossible to arrange at short notice. Why couldn't Christopher go with Heinz to Trier? Because, being together, they would call more attention to themselves. They might possibly be questioned. Heinz would be much less conspicuous alone. Christopher was to come straight to Brussels, and he wasn't to worry. If the lawyer's instructions were followed, everything would go smoothly.

So Christopher and Heinz packed and went to the station. They said very little. Perhaps the look in Heinz's eyes was fatalistic, not reproachful. But Christopher read a reproach in them: "You're sending me away. We shall never see each other again." This was the final move on the chessboard, the one Christopher had never allowed himself to contemplate. At that moment, it seemed to have been inevitable from the beginning.

Then Christopher got into his own train. It was half empty and he was alone in his compartment. It approached the Belgian frontier through thick woods. Passportless rabbits were hopping about; visaless birds flew hither and thither, not even knowing which country they were in. They crossed into Belgium and back again, finding the grass and the trees no different.

The lawyer had suspected that Christopher was toying with the idea of smuggling Heinz into Belgium. His last words had been a warning: "Don't do anything silly. You'd only get Heinz into much worse trouble than he's in now." When the train stopped at the frontier, Christopher took out his passport, ready for inspection. But no one came into the compartment. The train moved on again. For the first time in his life, he found himself entering a foreign country without official permission. If Heinz had been with him, what could the lawyer have done but accept the accomplished fact and somehow arrange for Heinz to remain in Belgium?

Next morning, the lawyer left Brussels by car for Trier, as he had promised. That night he returned, alone.

He told Christopher that he had duly met Heinz at the hotel. Heinz had assured him that he hadn't been questioned, hadn't aroused anybody's curiosity. They had gone to the consulate and got the visa. Then, just as they were about to start on their return journey, some Gestapo agents had appeared. They had asked to see Heinz's papers and had then taken him away with them. They had told the lawyer that Heinz was under arrest as a draft evader. Before leaving Trier, the lawyer had consulted a German lawyer and engaged him to defend Heinz at his forthcoming trial.

A day or two after the arrest, the German lawyer came from Trier to Brussels to discuss the tactics of Heinz's defense. He was a Nazi Party member in good standing and had the boundless cynicism of one who is determined to survive under any conceivable political conditions. Christopher, in his present hyper-emotional state, found a strange relief in talking to him, because he seemed utterly incapable of sympathy.

Heinz was now in four kinds of potential trouble:

He had attempted to change his nationality. (This could almost certainly be concealed from the prosecution.)

He had consorted with a number of prominent anti-Nazis, most of them Jews. (This could probably be concealed or, at worst, excused as having been Christopher's fault.)

He had been guilty of homosexual acts. (This couldn't be concealed, since Heinz had already confessed to them, but it might be partially excused, if the defense was properly handled.)

He had disregarded the draft call in Portugal. (This couldn't be concealed or excused.)

Before their parting in Luxembourg, Christopher had said to Heinz: "Just suppose that something goes wrong and you get arrested, you're to put all the blame on me. Tell them I seduced you. Tell them about our having sex together. Stick to that. Don't show any interest in politics, or they'll suspect you of staying away from Germany because you're anti-Nazi. Make them believe that you're completely stupid." And this was what Heinz, with considerable cunning and nerve, had managed to do.

Christopher and the German lawyer fully agreed that Christopher's character must be blackened at the trial in order to whiten Heinz's. Christopher must be represented to the court, in his absence, as a totally debauched creature, too effete to be anti-Nazi even, who had seduced this silly German boy at an early age and had persuaded him to leave Germany and live abroad with him by giving him large sums of money. What sexual act had they performed together? Obviously, they must have done *something;* otherwise, Christopher's association with Heinz might seem inexplicable to the police and therefore, perhaps, suspicious in some other way. The German lawyer proposed to reduce Heinz's guilt to a minimum by having him confess only to the least of all punishable sexual acts. He was to say that he and Christopher had had *"eine ausgesprochene Sucht zur wechselseitigen Onanie"*—"a pronounced addiction to reciprocal onanism." This was the name which their love was to dare to speak, in the face of its enemies! The German lawyer's tone was matter-of-fact; to him this was merely legal phraseology. Gerald Hamilton, who was present, appeared genuinely embarrassed and murmured, "Well, *really!*" Christopher laughed out loud, because, yes, it *was* funny—and laughter was the only alternative to futile screaming hate.

Christopher's diary, May 26:

Unbelievable as it seems, it's just a fortnight since I said goodbye to Heinz at the Luxembourg railway-station.

How have I got through the time? It's difficult to say. To those who find themselves in a situation like mine, I can't recommend masturbation too highly. Judiciously practised, it dulls your feelings almost completely. Only, if you do it too much, you feel more miserable than ever.

At first, I didn't think about Heinz at all. Or tried not to. I felt like a house in which one room, the biggest, is locked up. Then, very cautiously, I allowed myself to think of him in little doses—five minutes at a time. Then I had a good cry and felt better. But it is very hard to cry, when you know in advance that crying will do you good.

The most painful is to remember him with animals. I think of him stroking a rabbit, giving a new-born chicken its first drink of water, playing with Teddy. That's the worst. At meal-times I remember him, too, and wonder what he's eating. It's so monstrous to think of him locked in that stone room—so unnatural. I see him, for some reason, dressed rather smartly, in his best suit, sitting on the edge of his hard narrow bed, staring dully at his shoes. I don't imagine him fidgeting or pacing the cell or beating the door with his fists. He'll take it all quite fatalistically—just as he took our parting.

Meanwhile, I sit alone in a nice back-bedroom of the Hotel du Vallon, listening to the wireless which never stops playing in the courtyard below, and thinking: Now I must pull myself together. I must work.

My book is three quarters finished. The weather is stifling.

In Christopher's diary there is no mention of his more secret reactions. These were caused by his frustration, which demanded a responsible villain. He had no difficulty in finding one.

There was an incident to which his mind kept returning. On the night of May 13, after the lawyer had arrived back from Trier with the news of Heinz's arrest, Christopher had gone to his own room, wanting to be by himself. Almost at once, a boy—one of Gerald's friends—knocked on his door. Christopher was in no mood to talk and he made this clear. But the boy, though obviously embarrassed, wouldn't go away. At length he confessed that Gerald had told him Christopher mustn't be left alone, lest he should do something "dreadful."

The more Christopher thought about Gerald's behavior on this occasion, the more peculiar—and the more sinister—it seemed. The voice of his suspicion whispered: "Gerald knows you far too well to imagine that you'd ever commit suicide. Then what made him get into that sudden panic? There's only one explanation: *he felt guilty!* Remember that Irish Catholic background of his. He's still superstitious, still afraid of hell-fire. He must have done something which made him feel that, if you'd killed yourself that night, your blood would have been on his head . . . Now that he realizes you aren't going to do it, he's stopped worrying."

Suppose that there had never been any negotiations with Mexico. Suppose that the passport—which, the lawyer claimed, had at last arrived and was waiting for Heinz whenever he returned to Brussels—didn't exist at all. Suppose that the man who had represented himself as a member of the Mexican legation was just an accomplice of Gerald and the lawyer. Suppose that the two of them had planned from the beginning to avoid a showdown by getting Heinz arrested and sent back to Germany. Suppose that the Englishwoman who called in the police at the café in Paris was another accomplice. Suppose that whoever stole Heinz's identity card had been bribed to do it, and also the girls at the hotel who spoke against him. Suppose that Gerald had come to Luxembourg on May 4 to arrange for the police there to expel Heinz and tip off the Gestapo in Trier to be on the lookout for his arrival. Suppose—

Christopher would go on like this to himself until he ended by having to admit that his suspicions were mere fantasies. Nevertheless, against all reason, he continued to feel that Gerald—but not the lawyer—was somehow guilty. This, in itself, was unreasonable; either the two of them must have been partners in the crime, or they were both innocent. But Christopher was relying on his intuition, not his intellect, as he always ultimately did. His intuition told him that the lawyer was too prudent, too conventional to join in such a hazardous conspiracy; especially when the reward was no more than a half share, presumably, of the thousand pounds, minus considerable payments for accomplices and other items.

And surely only an innocent man could have the thick skin and the emotional stupidity to say what the lawyer said to Christopher, just a few days after Heinz's arrest: "Mr. Isherwood, we're both men of the world—frankly, don't you think you're well out of this? After all, you've done everything you could for Heinz. And he *has* caused you and your mother a great deal of trouble and expense."

The lawyer further demonstrated the thickness of his skin during a visit which he paid Kathleen in London on May 20. He began—according to Kathleen's diary—by deploring Heinz's indiscretion in bringing Christopher's name into the case. The lawyer, of course, knew perfectly well that Heinz had only done what Christopher had told him to do. He was lying to Kathleen because, I suppose, he thought it would please her to hear Heinz blamed. Kathleen might well have been pleased, if she hadn't known that he was lying; she had already been told the true facts by Christopher. Unaware of his blunder, the lawyer went on to make a bigger one. He told Kathleen that he wished Christopher would get rid of his present set of friends; they were a great handicap to him in his career, despite all his cleverness. Kathleen doesn't comment on this in her diary, but she must have resented the lawyer's tone extremely. Here was this (from her point of view) "shady" little person talking to her as though he were Cousin Graham! And what impudence to criticize Christopher's "present set" when he himself was one of them!

When Christopher said to himself that Gerald was somehow guilty, what he actually meant was that Gerald was *capable* of this crime. Gerald's dishonesty wasn't prudent, it was pathological. There was no question, in his case, of the sum at stake being too small, or of the risk of losing a friend too great. He would betray a friend without hesitation and immediately feel terrified of being found out and punished for it, in this and the next world. Christopher was forced to believe him technically innocent. And Heinz, when they discussed the question many years later, believed him innocent too. Yet the fantasy-making part of Christopher's mind harbored, from that time onward, a resolve. If Christopher was able to be present at Gerald's deathbed, he would kneel beside it and ask, "Gerald, did you do it?" If Gerald answered, "Yes," Christopher would forgive him; if "No," Christopher would believe him but would feel subtly disappointed. I can't understand the intent of this fantasy, unless it was that he loved Gerald and would want to give him a sort of going-away present. But when Gerald did die, in 1970, Christopher was elsewhere.

Arising out of the imagined question to Gerald, there was another which Christopher now began to ask himself. Am *I* guilty? Did I do all I might have done to save Heinz? He thought how Brian Howard, for example, would have behaved. Instead of becoming helpless with misery and obeying the lawyer's instructions, Brian would have risked taking Heinz with him on the Brussels train. And, if Brian hadn't had Christopher's luck at the

Belgian frontier, he would have fought to the very end
—demanding to see the British consul, telephoning the
Foreign Office, throwing himself at the Grand Duchess's
feet. How noble Brian's recklessness seemed! Why had
Christopher failed to rise to the occasion? I'm not a man
of action, he said to himself. But it wasn't quite as simple
as that.

Meanwhile, he worked on *Lions and Shadows,* finishing
that draft of it. William Robson-Scott came to stay with
him at the Hotel du Vallon. Christopher felt so grateful
for the moral support which William's mere presence
gave him that he dedicated the book to William when it
was published.

Heinz's trial was held in the middle of June. Christopher's name appeared in the transcript of the proceed-
ings, incorrectly spelled. "The English citizen Ischer-
vood, who unfortunately cannot be brought to justice,"
was accused of having committed reciprocal onanism
with the prisoner in fourteen foreign countries and in the
German Reich. The judge observed that, since he was
ignorant of the various penalties for the prisoner's crime
in these other countries, he would have to punish him
according to German law. This remark may or may not
have been meant as a joke, but its tone does suggest that
the attitude of the court was relatively unhysterical, un-
Nazi. Heinz got what was in those days considered a light
sentence: six months in prison, to be followed by a year
of labor service for the state and two years in the Army.

During the trial, Christopher had been mercifully ignorant of the greatest danger which had threatened
Heinz. Instead of being sentenced to a fixed term in a
regular prison, Heinz might easily have been sentenced
to an indefinite term in a concentration camp, as many
homosexuals were. In camp, Heinz would have been
treated as an outcast of the Reich who differed from a Jew

only in having to wear a pink triangle on his clothes instead of a yellow star. Like the Jews, homosexuals were often put into "liquidation" units, in which they were given less food and more work than other prisoners. Thus, thousands of them died.

After Heinz had been sentenced, all Christopher could do for him was to send him letters so discreetly worded that they were no more than tokens and to provide him, through the German lawyer, with cigarettes and with food that was better than the regulation prison fare. There was no hope, now, of the two of them being able to see each other before 1941, when Heinz finished his military service, and very little hope that he would be allowed to leave Germany, even then.

In July, Christopher was living at Kathleen's house in London. He had been hired to work on a screenplay based on a story by Carl Zuckmayer. I remember almost nothing about it, except that it was set in Austria. Ludwig Berger was to direct it.

Since the dialogue was being written in English, one of their first problems was: What kind of British dialect is the best equivalent to the speech of Austrian peasants? Should there, for example, be a suggestion of West Country, or Yorkshire, or Highland Scots? The question was referred to the producer, Alexander Korda. Berger asked him, in German: "What do the peasants speak?" and received the lapidary answer: "Little."

The film was never made.

In August, Wystan and Christopher went to Dover together and stayed there until the middle of September. They had rooms in a house on the harbor, 9 East Cliff. The gulls which nested in the cliff face behind the house kept up a frantic squawking. Christopher found it cheerful and absurd, but Wystan called it "sad like work" in the poem about Dover which he wrote during their visit. It was then that Christopher finished the final draft of *Lions and Shadows* and they wrote the first draft of their new play, *On the Frontier*. In a sense, it was about the Heinz situation: lovers who are separated by a frontier. But when Wystan wanted to write a ballad describing Christopher's life with Heinz and their parting, Christopher objected absolutely. Having read "Miss Gee," Christopher hated to imagine his private tragedy being retold in the heartless comic style of the Auden ballads. Nothing that Wystan said could convince him that this one would be different. A year or so later, Christopher withdrew his veto, fearing that he might have aborted a masterpiece. Wystan, however, said he had now forgotten all his ideas for it.

Dover's chief charm for Christopher was that it was a place of transit: channel steamers coming and going, travelers arriving and departing, all of them in a hurry. He watched them and felt relaxed because he wasn't in a hurry and didn't have anywhere to go. These anxious people seemed to belong to another life—the life he had been leading up to the time of Heinz's arrest.

Earlier that summer, Faber and Faber and Random House—the British and American publishers of their plays and Auden's poems—had offered them a contract to write a travel book about any Asian country or countries they chose to visit. (Maybe this idea had been suggested to the publishers by the pseudo-Asian setting of *F6*!) Wystan and Christopher would probably have chosen China anyway, because of its exotic appeal. If they had hesitated at all, it was because mere sightseeing seemed dilettante and escapist in the crisis atmosphere of the late thirties. Then their minds had been made up for them by the Japanese Army. It had invaded southward from Peking in early July and had attacked Shanghai a month later. China had now become one of the world's decisive battlegrounds. And, unlike Spain, it wasn't already crowded with star literary observers. (How could one compete with Hemingway and Malraux?) "We'll have a war all of our very own," said Wystan. They planned to leave England toward the end of the year.

From Christopher's diary, October–November:

Heinz is always the last person I think of at night, the first in the morning.

Never to forget Heinz. Never to cease to be grateful to him for every moment of our five years together.

I suppose it isn't so much Heinz himself I miss as that part of myself which only existed in his company.

I had better face it. I shall never see him again. And perhaps this is the best for us both.

What should I feel, now, if, by some miracle, Heinz was let out of Germany? Great joy, of course. But also (I must be absolutely frank) I should be a little bit doubtful; for what, really, have I to offer him? Not even a proper home or a place in any kind of social scheme.

There are times—in publishers' offices, at cocktail parties—when the little patent leather devil of success whispers in my ear: "He travels furthest who travels alone!" I wish I could accept this or any other consolation, however base.

This existence in London is having a curious and bad effect on me. I am getting ludicrously ambitious. I want to be known, flattered, talked about; to see my name in the papers. And, the worst of it is, I can. It's all so cheap and easy.

Here, alone, I am at any rate stronger. I want, above all, to be strong—to give protection like a tree. This isn't mere conceit. It is part of my deepest nature.

In this mirror of a diary, Christopher reveals a few frank glimpses of himself. The rest is posing.

His instinct to stop himself moping, no matter how, was a healthy one. His moping wasn't of the smallest use to Heinz. Far better to indulge his vanity as a celebrity or to entertain himself with other people's worries by advising them about their love troubles or their literary work—this is what he calls giving protection like a tree. Never mind if he thus forgot Heinz altogether for an hour or two; the alternative was to play the unhealthy game of self-accusation, to dwell on the past and ask himself unanswerable questions. For example: Had some part of his will consented to Heinz's arrest? Had his helpless behavior, that last morning in Luxembourg, concealed a cold decision to let the police set him free from Heinz and his problems? Those moments of mysterious joy which came to him sometimes—why did they make him feel guilty? Wasn't it because this joy was joy in his new freedom? And then there was that old persisting question: Should he ever have taken Heinz out of Germany? Was Heinz now cursing him for this in his prison cell?

(Fifteen years later, when Christopher next saw Heinz, in Berlin, Heinz assured him that he wouldn't, for anything, have missed their travels together. But Heinz was then speaking with the maturity and generosity of an extraordinarily lucky survivor who had served in the German Army on both the Russian and the Western fronts and come out of the war with a whole skin. He alone had the right to blame Christopher. It had never occurred to him to do so.)

Everybody who knew Christopher and some who had only read his work had heard, by this time, about Heinz's arrest. Christopher's widowerhood lent glamour to his image. If Christopher had been parted from a wife, a few sympathetic girls would have been touched by his plight and asked themselves: "Couldn't I make him happy again?" In Christopher's case, the sympathizers were young men who asked the same question. He encouraged them all to try. He preferred to have two or three affairs running concurrently; in that way, he felt less involved with any particular individual. The young men didn't resent this; they were no more deeply involved than Christopher. In nearly every case, the affair would come to an end without hard feelings and leave only pleasant memories.

Christopher brought some of these young men to Kathleen's house. Kathleen describes one of them in her diary as "a dear little thing, very spruce, as if he came out of a bandbox," and another as "a nice little thing with gentle manners and a charming voice and interested in music and literature." Despite the condescension in her tone, it is clear that she approves. She finds them entirely suitable for Christopher. They are gentlemen, not working-class; Englishmen, not undesirable aliens. They can be relied on not to involve him in scandal or undue expense.

Toward the end of November, Christopher was invited to join a delegation which was to visit Spain and declare the solidarity of left-wing artists and intellectuals with the Spanish government. Several well-known people, including Jacob Epstein, Rose Macaulay, and Paul Robeson, had already accepted the invitation. Christopher explained that he would be unable to join because he was starting for China with Wystan in the near future. But the lady who had organized the delegation swept this objection aside. *She* would be leaving almost immediately, she said, and only staying a few days. She would get him back to England with plenty of time to spare.

Wystan was to be invited also. Christopher wanted to discuss the question with him before giving an answer.

He hated the prospect of group travel with celebrated companions, most of them strangers and some probably egomaniacs. He expected Wystan to agree with him. Wystan did, but felt that he himself ought to go. So Christopher said that of course he would come too: "The old war-horse will never again desert its mate."

The lady organizer was a forceful character. She was rumored to have sent white feathers to several young men who had failed to volunteer for the International Brigade. She was certainly on the lookout for any lack of team spirit among the delegates. At one of their meetings, a delegate suggested that each of them should say what it was that he or she was most interested in seeing, while they were in Spain. The organizer interrupted severely: "I don't think we need waste any time discussing *that*. We all want to go to the front." When she announced her plans for their transportation to Barcelona, Rose Macaulay said brightly: "You needn't bother about me. I'll just run down there in my little car." The organizer gave a snort of disapproval at such individualism and of scorn at the notion that you could behave like a tourist when you were in a theater of war.

Christopher happened to mention that he would need TABC shots before going to China. The organizer knew a distinguished biologist who was a supporter of the United Front and would therefore inoculate him without charge. Christopher's shots would be fired, so to speak, in the battle against Fascism.

When I went for my inoculation today, Dr. G. was busy with his white mice. He was transplanting a tumor. The tumor is dissected out of a dead mouse and bits of it are inserted into living mice with a cannula. All the mice will die. But if you grafted the same tumor on to another race of mice—the black ones—it wouldn't grow. This particular tumor was called "tumor 15" and it has been kept alive already for two years.

Christopher suspected that the hypodermic with which he was injected was also used on the mice; anyhow, the biologist kept it in the same drawer with the cannula and with a big piece of chalk and a rag which he used to wipe the blackboard when lecturing to students. But this was no time for squeamishness—this critical but still hopeful phase of the Civil War: Teruel had just been taken from the rebels. The biologist's dirty untidy lab seemed much better suited to the mood of wartime emergency than some nice clean clinic.

Christopher now began to assume the airs of a soldier on the eve of departure for the front. This was chiefly to impress his young men—some of whom were destined for far more dangerous adventures, three or four years later. They were duly impressed.

One night, when Christopher was with Forster and other friends, somebody told him he ought to make a will. A piece of paper was produced. Christopher, rather drunk and enjoying this semi-heroic scene, scribbled a couple of sentences, leaving everything to Kathleen and Richard. Forster was one of the witnesses to the document. After its signing was over, he was asked: "Why don't *you* go to Spain, Morgan?" He replied: "Afraid to," in his mild cheerful voice. His simplicity rebuked Christopher's posturing, but without a hint of malice.

The Spanish government's travel permits were delayed, however; so the delegation's departure date kept being postponed. At length, Wystan and Christopher decided not to wait any longer. They confirmed their bookings for the voyage to China.

I believe that the delegation did go to Spain eventually and that Rose Macaulay did manage to drive all the way down to Barcelona in her little car.

The night before Wystan and Christopher left, a good-bye party for them was held in a studio. Most of their friends were there. Hedli Anderson sang. A concertina was played. People danced. Forster and Bob Buckingham enjoyed the party but thought the wine cup vile. There were strained relations between certain guests. I remember Brian Howard starting one of his fights with the words, "I refuse to allow my friend to be insulted by the Worst Painter in London," but I can't remember who the Worst Painter in London was.

Next morning, January 19, 1938, Wystan and Christopher left on the boat train for Dover. Some of the daily newspapers had sent cameramen to record their exit. Christopher grinned eagerly at the lenses and, in one pose, put his arm round Wystan's shoulder. Wystan looked noncommittal and bored.

FIFTEEN

Wystan and Christopher spent the night of January 19 in Paris. They sailed from Marseilles two days later on the *Aramis,* a ship of the Messageries Maritimes line.

They were in the second class, and they found to their disgust that they had been given a cabin which was much too small and hadn't even a table to write on. Wystan decided that they must transfer to the first class, despite the added expense.

However, just as they were going into the purser's office to arrange this, they were hailed by a large fat man with peering spectacles: "Is one of you Auden?" He introduced himself as an admirer of Auden's poetry and a rubber merchant. I will call him Mr. Potter.

Mr. Potter was an obviously first-class first-class passenger. It pleased him to display his authority. He spoke to the purser on their behalf and they were promptly given two much larger second-class cabins, one to sleep in, the other with two tables to write on, at no extra charge. In gratitude for this favor, Wystan and Christopher willingly became Mr. Potter's captive audience:

He sees himself as a debunker, a buccaneer, a six-teenth-century pirate born out of his epoch. He tells his co-directors that what they need is the spirit of the merchant-adventurers. He hates the banks. He hates public companies, because they aren't allowed to take risks. He particularly enjoys ragging the pompous U.S.A. businessmen. Somebody once cabled him from New York: "Believe market has touched bottom." Potter cabled back: "Whose?" At board meetings he lies on a sofa—ostensibly because he once had a bad leg; actually because this position gives him a moral advantage. He and his colleagues tell each other dirty limericks and the very serious-minded secretary takes them all down in shorthand—because, as he once explained, he thought they might be in code.

Much less willingly, Wystan and Christopher also became the captive audience of a young man with whom they had to share their table in the second-class dining room. He was a rubber planter, returning from leave in England to a plantation near Singapore. I will call him White.

White showed us photos—men in shorts, with pipes; girls in shorts, with nauseatingly plump knees. An appalling atmosphere of suburban Surrey exuded from the album. Better face a thousand deaths in China than a fortnight of planters' hospitality. Nothing he tells us about Malaya lessens our horror. Everyone joins the Territorials and there are tarantulas. (As I write this, White is doing his best to annoy and interrupt me by pacing up and down in front of my deck chair. Imagining that I'm writing a story, he says: "Their lips met in one long kiss.")

They docked at Port Said on the morning of January 25. Francis, who was now living in Egypt, came down from Cairo to meet the ship. He seemed shakier and a bit shrunken but essentially unchanged.

Wystan and Christopher were eager to explore Port Said, being still under the spell of its legend as the sex capital of the world. Francis assured them that it was deadly dull. He suggested that they should drive back with him to Cairo and reembark on the *Aramis* early next morning at Port Tewfik, after she had passed through the Suez Canal.

Wystan and Christopher were disappointed in the pyramids. They looked messy and quite new; like the tip heaps of a quarry, Wystan said. But they were staggered by the Sphinx. It seemed so alive, so horribly injured, so malign. A passenger on the *Aramis* had told them that the ancient Egyptians must have psychically foreseen the future importance of America to the rest of the world; that was why they had placed the Sphinx facing westward. Back on the ship, a few days later, Wystan wrote a poem which declared that the Sphinx is "gazing for ever towards shrill America." But then both he and Christopher were troubled by doubts. *Did* the Sphinx face westward? Strangely enough, neither of them could remember. Finally—after their return to London—Wystan asked someone at the Egyptian embassy. With the result that his revised version of the poem reads: "Turning/a vast behind on shrill America."

In Cairo that evening, they drank with Francis at a street-side café. Every few moments, boys would thrust sex postcards, bow ties, lottery tickets, riding whips, and clockwork trains into their faces; now and then, an offered carpet or curtain would hide them from each other altogether and cut off their conversation, despite Francis's screams at the vendors. He became his Greek self again, except that here he screamed in Arabic.

Later he took them to visit a friend who was a professor at the university. The professor told them tale after tale of Egyptian dishonesty, treachery, bribability, and self-sale. Both he and Francis spoke of the country's corruption with disgust, but they would probably have been resentful if Wystan or Christopher had criticized it. Egypt was an addiction which only addicts had the right to despise.

When they said goodbye to Francis that night, it was to be for the last time. He died in Egypt, in 1942.

They steamed southward, heading for Djibouti, Colombo, Singapore, Saigon, and, ultimately, Hong Kong; heading for the warm seas sacred to Conrad and to Maugham, with dolphins leaping before their bows and sparks of phosphorus in their wake. Wystan endured the voyage glumly, sometimes grumpily; he disliked being at sea, deplored the tropics, felt uprooted from his chilly beloved North. But Christopher, the place snob, found a new enchantment in each port of call. *He was East of Suez!*

Meanwhile, they had frequent talks with White and with Mr. Potter. White had now confessed to them that he was having an affair with the wife of a fellow planter who was a neighbor and close friend of his, in Malaya. The wife had told White that she had never dreamed love could be like this, "something wild and dangerous." And White had discovered that she was his "complete physical, spiritual, and emotional counterpart." The husband suspected nothing. White felt like a cad, but he couldn't give her up. "If anyone were to tell me, 'You oughtn't to go on seeing her,' " White said, "I should scream and say, 'Don't be silly.' "

When asked why the two of them didn't run away together, White explained that the world of rubber planting consisted only of Malaya and Ceylon; it was very small—everybody knew everybody—and very strict. A man who stole another man's wife would be cut dead; he wouldn't be able to show his face in the club or play rugger or tennis or go to dances. He would be obliged to give up his job. And there was nowhere else for a planter to go. Rubber planting was all White knew or cared about. He hated the prospect of returning to England and getting some other employment. His life would be ruined and so would hers.

Wystan and Christopher were now no longer bored by White. He fascinated them, because he had turned into a Maugham character. And they themselves had become characters in his story, by introducing him to Mr. Potter. For Mr. Potter had told them that he was planning to start some rubber plantations in Siam; and that he was on the lookout for an experienced planter who would be prepared to leave his present job and manage his plantations for him.

White and Mr. Potter henceforth met daily for deck games and bridge, throughout the rest of their time on board. If Mr. Potter had indeed offered him a managership, White didn't tell them. But this might be due to discretion, or an unwillingness to admit, even to himself, that the future of his romance was now in his own hands. He and Mr. Potter left the ship together at Singapore . . . Had the impression made by Wystan's poems on Mr. Potter started a chain reaction which would end in White's lifelong happiness? Wystan and Christopher never knew.

On February 16, they reached Hong Kong. Both of them found the city hideous—which surprised me when I visited it in 1957 and thought it picturesque, to say the least. But no doubt Wystan and Christopher had been expecting something purely and romantically Oriental. They didn't appreciate the clash of architectural styles in this Victorian-colonial fortress.

They were invited to formal dinner parties at which they met government officials and millionaires. Wystan was not charmed by the food or the company. "The oxtail soup wasn't oxtail," he wrote. "The women were cows and wore mermaid dresses; Sir Blank Blank, a squat red-faced toad, was reputed to have the Eighteenth Century Mind." Speaking of the Japanese invasion of China, a businessman said to Christopher: "Of course, from our point of view, both sides are just natives." A lady told him that a formerly respected member of Hong Kong society had been seen furtively eating dog at a Chinese restaurant on the mainland, and that the pet dogs owned by her friends kept disappearing. When Wystan and Christopher tried to find out about the journey which was ahead of them, they were given the kind of advice intended to scare novices: Never mix with a Chinese crowd or you'll get typhus. Never go for a walk by yourselves or they'll shoot you as spies.

On February 28, they left Hong Kong by river boat for Canton. Their wanderings around China during the next three and a half months are recorded in *Journey to a War.* Here are a few impressions which come to me when I try to resmell, retaste, rehear, and resee that experience:

The sweetly perfumed smell of the dust—said to be poisonous because the wind blew it from the family grave mounds which occupied part of every peasant's land; some people wore masks to protect themselves from it. The taste of two kinds of tea—either very faint, clear water with a pale green sprig floating; or strongly fishy, dark brown. The pig squeal of wheelbarrows with unoiled wheels, "because the squeal is cheaper." The clatter of mah-jongg players' tiles in the inns at night. Blue-clad figures dotted all over a landscape—men in blue, women in blue, children in blue—whichever way you looked. And smiles, smiles all around you—did it cost them no effort to keep their mouths in that position? Your face ached from smiling back.

Despite some wild rides in chauffeured cars, I remember transportation as slowness. Slow trains, days late already, that stopped suddenly for hours on end, then restarted suddenly without the slightest warning; they would have left you stranded in the back of nowhere if you'd strayed too far away from them. Painfully slow hikes along cobbled roads as narrow as garden paths. Slow plodding through the rain on little furry horses. Slow careful descents in carrying chairs of nearly vertical mountain trails, when even your own terror was in slow motion. Being carried in chairs and pulled in rickshaws created a physical relationship which both Wystan and Christopher found indecent. Man has no right to make such use of manpower, they said. When their feet hurt sufficiently, they swallowed their scruples. On such occasions, the very toughness and willingness of their carriers and pullers shamed them—all the more so, if one of those lithe erect figures turned and showed, as sometimes happened, that the youthful trunk supported an aged wrinkled face.

When the two of them were traveling, they caused much curiosity and laughter. Wystan had a woolen cap and an immense shapeless topcoat, with carpet slippers to appease his corns. Christopher had a beret, a turtleneck sweater, and oversized riding boots which gave him blisters. Wystan dressed in the way that was natural to him. Christopher was in masquerade as a war correspondent.

He may have looked the part—correspondents can be a bit absurd—but he must often have betrayed his amateur status by his nervousness. The threat of air raids kept him keyed up, especially when he was on a train. If they were ordered to leave it and take cover, he couldn't restrain himself from hurrying. Wystan never hurried. At Tungkwan, when their train had to pass a place where some Japanese guns were mounted on the opposite side of the Yellow River, Christopher was the one who took precautions; he insisted on opening the window lest its glass should be blown in by an explosion.

Christopher was always more apt to be troubled by the threat of danger than by danger itself. When he first saw an air raid, he felt awe rather than fear—awe followed by exhilaration. He was awed by being in the presence of absolute, impersonal hostility. These planes had come simply to destroy.

The searchlights criss-crossed and suddenly there they were, flying close together and high up. It was as if a microscope had brought into focus the bacilli of a fatal disease.

Then, as the antiaircraft guns crashed out, the tracer bullets shot upward, buildings flamed, and the punching concussions of the bombs made Christopher catch his breath, he was aware only of a violent physical excitement; "something inside me was flapping about like a fish." He describes the spectacle as *"wrong,* an insult to Nature" but admits that it was also "as tremendous as Beethoven."

On such occasions, Wystan would say: "Nothing's going to happen, I know it won't, nothing like that ever happens to *me."* His bland irrational assurance irritated Christopher. Yet Christopher did find an equally irrational sense of safety in their being together. Their relationship seemed at all times more real than their surroundings—this country and this war. So much so that he could almost imagine they were invulnerable—just as Martians are sometimes said to be, in tales about their visits to our world.

Were the two of them ever in serious danger of being killed? Two or three times, perhaps. A shell might just possibly have hit their compartment when the train was passing Tungkwan; the Japanese often fired on the trains, though they seldom did them much damage. Then there was a daytime air battle over Hankow which Wystan and Christopher watched lying on their backs on the lawn of the British consulate. (This was Wystan's idea, to avoid getting a stiff neck.) During the battle, some sort of

302

missile did hit the ground quite close to them. And then there was their visit to the front, at Han Chwang. The Chinese started to bombard the Japanese lines and the Japanese fired back. Wystan and Christopher were told by their hosts that they must leave. As they were crossing a large empty field, just behind the trenches, several Japanese planes appeared and circled low overhead. The soldier who was escorting Wystan and Christopher urged them to lie down, although there was absolutely no cover. They were now subject to the whim of the Japanese pilots and might well have been machine-gunned. But all that happened was that Wystan took photographs, telling Christopher: "You look wonderful, with your great nose cleaving the summer air." After which he shuffled his carpet slippers impatiently, wanting to ignore the planes and hurry on to the village where their lunch was waiting.

This Chinese journey was the longest continuous confrontation which Wystan and Christopher were ever to have in the course of their lives. Here they were, nakedly exposed to each other, day after day. But they only became conscious of this when there was friction between them.

Wystan accused Christopher of sulking whenever his will was crossed. Christopher's despotism and sulks sometimes irritated Wystan. But more often he endured them good-naturedly and with humor, as he had been enduring them for years:

> *Who is that funny-looking young man, so squat with a*
> *top-heavy head,*
> *A cross between a cavalry major and a rather prim*
> *landlady,*
> *Sitting there sipping a cigarette?*

*If absolutely the whole universe fails to bow to your
    command,
How you stamp your bright little shoe,
How you pout,
House-proud old landlady.
At times I could shake you.*

(These are extracts from a poem—basically affectionate
in tone—which Wystan had written in a book he gave
Christopher, the year before. The book was D. H. Lawrence's *Birds, Beasts and Flowers;* hence Wystan's imitation
of Lawrence's style.)

Wystan was well aware of the sinister side of Christopher's character, and he didn't deny that it fascinated him
more than it repelled him. Christopher writes that "Wystan once told me, almost admiringly, that I was the cruel-
lest and most unscrupulous person he had ever met." It
seems to me that Wystan was incapable of cruelty but that
he had a streak of masochism in him which could invite
it from others.

After their return to England, Christopher wrote in his
diary:

In China I sometimes found myself really hating him
—hating his pedantic insistence on "objectivity,"
which was really a reaction from my own woolly-mindedness. I was meanly jealous of him, too. Jealous of his
share of the limelight; jealous because he'll no longer
play the role of dependent, admiring younger brother.
Indeed, I got such a *physical* dislike of him that I deliberately willed him to get ill; which he did.

Then, in New York and on the Atlantic crossing, we
had these extraordinary scenes—Wystan in tears, telling me that no one would ever love him, that he would
never have my sexual success. That flattered my vanity;
but still my sadism wasn't appeased. And actually—
believe it or not—when we got back to England I
wouldn't have him to stay the night, because I was

jealous of him and wanted to stage the Returning Hero act all by myself . . . Of course, I'm well aware that these confessions sound far worse than they are. My essential feeling for Wystan is untouched by all this, and will remain so.

Most of their arguments in China were games which they played with each other, to pass the time. It was only when they got onto metaphysics that they ceased to be playful. Then Christopher's "woolly-mindedness" clashed with Wystan's "pedantic objectivity," as Christopher declared passionately that he *knew* he hadn't got a soul.

According to Christopher's diary:

The more I think about myself, the more I'm persuaded that, as a *person,* I really don't exist. That is one of the reasons why I can't believe in any orthodox religion: I cannot believe in my own soul. No, I am a chemical compound, conditioned by environment and education. My "character" is simply a repertoire of acquired tricks, my conversation a repertoire of adaptations and echoes, my "feelings" are dictated by purely physical, external stimuli.

Christopher did well to call himself woolly-minded. All he has actually stated here is that he can't believe in his own individuality as something absolute and eternal; the word "soul" is introduced, quite improperly, as a synonym for "person."

A year later, when Christopher was in California, he would have long talks on this subject with Gerald Heard. (Gerald Heard and Chris Wood, together with Aldous and Maria Huxley, had left England for the States in April 1937.) As the result of his talks with Gerald and with Gerald's friend and teacher, the Hindu monk Prabhavananda, Christopher would find himself able to believe—as a possibility, at least—that an eternal impersonal presence (call it "the soul" if you like) exists within all creatures and is other than the mutable non-eternal "person." He would then feel that all his earlier difficulties had been merely semantic; that he could have been converted to this belief at any time in his life, if only someone had used the right words to explain it to him. Now, I doubt this. I doubt if one ever accepts a belief until one urgently needs it.

But, although Christopher wasn't yet aware that he needed such a belief, he may have been feeling the need subconsciously. This would explain his recently increased hostility toward what he thought of as "religion" —the version of Christianity he had been taught in his childhood. Perhaps he was afraid that he would be forced to accept it, at last, after nearly fifteen years of atheism.

When Christopher raged against religion, Wystan would laugh and say, "Careful, careful, my dear—if you keep going on like that, you'll have *such* a conversion, one of these days!" If Christopher did indeed hate Wystan at moments, it was because of the smugness of Wystan's Christian dogmatism.

During their arguments, Christopher sometimes invoked the example of Forster: Morgan, he said, was incapable of having any truck with "such Fascist filth." I wonder, now, if Wystan then believed what he stated in a letter to Christopher many years later, in explanation of Forster's declared agnosticism: "As I see him, Morgan is a person who is so accustomed to the Presence of God that he is unaware of it; he has never known what it feels like when that Presence is withdrawn." If Wystan did already believe this in 1938, he wisely kept his mouth shut. I can imagine the yell of protest Christopher would have uttered, on hearing such an outrageous accusation against his Master.

On May 25, they reached Shanghai. This was the last stop on their Chinese journey. They had been invited by the

British ambassador, Sir Archibald Clark-Kerr, and his wife, to stay at their house in the International Settlement. The four of them had first met in Hong Kong and again in Hankow. Archie was a big handsome humorous Scot, a pipe smoker with a collection of thirty-two pipes to choose from. Tita Clark-Kerr was a beautiful tiny blond Chilean, who read detective stories.

The house, with its columns and clipped lawns, its vases and lacquered screens, its Chinese servants in lemon silk jackets, was every inch a Residence. Archie and Tita didn't even pretend to feel at home in it. Their daytime lives were lived almost entirely in public, passing from one diplomatic or social duty to another, while many sharp eyes and ears interpreted their least gesture and lightest word. No doubt, it gave them some slight relaxation to entertain two guests who weren't official personages. Archie referred to Wystan and Christopher as the Poets, and the Poets did their best to reciprocate by behaving as poetically as good manners permitted. Still, it was a strain. And, all too often, when they had got Archie to themselves in his study and were laughing and joking, a secretary would enter to announce that it was time he left for some conference. Then the tall doors would be thrown open, an order would be barked out, the guard on the staircase outside would crash to attention, and Archie, now His Excellency, would slowly, gravely descend the stairs. Before their very eyes, he became the British Empire.

Within the International Settlement, the two extremes of the human condition almost touched each other. Here were the mansions and the banks, the elegant shops, the luxury restaurants, and the nightclub at the top of a tower, from which guests had watched the Japanese attack on the outer city, a few months earlier. And here were the refugee camps and the dozens of factories in which children were being literally worked to death by their employers. The refugees were packed into huts with triple tiers of shelves: one shelf for each family to cook, eat, and sleep on. The perimeter of the Settlement was guarded by a mixed force of foreign troops, confronting the Japanese troops who guarded their conquered territory of deserted ruins.

All this Wystan and Christopher dutifully inspected, described, photographed. They had seen ugly sights during their Chinese journey—wounded soldiers stranded at railway stations, without medical aid, some of them stinking of gas gangrene; mutilated corpses after an air raid. But misery in Shanghai seemed more miserable than elsewhere, because its victims were trapped between their Western or Chinese exploiters and their Japanese conquerors, without any apparent hope of escape.

Toward the end of their visit, Wystan and Christopher began taking afternoon holidays from their social consciences in a bathhouse where you were erotically soaped and massaged by young men. You could pick your attendants, and many of them were beautiful. Those who were temporarily disengaged would watch the action, with giggles, through peepholes in the walls of the bathrooms. What made the experience pleasingly exotic was that tea was served to the customer throughout; even in the midst of an embrace, the attendant would disengage one hand, pour a cupful, and raise it, tenderly but firmly, to the customer's lips. If you refused the tea at first, the attendant went on offering it until you accepted. It was like a sex fantasy in which a naked nurse makes love to the patient but still insists on giving him his medicine punctually, at the required intervals.

Every evening, when they met Archie and Tita for pre-dinner cocktails, Archie would ask what they had been doing that afternoon. If they had been to the bathhouse, they had to invent something. Archie accepted their lies without comment, but a certain gleam in his eye made them wonder if he was playing a game with them. Probably, they said to each other, they were followed whenever they went out, as a routine security measure, and a police report of their movements was placed on

Archie's desk. Of one thing they felt certain: if Archie did know about the bathhouse, he wouldn't be in the least shocked.

Wystan and Christopher had deliberately kept their travel plans vague, choosing one route rather than another as local circumstances suggested. Having now decided that they wanted to return to England by way of New York, they went to the U.S. authorities in Shanghai to ask for transit visas. It never occurred to them that they would have the least difficulty in getting these.

But it so happened that the official on duty that day was in a bad humor. He had just been harassed by an obstinate flock of White Russians who wanted to emigrate to the States and wouldn't take *nyet* for an answer. Having dismissed them with understandable but unnecessary brusqueness, he turned impatiently to Wystan and Christopher. They told him their business. He answered that they should have applied for the visas in England before they started. Could they *prove* to him that it was absolutely necessary for them to pass through New York? No? Then let them cross Canada and sail home from Halifax, as British subjects should.

As they turned to leave, frustrated and furious, the official ungraciously asked them what they were doing in Shanghai. Perhaps he suspected them of being undesirables who should be deported from the Settlement. Delighted at this chance to hit back at him, they replied demurely: "Staying with the British ambassador."

Tableau. The official's manner changed with indecent suddenness. They were granted special visas which allowed them to visit the States as many times as they cared to, during the next twelve months.

The ship on which they were to cross the Pacific would call at three ports in Japan. So now they were about to visit what they had come to regard as an enemy country. In China, the Japanese had been the Enemy, the bomb droppers, and as such non-human. They had seen only two at close quarters, as human beings—both of them prisoners. One was a loutish, pathetically scared youth, tied up with rope like a parcel. All they could do for him was to put a cigarette between his lips. The other was an ex-schoolmaster who answered questions in English with a sad natural dignity.

Then, in the International Settlement, they talked to a delegation of Japanese civilians, on a so-called fact-finding mission. These were either the blandest of hypocrites or the most childish of wishful thinkers. They declared that they loved the Chinese people and felt absolutely no bitterness toward them. This war was such a pity; it could have been avoided so easily, Japan's demands were very reasonable. They hoped that Wystan and Christopher had had no inconvenience while traveling. "Only from your aeroplanes," Christopher answered, and got a seemingly hearty laugh.

They sailed from Shanghai on June 12. Their Canadian Pacific liner was comfortable and old-fashioned, with an open coal-burning fireplace in the lounge. Her name evoked the days of Victorian imperial megalomania: *Empress of Asia*.

Two days later, they saw their first seaport on the Japanese coast. Christopher's immediate reaction was to exclaim: "Ibsen!" The psychological climate of the little town seemed Scandinavian; it looked so sad and drab and clean. The temple in its park made him think of a municipal office. He missed China's gaudy dirty picturesqueness. This was Nagasaki, seven years before the atomic bomb.

In Kobe, all the shops were lighted but the street lamps weren't—in case of air raids, they were told. But surely the Chinese were incapable of bombing Japan? The precaution seemed absurd; perhaps it was actually an attempt to encourage Japanese war-mindedness.

On the train to Tokyo, the car porter annoyed Wystan by flicking continually around his feet with brush and dustpan, collecting his cigarette ash. This was a vicious circle, since Wystan kept dropping it, out of more or less deliberate aggression. They were lucky enough to get a calming glimpse of benign Mount Fuji lit by the setting sun, before the night clouds closed around it. But, when they arrived in Tokyo:

A raving screaming mob with banners was seeing a troop train out of the station to the front. The sight so shocked poor Wystan that he dropped and broke his only pair of glasses, and so will travel blind to New York. [Wystan, being nearsighted, would still be able to read, however.]

They spent the night of June 17–18 at the Imperial Hotel. I have a memory connected with this which I suspect. It isn't recorded in Christopher's diary and it is rather too symbolic to be strictly true:

While Christopher is sitting waiting for Wystan in the lobby of the hotel, next morning, he witnesses a ceremonious meeting between two officers in uniform, a Nazi and a Japanese—the Berlin–Tokyo Axis personified. They exchange Nazi salutes, then bow Japanese-style, then shake hands. They are standing beneath a big chandelier; and, as they greet each other, the chandelier begins to sway. It is Christopher's first, very slight, earthquake.

That afternoon, they sailed from Yokohama, bound for Vancouver. Christopher had never before seen the farewell ritual of throwing one end of a paper streamer from the ship to the shore, thus linking yourself for a few last moments with someone you are leaving behind. As the ship began to move, Christopher suddenly imagined Heinz standing down there on the dock, the streamer pulling tight between them, then snapping . . . The experience was almost physically painful.

The North Pacific was cold, even now at midsummer, and very calm. They got glimpses of the Aleutian Islands. Beyond these, there was a pale frore brightness in the sky which suggested the gleam of the icecap. Somebody died on board and was buried at sea. I remember flowers being scattered at the end of the ceremony—happy-landing flowers collected from the staterooms, already faded. They floated away behind the ship, on the smooth gray surface of the water, far far to westward. They were out of sight before they sank.

This eventless ten-day voyage was an ideal opportunity for physical and mental convalescence. Both Wystan and Christopher had suffered from dysentery throughout their journey. While they were staying with the Clark-Kerrs, Christopher's stomach cramps had once made him roll on the bedroom floor grunting with pain and jerking his body like an opening and shutting jackknife. Later, in England, he was told by the doctor that his intestines still retained souvenirs of China, at least twenty kinds of internal parasite.

The mental souvenir was odder than these. For some months after leaving China, he had a recurrent dream of being in an air raid. But the air raid—or whatever it represented—was always pleasantly exciting, never terrifying. Without being able to interpret this dream exactly, he became aware that he had now lost much of his neurotic fear of "War" as a concept. A very little exposure to danger will go a long way, psychologically; he had learned from it that his fear in China had been a healthy fear which he needn't be ashamed of. He now no longer dreaded that he would behave worse than most other people in a crisis, though he didn't expect to behave better. This self-knowledge would influence his future decisions, making him less inclined to worry how the world might judge them.

The entrance to Vancouver harbor was superb; and the immigration official said, "Welcome to Canada!" To Christopher, who had come to regard all such officials in Europe as his natural enemies, this formal tourist-conscious greeting had a cheering novelty; the New World seemed full of good will. And the Canadian Pacific train obligingly stopped to let them stroll around and admire the Great Divide and Lake Louise. The country was vast, magnificent, cold, clean, and empty, yet with a reassuring Scottish snugness of oatmeal, cream, rich wholesome food.

Then down into the United States at Portal, North Dakota—a dismaying contrast. The hot shabby prairie was blowing itself away in clouds of dust. And the prices in the dining car shocked them. Driving through Chicago after dark, they hoped for glimpses of gangsters but were shown only a flower shop which had supplied wreaths for their funerals. On the last leg of the ride to New York, the landscape became stately with cliffs and the broadening Hudson. Then they arrived and found themselves in a station built like an oversized Roman temple. Wystan said, "We ought to be wearing togas."

Waiting to greet them was George Davis, novelist and literary editor of a fashion magazine and their friend already; they had met him in London the year before. Small, plump, handsome, sparkling, he gaily stuffed into their pockets the wads of dollar bills he had earned for them by selling their travel articles to his own magazine and others. Utterly at their disposal as host, guide, and fulfiller of all their desires, he was there to make them feel that New York was a theatrical performance staged expressly for them and that everybody in this city had been yearning for their arrival. He never left them for long throughout the nine days' wonder of their visit.

George's showmanship created a delirium of impressions. The Rainbow Room, balanced on a fountain jet of lights shot skyward, sixty-five stories high. (Perhaps it was there that Christopher first heard, "Jeepers, creepers, where'd ya get those peepers?" which would become as magic for him as the long-ago songs of Berlin, when he had found a boy to dedicate it to.) Maxine Sullivan in Harlem swing-singing "Loch Lomond" into a live darkness of black faces and white eyeballs. Coney Island on the Fourth of July, crammed to the water's edge. A Bowery dive where a fight broke out and the bartender vaulted the bar with a club and they were hurried away as the police drove up with screaming sirens. (George apologized profusely, saying he'd never known such a thing to happen there before. But Wystan and Christopher took it all for granted; it was exactly what the movies had taught them to expect of New York.)

They were interviewed and photographed. They were taken to parties and introduced to celebrities: Maxwell Anderson, Muriel Draper, Orson Welles, Kurt Weill and his wife, Lotte Lenya (whom George would later marry). They took Benzedrine every morning to give them energy for these encounters, Seconal every night to make them sleep. Wystan later made the use of uppers and downers part of his routine; he called it "the chemical life."

George also offered to make sexual introductions for them. "All right," said Christopher, half in joke. "I want to meet a beautiful blond boy, about eighteen, intelligent, with very sexy legs." Such a boy was instantly produced; he was almost too suitable to be true. I will call him Vernon.

Christopher reacted to Vernon much as he had reacted to Bubi, on his first Berlin visit. Both were infatuations based on a fantasy; only, this time, Christopher was looking for the American, not the German, Boy. The earlier infatuation had been stronger but less serious, and it had owed a great deal of its strength to difficulty in communication. This time there was no language barrier and a lot more for the two of them to talk about; Vernon really was intelligent and eager to educate himself. He was also good-natured, tough, and independent. He radiated health and physical energy. Comparing him with those exquisite but remote, almost otherworldly-looking attendants at the Shanghai bathhouse, Christopher found him wonderfully human-smelling, muscular, hairy, earthy.

Vernon himself certainly wasn't infatuated, but I think he was attracted. Christopher, at that particular moment, could easily be regarded as a romantic figure, just returned from dangerous exotic adventures and worthy of this young city dweller's admiration and envy.

Vernon was tired of New York and longed to leave it; Christopher, who would be forced to leave it within a few days, had fallen under its spell. However, its spell was now largely Vernon's, the American Boy's. The American Boy is also the Walt Whitman Boy. And the Walt Whitman Boy is, by definition, a wanderer. So Christopher found it natural to indulge in daydreams of a future wander-comradeship with Vernon in the Whitman tradition:

> *We two boys together clinging,*
> *One the other never leaving,*
> *Up and down the roads going, North and*
> *   South excursions making . . .*

Auden has left it on record, in an interview given to the BBC many years later, that it was during this first visit to New York that he and Christopher decided to return and settle in the States for good:

I would say that I felt the situation in England for me was becoming impossible. I couldn't grow up. That

English life . . . is for me a family life, and I love my family but I don't want to live with them.

I don't remember that Christopher was so positive in making up his mind to emigrate, at that time. But then, Christopher's feelings about England were different from Wystan's. He didn't think of England as his family. And, much as he was often able to enjoy himself there, he continued to feel the old hostility. For him, it was still the land of the Others. And in rejecting Heinz, it had rejected him too.

(Not until after the Second War, when England had ceased to be imperial and had become a minor power with a cosmopolitan population, did Christopher begin to love it, for the first time in his life. It had turned into the kind of country he had always wanted it to be.)

Besides, Christopher had moved, or been moved, around so much already that another change of country would have far less emotional significance for him than it would have for Wystan. So it was for Wystan to decide. His own attitude was passive. If Wystan chose to emigrate, then he would too. Despite their occasional frictions, he felt closer to Wystan than ever. While nearly all of his other friends were gradually withdrawing from him, into long-term relationships or careers or both, life seemed to be binding the two of them together.

SIXTEEN

Wystan and Christopher got back to London on July 17 —to find that this was the evening when Beatrix Lehmann would give a one-night-only performance of Cocteau's *La Voix Humaine.* (In the English-language production by the Group Theatre, it was called *The Telephone.*) They were lucky indeed not to have missed this—it was one of her most daringly imaginative stage images. Transforming herself into a sort of Laocoön, she made the telephone cord seem to writhe around her body like a serpent of jealousy which would end by killing her. When Christopher talked to her afterwards, she told him that she had caught sight of them in the middle of the performance. She had supposed them to be still in China, and the joyful shock had nearly startled her out of her character.

Toward the end of July, Christopher went to stay with John Lehmann and his mother at Totland Bay on the Isle of Wight. This was a place of nostalgia for John, who had spent his holidays there as a child, and for Christopher, who had worked on *All the Conspirators* at nearby Freshwater Bay and been visited there by Edward and Wystan and Hector Wintle. The landscape of the Past remained almost unaltered, with its smells of sea salt and pines and sunburned turf. But the Present was already within the shadow of the immediate Future, in which a showdown with Hitler over Czechoslovakia was surely unavoidable.

During August, Christopher was in Ostende and in Dover. He went to Ostende with Jimmy Younger. The two of them had started a duet of their own which was independent of Christopher's friendship with Stephen. Memory of their life at Sintra had drawn them together. It was important to both of them that Jimmy had known Heinz, had even had sex with him on one occasion. But Jimmy and Christopher each declared that the other had changed for the better, since those days. Jimmy admitted that he had sometimes hated Christopher. Christopher remembered how, in his diary, he had viciously referred to "Jimmy's primly-composed rabbit-mouth and the thick inflamed nape of his neck." Christopher now found him desirable as well as companionable. They made love often, with the warmth of friendly affection.

At Dover were Forster, Bob and May Buckingham and their small son Robin, Cuthbert Worsley, Joe Ackerley, William Plomer. I have the snapshots Christopher took of them, then. It seems poignant to me, now, that they are all smiling, under that growing war threat of which they must all, except Robin, be continually aware. But doesn't one always smile when one is photographed on holiday?

Forster, as so often, has an air of being amused in spite of himself. Bob is gaining weight and grins as if he knows this and doesn't care. May, with her hair smooth like a Madonna's, smiles demurely; you would never guess that she can drink and tell dirty stories. Robin has Bob's grin and looks exactly like him. (When Christopher saw the

Buckinghams for the first time after the war, in 1947, Bob told how funny May had looked, being blown down the passage of their house by the blast of a bomb. And both of them roared with laughter, as though they were actually watching her in this undignified situation. Bob had been decorated for his bravery during the Blitz.)

Cuthbert Worsley, a big blond bespectacled athlete, smiles more broadly than any of them. But it is a smile of intelligent courage, not of the optimism of mere good health. He has already seen what war is like, while serving with an ambulance unit in Spain. Joe Ackerley smiles enigmatically, by simply baring his teeth around the mouthpiece of his pipe. He has fought in World War I and been wounded and taken prisoner by the Germans. At forty-two, he is one of the handsomest men of his generation and one of its most obstinate pessimists. When he talks, his gloom has such charm that it cheers up everybody except himself. He thinks that life is altogether vile.

William Plomer is the only one who may possibly agree with Ackerley; but there is no way of knowing this. Up on the surface, as always, he is full of fun. In the rooms he rents here every summer, there are Victorian landscape paintings, with houses, trees, and a few cows. Or rather, that was how they used to be. Lately, some small figures, painted perfectly to scale, have begun to appear in the background amongst the trees, or looking out of the windows of the houses. William introduces them into the pictures with loving care; there is never a clash of colors or a brushstroke which calls attention to itself. These trespassers are so discreet that you scarcely notice them. If the landlady has noticed, she has never said anything about them to William.

When Christopher returned to London after this holiday, he decided to keep a record of the crisis:

> The situation is so serious that I must force myself to be interested as well as merely horrified by it.

Beginning on August 20, he made fairly regular entries in his diary, right through to the end of September. (They are quoted from extensively in *Down There on a Visit*.)

These entries are actually more often about Christopher than about the political situation. His diary-keeping was a discipline designed to shame himself out of giving way to panic-depression, sloth, overdrinking, oversmoking, masturbation, and nervous pottering around. Another such discipline was his work on the prose section of *Journey to a War*. This would have been hard enough at any time. Transcribing the travel diary kept by Wystan and himself was boring toil, but it had to be done before he could edit and rewrite the diary as a coherent narrative. And, whenever his will weakened, there was an inner saboteur voice which asked: "What's the use of all this? Who'll want to read about your faraway out-of-date war when the bombs start falling on London?"

On his days of weakness, Christopher thought of the crisis as a jealous god which demanded his total attention and was angered by his efforts to work. He bought newspapers in a superstitious attempt to appease the god, feeling that the news would get worse if he missed one single edition; but he barely glanced at their headlines before throwing them away.

The crisis made Heinz seem more remote, although he continued to write letters and although John Lehmann had just brought back a first-hand account of him. John had gone to Berlin to visit Heinz; he was now working off his year of labor service, helping put up a building on the Potsdamerplatz. John reported that he appeared to be much tougher and more politically conscious than before his return to Germany. This glimpse of a new self-reliant

Heinz was inspiring, but Christopher wasn't comforted by it. He thought how hopelessly isolated Heinz must be feeling, in the midst of his Nazi countrymen . . . But Heinz, after all his misfortunes, was to be marvelously fortunate. Not long after this, he would meet someone he could love and confide in—the girl he would eventually marry.

Christopher thought of Vernon, too. Vernon seemed even more remote than Heinz. He was a citizen of the New World which Christopher had begun to hope might be the homeland he had failed to find in Germany. But would he ever see Vernon or New York again? The crisis seemed more and more likely to end in war, and he couldn't leave England while it continued. Patriotism? Definitely not. This was largely apathy. He felt possessed by the crisis. It had become his world. He couldn't imagine himself living elsewhere, outside it.

Christopher had his worst moments of depression when he was with the weak. In ordinary life, he enjoyed their company; they made him feel protective, especially when they were charming and young. But now he needed to be with the strong. All his close friends had strength of some kind and could transmit it to him.

Edward and Hilda Upward, Olive Mangeot, and Jean Ross drew strength from their Marxism. They were able to see the crisis calmly and ideologically as one phase of an evolving situation, which might further their cause. Therefore, though they hated and feared the prospect of war, they couldn't be hypnotized by it into helplessness.

Beatrix Lehmann had to be strong; it was a necessity of her life as an actress. She was constantly being forced to rise to occasions, deal with emergencies, become greater than herself. War might present itself to her as a new kind of emergency, an air raid during one of her performances. She would deal with that, too. In her humorous way, she was heroic.

Hector Wintle and Robert Moody (Lee, in *Lions and Shadows*) drew strength from their professional status. In peace or in war, under capitalism or Communism, doctors always know what they should be doing; and everybody agrees that they should be doing it. Into the world of Hector and Robert, the Enemy can only enter as a patient—even though he may have been bombing the hospital when he was shot down. Christopher admired and envied them. It was too late for regrets, but the thought kept arising: he might have been their colleague now.

Stephen's peculiar kind of strength lay in his emotional flexibility; faced with an emergency, he sometimes laughed, sometimes wept, always with violence. Stephen was rather proud of his ability to weep, and rightly so. A grown man who can shed tears without embarrassment is like a yogi who has learned to expel toxic matter from his body by consciously speeding up the peristaltic rhythm. He can eliminate many of life's poisons.

(People like Stephen are unusually well equipped to deal with danger. During the war, he was to join the Fire Service, which would have seemed to Christopher a terrible ordeal; not only because of the fires themselves but also the dizzyingly tall ladders you had to climb.)

As for Forster, I have already made clear what the nature of his strength was. A meeting with him never failed to restore Christopher's morale.

But it was from John Lehmann that Christopher got support of the most practical kind; thanks to John, he was able to start preparing his mind for the worst. Kathleen and Richard had now left London to visit some cousins in Wales. If war broke out, they would remain there and Kathleen's house would be closed. When that happened, said John, Christopher must come and share his flat with him. Already, they were planning a wartime life together. They had written to the Foreign Office, offering their services for propaganda work. (I cannot now believe that Christopher would have been able to stick at this for long.) Privately, he made one reservation: if Wystan offered him some other course of action, then he would probably go along with Wystan. But Wystan was still away, on holiday in Belgium.

This is an account of the final day of the crisis, September 28, taken partly from Christopher's diary, partly from *Down There on a Visit*, which contains added details, remembered, not invented:

The last shreds of hope are vanishing down the drain. Wilson came back from Berlin, snubbed. The German Army mobilizes this afternoon. Parliament meets, to introduce conscription. Chamberlain spoke last night, like a wet fish, saying: How dreadful, how dreadful.

London is all gas-masks and children screaming when they're fitted on. Everybody is enlisting or running away from town. Nanny is wonderful. She trots up and down stairs, with cups of Ovaltine.

Later. I went to Victoria to meet Wystan, returning from Belgium. The boat-train was late. Newspapers appearing every 20 minutes. The station full of sailors, going down to join the mobilized fleet. A few women in tears. One ray of hope: Berlin denies their reported ultimatum to mobilize at 2 P.M. Stolid with misery, I chewed gum.

Wystan arrived at last, very sunburnt and in the highest spirits, wearing a loud, becoming check suit. "Well, my dear," he greeted me, "there isn't going to be a war, you know!" For a moment, I thought he must have some stop-press information—but no. He had merely met a lady at the British Embassy in Brussels who could read cards, and she had told him that there will be no war this year.

Even as we drove away from the station, the placards appeared: Dramatic Peace Move. I yelled to the driver to stop—Wystan found my excitement a bit excessive

—and we read how Hitler, Mussolini, Daladier, and Chamberlain are to meet in Munich tomorrow.

Later came the news of the super-scene in the Commons. Chamberlain's voice breaks. Queen Mary in tears. Only the Communist Gallagher spoke up and said it was all a sell-out.

As far as Christopher was concerned—I won't venture to speak for anybody else—this post-Munich autumn of 1938 was a period of relief disguised as high-minded disgust. Like all his friends, and thousands of other people, Christopher declared that England had helped betray the Czechs. He meant this. It seemed to him absolutely self-evident. Yet his dead-secret, basic reaction was: What do I care for the Czechs? What does it matter if we are traitors? A war has been postponed—and a war postponed is a war which may never happen.

Wystan and Christopher were now intending to go back to the States, sometime in the near future. But they were in no hurry. First, they wanted to finish *Journey to a War* and see *On the Frontier* staged. The special visa they had got from the Americans in Shanghai made them feel all the more relaxed. Because of it, they would have no further formalities to go through. They could leave at short notice, whenever they decided to.

At the beginning of November, Christopher was invited by Lady Sibyl Colefax, one of the most celebrated arts-and-letters hostesses of the day, to a dinner party. Among the guests was Virginia Woolf. By now, she and Christopher had met several times. In her mid-fifties, Virginia was perhaps more beautiful than she had ever been. Her features had the nobility of a princess in a tragedy, a doomed princess who was nevertheless capable of saying, like the Duchess of Malfi: "I prithee, when were we so merry?" When Christopher saw her, she was full of wit and gossip and delicately malicious laughter.

On an earlier occasion, when Christopher had been asked by the Woolfs to tea, he had stayed on, at Virginia's suggestion, to supper, remaining happily under her spell, hardly talking at all, just watching her and listening and laughing. Then suddenly, at about ten o'clock, he remembered with a start of dismay that a young man must already be waiting for him at a hotel near Croydon Airport—from which they were due to fly, next morning, on a romantic two-day visit to Paris. Christopher had hardly expected the young man to agree to make this trip and regarded him as a conquest to be proud of. Yet Christopher had absolutely forgotten his existence for several hours and was now actually sorry to have to leave Virginia. Could any hostess earn a sincerer tribute? She wasn't aware of the situation, of course. Indeed, she doesn't seem to have been much aware of Christopher himself. In her diary, referring to the Colefax dinner party, she describes him as though he were still a stranger:

> Isherwood and I met on the doorstep. He is a slip of a wild boy: with quicksilver eyes: nipped; jockeylike. That young man, said W. Maugham, "holds the future of the English novel in his hands."

(The jockey impression was probably made, as Robert Craft has guessed, by Christopher's small stature and "bantam-weight, somewhat too short legs, and disproportionately, even simianly long arms." "Wild" seems flattering, applied to timid cautious Christopher. The adjective "nipped" is the most apt, in my opinion; it is confirmed by Keith Vaughan's verdict, about ten years later: "a dehydrated schoolboy.")

Maugham was at this party. So was Max Beerbohm, plump but fragile, with red-ringed pouched blue eyes. He was only ten years older than Virginia but seemed helplessly becalmed in the past. Christopher could think of no remark which would blow wind into his sails. Maugham, at nearly Beerbohm's age, was still briskly cruising the present. Maugham and Christopher already knew each other slightly; they had had lunch together at Maugham's club. His dark watchful bridge player's eyes intimidated Christopher; also his stammer, which somehow made you feel that you were stammering, not he. But, behind the grim, vigorously lined mask of the face, Christopher was aware of a shy warmth, to which he was eager to respond. He would be honored to adopt Maugham as his Uncle Willie, if only Maugham would let him.

Having got rather drunk at dinner, Christopher decided to improve their relations. But the drink had been sufficient only to interfere with his timing; it didn't steady his nerves. He interrupted what Maugham was telling his semicircle of listeners, with a fatally tactless opening line: "Mr. Maugham, on the boat to China, last winter, we had an experience which was exactly like one of your stories—"

From then on, all was nightmare. Christopher heard his own thickened stumbling voice trying to describe the characters of Mr. Potter and White and explain the dramatic significance of their meeting. But he kept leaving out important details; the anecdote simply would not come to a point. Breaking off abruptly, he excused himself and hurried from the room. As he was about to let himself out of the house, a parlormaid came forward, offering a pen. She asked him to sign Lady Colefax's guestbook. With a shaking hand, he scrawled his signature, putting so much pressure on the pen that it snapped in half. Then he fled, never to return.

(I have described what I remember Christopher felt. But his disgrace can't have been as total as he supposed.

Perhaps Maugham found his awkwardness touching and sympathetic. In any case, it must have been after Christopher's exit that Maugham made that remark about him to Virginia Woolf. And Maugham continued to praise Christopher's work to other people on many occasions. Though he never quite became Uncle Willie, he was a helpful, hospitable, and outspoken friend to Christopher for the rest of his life.)

On the Frontier opened at the Arts Theatre, Cambridge, on November 14. Maynard Keynes was its sponsor. Keynes, that aristocrat of Bloomsbury and the Stock Exchange, referred to economics as though they were a branch of academic philosophy, quite unrelated to mere money. It seemed indelicate to remember the fact that his financial know-how had made his college, King's, the richest of the Cambridge colleges and had funded the building of this theater.

Keynes's wife, the former Lydia Lopokova, was the play's leading lady. As before, Doone directed, Britten composed, Medley designed.

Rupert had to cope with the usual problems. When he asked the electricians to create the effect of an offstage torchlight procession, he was told that this was forbidden by the fire regulations. "Ridiculous!" cried Rupert. "All I want is lights that flicker." "Can't have them." "But I *must* have them!" "Can't have them." Deadlock. Then someone murmured: "Course, we *might* do the orphanage being burnt in *Ghosts.*" This proved to be exactly what Rupert had been asking for . . . Although Britten had written music for the song "Industrialists, bankers, in comfortable chairs—" Wystan insisted that it must be sung to the air "Sweet Betsy from Pike." Britten was rather hurt but gave way with a good grace . . . Medley's divided set, "The Ostnia-Westland Room," was so striking that the whole audience applauded it when the curtain rose.

What became evident in performance was that Wystan and Christopher had made their two villains, Valerian and the Leader, more entertaining, more sympathetic even, than any of the other characters. The play was overbalanced by Valerian's charm and humor and the Leader's clowning. The tragic love story, despite its beautiful verse, seemed a tiresome interruption. Ernest Milton, who played the Leader, had the reputation of being the only actor in England who could say "gold" as a four-syllable word: "goo-oo-oo-oold." He was alleged to have done so in *Timon of Athens*. They were willing to believe this, though they hadn't the nerve to ask him for a demonstration. They both reveled in his larger-than-life gestures and intonations.

The first-night audience was friendly. It laughed whenever it could and treated the rest of the play with polite respect. *On the Frontier* wasn't a harrowing disaster; it passed away painlessly.

At the end, Wystan had been asked to make an appeal from the stage, for aid to the children of Spain. His speech began with one of those nonsensical utterances which sometimes become legendary. They are produced by speakers who are trying to talk about two different subjects simultaneously—in this case, the play and the children. Wystan had evidently intended to say that worse things were happening in the outside world at that moment than anything they had been shown in the play. What he did say was: "As you all know, worse things have been happening in the audience tonight than on the stage." This was the biggest laugh of the evening.

Wystan and Christopher went to Brussels in mid-December and were there with a few friends until the end of the first week of January 1939. While there, they finished work on *Journey to a War*.

The date of their departure for New York was now fixed; they were to sail on January 19. This would be the first anniversary of their departure for China. I suspect that Christopher chose the French liner *Champlain* because she happened to be sailing on that day. I know that he deliberately left Los Angeles on January 19, 1947, when he was making his first return visit to England, after the war. Christopher liked to bet on his luck, so to speak, by beginning a journey or a writing project on the anniversary of a previous one which had turned out well. He also kept a lookout for omens. He had thought he had a favorable one when he noticed that their lodgings in Brussels were inside the map square *F6*.

This omen deceived him, however. While in Brussels, he caught clap, for the first time in his life. In those pre-penicillin days, the treatment was painful; when the doctor washed out his urethra with strong stinging disinfectant, he yelled. But he was cured again before Christmas. Wystan refers to Christopher and his clap in "The Novelist":

> *And in his own weak person, if he can,*
> *Dully put up with all the wrongs of Man.*

In "Rimbaud," another sonnet written at that time, Wystan refers to a domestic accident of his own: the radiator in his room had burst and he had had to sit writing in his overcoat. Forster, on being told of their troubles, wrote back:

> My life is a watercolor rendering of yours: a burst water-pipe instead of a radiator, cough and cold instead of clap.

Wystan introduced Christopher to the psychic lady at the British embassy who had told him, during his earlier visit, that there wouldn't be a European war in 1938. The lady read Christopher's palm and saw the letter H in it. This letter, she said, was of great importance in his life.

Christopher was impressed. Apart from the obvious reference to Heinz, there was Vernon, whose real name also began with an H. (Christopher was even more impressed when, in 1940, he reflected that he was now in Hollywood; that he had met Heard again and, through him, Huxley; that he had embraced Hinduism; that he was living on Harratt Street; that he had just written a screenplay based on the novel *Rage in Heaven* by James Hilton!)

Perhaps Wystan and Christopher had lingered in Brussels to shorten their English goodbye-saying as much as was decently possible. When Christopher did return to London, his days were filled with farewell lunches, drinks, dinners, parties, lovemakings. Kathleen's diary records his many social engagements—rather wistfully, for she herself wasn't able to see much of him. My own memory records nothing. Christopher must have found this gradual parting painful and therefore chosen to forget it.

Did he think of himself as a deserter? He had left England often enough before this and for indefinite periods, with only a vague intention of returning some day or other. He couldn't have known definitely yet that he would want to stay in the States; he might well find that he couldn't take root there. Certainly, his closer contact with his friends during the Munich crisis—the feeling that they were all in the same sinking boat—had made it harder for him to leave them, this time. But I doubt if any of his real friends reproached him for it. They had grown used to thinking of him as a chronic wanderer.

I believe that what Christopher then experienced was only the natural apprehension one feels before taking any big step: Isn't this all a terrible mistake?

Although the *Champlain* wasn't going to sail until next day, Wystan and Christopher had arranged to take the boat train to Southampton in the late afternoon of January 18 and spend that night on board. This was possibly another excuse to cut the partings short—particularly Christopher's parting from Kathleen and Richard.

I have written very little about the relations between Christopher and Richard in the years since Christopher left Berlin. There is very little to write. The brothers remained intimate, but within narrow limits. Christopher would tell Richard anything about himself that Richard cared to ask, but their private conversations were brief; they took place chiefly in the bathroom, while Christopher was shaving. They seldom went out together alone. They almost never visited Christopher's friends. It seems to me now that, if Christopher had involved Richard more deeply in his life, he would have upset the delicate balance of his improved relations with Kathleen. And Richard didn't really want to be involved. He was a very private person, though full of curiosity about others. He preferred to be with Christopher's friends only when they came to the house, and then ask questions about them after they had gone.

On October 7, 1938, Kathleen had become seventy years old. Up to then, Christopher had remained vague about her age. I can still remember the shock which the news gave him; she always looked much younger than she was. He told her jokingly that no doubt her youthfulness was due to his never having treated her as an old lady; this was his way of apologizing for his past unkindnesses.

Kathleen and Christopher both cried a little when they said goodbye. The thought that they might not see each other again was in their minds. But Christopher's departure for China may well have seemed gloomier to Kathleen than this one, for then he was going into some danger. A young man Christopher had grown very fond of came with him in the taxi to Waterloo Station. On the way there, he gave Christopher a keepsake—the cork from his first bottle of champagne—over which more tears were shed. Forster, who had come to see them off, asked Christopher, "Shall I join the Communist Party?" I am sure Christopher's answer was no, but I forget the reason he gave. Probably the conventional one: You can be more useful outside it. In any case, Forster's question was less than half serious. The departing, like the dying, are credited with psychic wisdom; you feel you ought to ask them something.

It was sad, sad as dying, to leave these loved ones behind. But neither Wystan nor Christopher wanted to admit that this was in any sense a death or that they were the objects of a wake. As the boat train pulled out of the station and they need wave no longer, Christopher felt a quick upsurge of relief. He and Wystan exchanged grins, schoolboy grins which took them back to the earliest days of their friendship. "Well," said Christopher, "we're off again." "Goody," said Wystan.

Now, on board the *Champlain,* they were really alone together, as they hadn't been since the China journey. In Brussels, there had always been other people in the background. In London, they had been leading public lives.

Wystan was embarrassed by Christopher's public self —the Isherwood who would put an arm around his shoulder when cameras or other eyes were watching. Isherwood was good at self-exposure; he knew all the tricks of modesty and never boasted except in private. (When he did boast, mostly about his sex life, it was with a vulgarity which showed that he was truly Uncle Henry's nephew.) Wystan was shyer and more fastidious; this sometimes had the odd effect of making his public self seem aggressive, dogmatic, arrogant. (It was only much later, in America, that he began to love and be loved by his audiences.) In public, Wystan and Christopher were as polite to each other as mere acquaintances. If Wystan disagreed strongly with something Christopher had said, a furrow would appear between his eyes and his mouth would begin to twitch. But he never contradicted Christopher when strangers were present.

Now, communication between them was reestablished. This, to Christopher at least, meant an unaccustomed freedom. Alone with Wystan, he was able, literally, to speak his mind—to say things which he hadn't known were in it, until the moment of speaking. One morning, when they were walking on the deck, Christopher heard himself say: "You know, it just doesn't mean anything to me any more—the Popular Front, the party line, the anti-Fascist struggle. I suppose they're okay but something's wrong with me. I simply cannot swallow another mouthful." To which Wystan answered: "Neither can I."

Those were not their exact words, but, psychologically, it was as simple as that. They had been playing parts, repeating slogans created for them by others. Now they wanted to stop. Christopher felt almost equally surprised by his own statement and by Wystan's agreement with it. The surprise was mutual. Their agreement made them happy. Now, more than ever, they were allied. Yet their positions were really quite different.

Wystan had been aware of his own change of attitude for some time already. He hadn't spoken of it to Christopher because he had expected that Christopher would be horrified by it. As I have said earlier, Wystan's left-wing convictions had always been halfhearted and at odds with his religious feelings. While in Spain, he had been disgusted by the burning of churches and the anti-religious propaganda permitted by the government. Nevertheless, he had believed that the government's cause was mainly just. He had been willing to fight against Franco. He wasn't a pacifist and would never become one. Back in England, he had attended meetings and made public statements because he still believed that Franco must be fought, and because he wanted to show his solidarity with left-wing friends he admired and loved. Now, however, he was about to start a new life in another country. His obligations wouldn't be the same in the States. He wouldn't be a member of a group. He could express himself freely as an individual.

Christopher had taken longer than Wystan to become aware of his own change of attitude because he was embarrassed by its basic cause: his homosexuality. As a homosexual, he had been wavering between embarrassment and defiance. He became embarrassed when he felt that he was making a selfish demand for his individual rights at a time when only group action mattered. He became defiant when he made the treatment of the homosexual a test by which every political party and government must be judged. His challenge to each one of them was: "All right, we've heard your liberty speech. Does that include us or doesn't it?"

The Soviet Union had passed this test with honors when it recognized the private sexual rights of the individual, in 1917. But, in 1934, Stalin's government had withdrawn this recognition and made all homosexual acts punishable by heavy prison sentences. It had agreed with the Nazis in denouncing homosexuality as a form of treason to the state. The only difference was that the Nazis called it "sexual Bolshevism" and the Communists "Fascist perversion."

Christopher—like many of his friends, homosexual and heterosexual—had done his best to minimize the Soviet betrayal of its own principles. After all, he had said to himself, anti-homosexual laws exist in most capitalist countries, including England and the United States. Yes —but if Communists claim that their system is juster than capitalism, doesn't that make their injustice to homosexuals less excusable and their hypocrisy even viler? He now realized he must dissociate himself from the Communists, even as a fellow traveler. He might, in certain situations, accept them as allies but he could never regard them as comrades. He must never again give way to embarrass-

334

ment, never deny the rights of his tribe, never apologize for its existence, never think of sacrificing himself masochistically on the altar of that false god of the totalitarians, the Greatest Good of the Greatest Number—whose priests are alone empowered to decide what "good" is.

(Wystan was much more apologetic about his homosexuality than Christopher was, and much less aggressive. His religion condemned it and he agreed that it was sinful, though he fully intended to go on sinning.)

The change in Christopher's attitude was also related to Heinz and the Nazis. As long as Heinz had been outside their power but menaced by them, Christopher's attitude to them had been one of uncomplicated hatred. But now Heinz was about to become an unwilling part of the Nazi military machine. Soon he would be wearing Hitler's uniform. Christopher didn't for one moment wish him to do otherwise. Heinz had plenty of courage but he wasn't the type who could be expected to disappear and join the underground, or to take a stand as a pacifist in a country where pacifists would probably be executed.

Suppose, Christopher now said to himself, I have a Nazi Army at my mercy. I can blow it up by pressing a button. The men in that Army are notorious for torturing and murdering civilians—all except for one of them, Heinz. Will I press the button? No—wait: Suppose I know that Heinz himself, out of cowardice or moral infection, has become as bad as they are and takes part in all their crimes? Will I press that button, even so? Christopher's answer, given without the slightest hesitation, was: Of course not.

That was a purely emotional reaction. But it helped Christopher think his way through to the next proposition. Suppose that Army goes into action and has just one casualty, Heinz himself. Will I press the button now and destroy his fellow criminals? No emotional reaction this time, but a clear answer, not to be evaded: Once I have refused to press that button because of Heinz, I can never press it. Because every man in that Army could be somebody's Heinz and I have no right to play favorites. Thus Christopher was forced to recognize himself as a pacifist—although by an argument which he could only admit to with the greatest reluctance.

Other thoughts and emotions related themselves to this argument. Remembering those hapless homeless Chinese crowds, pushed helplessly by the war tide, clinging to the roofs of trains or huddled beside the tracks, Christopher felt ashamed of all the militant lectures on China he had been giving, right up to the time he sailed. How could he have dared to suggest that any of these people—or any people anywhere—*ought* to fight, *ought* to die in defense of *any* principles, however excellent? I must honor those who fight of their own free will, he said to himself. And I must try to imitate their courage by following my path as a pacifist, wherever it takes me.

The above description of Christopher's reactions is far too lucid, however. What had actually begun to surface in his muddled mind was a conflict of emotions. He felt obliged to become a pacifist, he refused to deny his homosexuality, he wanted to keep as much of his leftism as he could. All he could do for the present was to pick up his ideas one after another and reexamine them, ring them like coins, saying: This one's counterfeit; this one's genuine, but I can't use it; this one I can keep, I think.

Wystan had his mother's Christianity to fall back on. Christopher had nothing but a negative decision—if war came, he wouldn't fight. He was aware, of course, that pacifism had its positive obligations—you had to do something instead of fighting. Heard and Huxley were the only two articulate pacifists he could contact. They might be able to restate pacifism for him in terms of reason, instead of emotion. He had been told that they had entangled themselves in some Oriental religion; but he could reject the religion and still adopt their pacifist ideology. He would write to Heard as soon as he landed

336

in New York. Later, perhaps, he would go out to California and consult them both.

The voyage was stormy. The *Champlain* seemed very small, slithering down the long gray Atlantic slopes, under a burdened sky. On this voyage, Wystan and Christopher had no literary collaboration to occupy them. Wrapped in rugs, they lay sipping bouillon, or they paced the deck, or drank at the bar, or watched movies in the saloon, where French tapestries flapped out from the creaking, straining walls as the ship rolled. They amused themselves by taking over the puppet show in the children's playroom and improvising Franco-English dialogue full of private jokes and double meanings. Their audience of children didn't care what the puppets said, as long as they kept jumping about. Off the coast of Newfoundland, the ship ran into a blizzard. She entered New York harbor looking like a wedding cake.

At the end of Christopher's brief visit in 1938, he had felt absolutely confident of one thing, at least. If he did decide to settle in America—and, by America, he meant New York—he would be able to make himself at home there. This, he said to himself, was a setting in which his public personality would function more freely, more successfully than it could ever have functioned in London. Oh, he'd talk faster and louder than any of the natives. He'd pick up their slang and their accent. He'd learn all their tricks. Someone had repeated to him a saying about the city: "Here, you'll find sympathy in the dictionary and everything else at the nearest drugstore." This delighted him. He had accepted it as a challenge to be tough.

But now New York, on that bitter winter morning, appeared totally, shockingly transformed from the place

337

he had waved goodbye to, the previous July. Christopher experienced a sudden panicky loss of confidence.

There they stood in the driving snow—the made-in-France Giantess with her liberty torch, which now seemed to threaten, not welcome, the newcomer; and the Red Indian island with its appalling towers. There was the Citadel—stark, vertical, gigantic, crammed with the millions who had already managed to struggle ashore and find a foothold. You would have to fight your way inland from your very first step onto the pier. Already, it was threatening you with its tooting tugboats, daring you to combat.

God, what a terrifying place this suddenly seemed! You could feel it vibrating with the tension of the nervous New World, aggressively flaunting its rude steel nudity. We're Americans here—and we keep at it, twenty-four hours a day, *being* Americans. We scream, we grab, we jostle. We've no time for what's slow, what's gracious, what's nice, quiet, modest. Don't you come snooting us with your European traditions—we know the mess they've got you into. Do things our way or take the next boat back—back to your Europe that's falling apart at the seams. Well, make up your mind. Are you quitting or staying? It's no skin off *our* nose. We promise nothing. Here, you'll be on your own.

Christopher, trying hard to think positive thoughts, declared that he was staying. But the Giantess wasn't impressed. The towers didn't care. Okay, Buster, suit yourself.

Now, however, the quarantine launch arrived. On it were Erika and Klaus Mann, come out to welcome them. They were full of liveliness and gossip. And, at once, the Giantess stopped threatening, the towers no longer appalled. Christopher felt himself among friends, cared for, safe. And Vernon would be waiting for him on shore; Christopher had cabled to him from the *Champlain*. A couple of hours from now, somewhere within the grimness of that icebound Citadel, in a place of warmth and joy, the two of them would be in each other's arms.

This is where I leave Christopher, at the rail, looking eagerly, nervously, hopefully toward the land where he will spend more than half of his life. At present, he can see almost nothing of what lies ahead. In the absence of the fortune-telling lady from Brussels, I will allow him and Wystan to ask one question—I can already guess what it is—and I will answer it:

Yes, my dears, each of you will find the person you came here to look for—the ideal companion to whom you can reveal yourself totally and yet be loved for what you are, not what you pretend to be. You, Wystan, will find him very soon, within three months. You, Christopher, will have to wait much longer for yours. He is already living in the city where you will settle. He will be near you for many years without your meeting. But it would be no good if you did meet him now. At present, he is only four years old.

A pioneer in exploring gay themes in his writing, **Christopher Isherwood** (1904–1986) is best known for his classic *Berlin Stories,* the basis for the stage and movie successes *I Am a Camera* and *Cabaret.* His books *Down There on a Visit, Lions and Shadows, A Meeting by the River, The Memorial, My Guru and His Disciple, Prater Violet, A Single Man,* and *The World in the Evening* are also published in paperback by the University of Minnesota Press.